W9-CQD-519

Children's Literature Association Centennial Studies

1. *Beatrix Potter's* Peter Rabbit: *A Children's Classic at 100*, edited by Margaret Mackey. 2002.

Beatrix Potter, *The Tale of Peter Rabbit,* p.11 (1902 edition).

Beatrix Potter's *Peter Rabbit*

A Children's Classic at 100

Edited by Margaret Mackey

Children's Literature Association Centennial Studies, No. 1

The Children's Literature Association
and
The Scarecrow Press, Inc.
Lanham, Maryland, and London
2002

SCARECROW PRESS, INC.

Published in the United States of America
by Scarecrow Press, Inc.
4720 Boston Way, Lanham, Maryland 20706
www.scarecrowpress.com

4 Pleydell Gardens, Folkestone
Kent CT20 2DN, England

British Library Cataloguing-in-Publication Information Available

Library of Congress Cataloging-in-Publication Data

Beatrix Potter's Peter Rabbit : a children's classic at 100 / edited by Margaret Mackey.
p. cm. — (Children's Literature Association centennial studies ; no. 1)
Includes bibliographical references.
ISBN 0-8108-4197-5 (alk. paper)
1. Potter, Beatrix, 1866–1943. Tale of Peter Rabbit. 2. Potter, Beatrix, 1866–1943—Characters—Peter Rabbit. 3. Children's stories, English—History and criticism. 4. Peter Rabbit (Fictitious character). 5. Rabbits in literature. 6. Rabbits in art. I. Mackey, Margaret. II. Series.

PR6031.O72 T333 2002
823′.912—dc21 2001049620

∞ ™The paper used in this publication meets the minimum requirements of American National Standard for Information Sciences—Permanence of Paper for Printed Library Materials, ANSI/NISO Z39.48–1992.
Manufactured in the United States of America.

Contents

Acknowledgments

It has been an exciting project to work on this book, and I would like to thank the Children's Literature Association for offering me the opportunity. People too many to name helped me assemble the list of contributors and provided contact information; I thank them all. I owe a great debt to all the contributors for their lively and fascinating contributions, as well as for their cheerful and professional approach to deadlines; they collectively provide living testimony to the idea that the most effective way to work is to find good people and then stand back!

It was a pleasure to work with everyone who was involved with this book, but one contributor stands out in particular for her generous support and apparently bottomless font of good ideas. That person is Judy Taylor, who put me in touch with many of the people whose chapters appear in this collection, and who offered much good advice both to me and to other contributors. Her dedication to the cause of preserving and propagating the works of Beatrix Potter is exemplary; every children's author should wish for such careful and loving guardianship. Of course, all the responsibility for errors and problems in this collection is mine alone.

At a more local level, I would like to thank Jackie Seidel for all her work with the manuscripts. She has taken on a range of editorial duties with good will, enthusiasm, and acumen. Her perceptiveness made many contributions to this book.

Raymond E. Jones, chair of the publication committee of the Children's Literature Association, put in many heroic hours of copyediting, and also provided much highly helpful advice in many other areas. I would like to thank him, as well as Sarah Cooke, who worked on details of documentation. I am also grateful to David Russell, a previous chair of the publication committee, who helped in the early stages of this project.

More official acknowledgments are in order. The illustrations in this book come from several sources. Frederick Warne & Co. is the owner of all rights, copyrights, and trademarks for Beatrix Potter character names and illustrations. The company kindly granted permission for the reproduction of six pictures by Beatrix Potter. It is important to note that the views contained in these essays are those of the individual contributors and not necessarily those of Frederick Warne & Co. The reproductions of two pictures by John Everett Millais are courtesy of the Victoria and Albert Picture Library in London. The Huntington Library Art Galleries and Botanical Gardens in San Marino, California, granted permission for the reproduction of Thomas Gainsborough's *Blue Boy*. The Peter Rabbit™ Barbie Doll® is reproduced with permission of Mattel, Inc. Thanks also to the Osborne Collection of Early Children's Books at the Toronto public libraries for access to the *Peter Rabbit Almanac* for 1929. We are grateful to all these publishers and owners for helping us make our independent tribute to a great writer and illustrator as complete as possible.

Finally, I would personally like to thank the Social Sciences and Humanities Research Council of Canada for their ongoing support for my work with Peter Rabbit, in this and other forms.

Introduction

Peter Rabbit is unarguably a "classic" story for little children. Ever since its original publication, it has generally been agreed that this book succeeds artistically just as comprehensively as it does in terms of ongoing appeal to children. After a book has been so significant, so triumphant for a whole century, how can there possibly be anything left to say about it?

The thirteen authors in this book address that question from many perspectives. In their diverse and fascinating approaches to a very familiar story, they provide new insights into the phenomenal success of Beatrix Potter over many decades. At the same time, they also offer a multifaceted view into the dynamic world of the study of children's literature. All the contributors to this book deal with a single, small, and very well-known title: very tight constraints indeed. Yet it is astonishing to see how rich, varied, and illuminating their observations are.

This book provides insights into Potter's little story and, at the same time, provides a snapshot of the state of the scholarly study of children's literature as we move into another century. The contributors to this book represent a broad sampling of the diverse world of children's literature. Biographers, translators, and museum specialists rub shoulders with academic teachers and scholars from English departments, library schools, and teacher education faculties. Experts who have spent a lifetime working on the aesthetic achievements of Beatrix Potter are represented here, as are both established and new scholars in many related fields. Children also have a voice in this book, thanks particularly to the careful work of Lawrence Sipe and his teacher colleagues. Through the lens of a single title, we can see a rich tapestry of interweaving interests and priorities, and gain insight into the appeal and importance of the study of children's literature. The multi-disciplinary roots and discourses of the field are amply demonstrated in the very different approaches of the different contributors.

THE APPEAL OF *PETER RABBIT*

For a century, this little book has been given to children by adults who love both the children and the story. For many decades of that century, the majority of the adults who share the book with children remember it with affection from their own childhood. Paradoxically, the book is very accessible to small children but only as long as they have adult help. Thus the adults reading at their child's bedside are often reading in the light of their own recollections of the book being read to them, often in very similar circumstances by their own parents. Few nursery books bear such a historical patina of ongoing delight communicated between parents, grandparents, and small children over so many generations.

At one level the book represents, even seems to embody, a core domestic value of children being cared for by grown-ups who themselves were once small. Yet the hero of the story moves from that home-based security into a dangerous and threatening world, far from any place where adults can help or look after him. This contradiction shapes the story, and it affects the kinds of attention paid to this book over the past hundred years.

SELLING THE STORY

Over the course of a hundred years, a book can reinvent itself or be reinvented by others in many ways. One of the most intriguing qualities of *Peter Rabbit* and Potter's other little books is that they have remained so true to themselves at the same time that they have been translated, adapted, reworked, and otherwise transmogrified.

As Judy Taylor recounts in her chapter outlining the history of *The*

Tale of Peter Rabbit, the story changed in small ways through its first few incarnations. Like many children's classics, it developed out of a story created for a single child, and the early editions marked stages of its development into the text we now take for granted as the "true" version. But the parameters of the classic story are not entirely fixed, even today. Indeed, as this book was going to press, Frederick Warne announced that their plans for celebrating *Peter Rabbit*'s centennial include a "redesign" of all Potter's little books, working to recreate the original productions in terms of typeface, paper, page design, and so forth. *The Tale of Peter Rabbit* will be further altered by the restoration of the four pictures that were left out in 1903 and the addition of two others that were never used. As cinema versions of a movie are now sold in video and DVD in the different edition of a "director's cut," so we will come closer to the *Peter Rabbit* that previously existed only in Potter's studio.

We are, of course, used to seeing different versions of *Peter Rabbit.* The ongoing cycle of parents, grandparents, and small children engaging with this book is intimate and appealing, but the very delights of that cycle have opened vast marketing opportunities. Beatrix Potter herself, as Lissa Paul suggests in this book, was usually open to new ways of selling her small characters, but even she would surely be surprised at the scale of the contemporary market. In many cases, what is being sold is a physical manifestation of that ongoing link between the generations provided by the little stories; the christening cup or porringer that Grandma buys for Baby is surely rooted in this tradition. At the same time, *Peter Rabbit* is utterly contemporary in its plurality, its multiple manifestations and reworkings. In terms of ownership, the Potter books also participate in a very contemporary story. Beatrix Potter published with the relatively small company of Frederick Warne and actually left the copyright to her publisher on her death. Today, after a series of purchases, Warne is owned by Pearson, one of the major media conglomerates of the twenty-first century. Peter Rabbit has been transformed into clothing, china, toys, games, and souvenirs of all kinds, as well as continuing a very successful existence in his original incarnation within the covers of the little book.

Similarly, Peter's story is now told through an enormous range of media. The official *Peter Rabbit* website has won awards; the CD-ROMs were among the first for children to include a 360-degree surround-space; the official animations were greeted with enthusiasm when they first appeared on television; the film of the ballet is a little masterpiece in its own right. The activity books, the audio books, and the bath and board books all take their place in the proliferating world of versions of this little story. It is a tribute to the power of the original telling that Potter's own books still command pride of place among all these reworkings—though it will be interesting to see if the video versions ever triumph in terms of being more widely accessible to children. After all, a toddler needs help to read the story, but not to run the video.

In addition to the commodities and the different media reworkings, there is a third category of alternative texts. The original story, right from its inception, has provided the inspiration for a huge range of pirate imitators and retellers, again in many media. However aesthetically reprehensible some of these versions may seem to a purist eye, they have made their own contribution to another element of the century of *Peter Rabbit* in terms of their contribution to the accelerating market of collectibles: out-of-print pirate editions command high prices. The pirate copies have also played a role in the global history of *Peter Rabbit* in a variety of ways; in the last chapter of this book, Shin-ichi Yoshida describes the importance of pirate editions in Japan, where they appeared long before the original was available.

Another part of the success story of *The Tale of Peter Rabbit* is its worldwide appeal. It has appeared in 36 languages over the past century. This celebratory book does not spread its wings quite so far, but it does contain contributions from four different countries: seven from the United States, three from the United Kingdom, two from Canada, and one from Japan, a tribute to the ongoing fascination of the story, even to those who have never seen the English countryside it celebrates.

Given the complexity and interest of the world of *Peter Rabbit,* it is not surprising that there is a society exclusively devoted to the works of Beatrix Potter. Founded in 1980, the Society includes people professionally involved with Potter's works and people who simply love them. It collects Potter materials, often storing them in the vaults of Frederick Warne; it produces newsletters and other publications; it organizes an annual lecture and a biennial Study Conference, and generally contributes to the ongoing enjoyment and study of Potter's achievements in a variety of interesting ways.[1]

In short, the story is reframed in different institutional and international ways. Yet after a century, what still matters most of all is the strength of the ties created among children and adults to the little book of *The Tale of Peter Rabbit.*

THE ORGANIZATION OF THIS BOOK

The century-long life of *The Tale of Peter Rabbit* is thus a complex phenomenon. Not surprisingly, the variety of perspectives offered by the contributors to this book is also rich and pleasing.

In order to arrange these articles usefully for readers, I have borrowed terms from David Rudd's recent account of the works of Enid Blyton.[2] Rudd talks about the pre-texts, the con-texts (the contemporary issues and the more enduring themes associated *with* the works), and the post-texts or rewrites, adaptations, and sequels. I have found this framework helpful in sorting a set of thirteen papers that all have an excellent claim for pride of place.

I have also added a category of my own that takes precedence over all those three headings just described. So this book opens with a section on "Text" in which we explore readings of the book itself. The first chapter offers us a new perspective on children's responses to the story. Lawrence Sipe, who has done a great deal to open our eyes to the creative interpretive powers of very young children, works with teachers to investigate the responses of 346 urban African-American children aged five and six. Their enthusiastic yet serious reaction to the book confirms that the story still speaks with a living voice, even when transplanted from its original rural, Victorian and English context. In the second chapter of this section, Carole Scott, an English professor in San Diego who has written widely on children's literature and recently published a book on picture books, provides a different approach: a close reading of the dynamics of word and picture in the little story. No doubt most readers of this book will have read *The Tale of Peter Rabbit* many times already, but her deft and illuminating interpretation invites us all to look again.

Next we have the "Pre-Text" section. What factors contributed to the creation of this story? In this part of the book, Judy Taylor, noted Potter biographer and a well-known expert on many different aspects of the little stories, addresses the question of how *The Tale of Peter Rabbit* came to be and how it developed into the book so familiar to us today. Joyce Irene Whalley, who worked for years at the Victoria and Albert Museum and has been involved with many exhibitions of Potter's work, offers an illuminating historical analysis of Potter's illustrations. Lissa Paul, who is a professor in the Education Faculty at the University of New Brunswick and known for her wide-ranging explorations of children's literature, takes a provocative look at Potter as a "coolhunter."

She explores Potter's understanding and use of new technologies of her time, as well as analyzing her appropriation of new forms of circulation and distribution.

The "Con-Text" section is more variegated in its make-up, looking at different ways of reading Potter in terms both of contemporary issues and also of enduring themes. The essays in this section broadly and variously address the question of "What qualities have enabled this book to work so well and for so long?" The variety of approaches among these essays is a testimony to the strength and diversity of the field. June Cummins, a well-known scholar of children's literature at San Diego State University, reads the story alongside and against *Goblin Market,* a poem written for children by Potter's contemporary, Christina Rossetti. Her account of how this double reading extends and enriches both texts offers interesting insights into reading processes. Eliza Dresang, a professor of library and information studies who has made an extended study of changes in children's literature in a digital age, analyzes *Peter Rabbit*'s qualities as a "radical" text. She shows how Potter's century-old book addresses readers in ways that seem completely contemporary. Kara Keeling and Scott Pollard, who work at Christopher Newport University, combine, as they have done before, in a productive scholarly partnership to look at *The Tale of Peter Rabbit* as a story about appetite. Their perspective on physiological and social qualities of eating experiences provides stimulating new ways of thinking about the story. Alice Byrnes, from Molloy College in New York, looks at the book from the perspective of a psychologist and explores the archetypal elements of both Potter's and Peter's stories, drawing connections between the two by means of a Jungian framework. Melissa Gross, who works in the School of Information Studies at Florida State University, also looks at universal elements of appeal in *Peter Rabbit,* but explores these questions through a comparison with another acknowledged classic picture book for children, *Where the Wild Things Are* by Maurice Sendak.

One fascinating element that unites these five chapters in the "Con-Text" section is the illumination they shed on how we read. A single story almost never exists in isolation; whether we read *Peter Rabbit* alongside *Goblin Market, Where the Wild Things Are,* the *Harry Potter* books, a Jungian account of childhood, or a recipe for rabbit pie does affect what we take away from it. Fortunately, one kind of reading need never rule out another, and the variety of perspectives in this section shows how a range of personal and disciplinary approaches can enrich our understanding. The field of children's literature is productively cultivated by different ways of thinking and writing, as well as reading.

The last section brings us to the theme of the Post-Text. The three essays in this part of the book address very different forms of life after publication. Peter Hollindale has been well known for many years for his work in children's literature; he recently retired as Reader in English and Educational Studies at the University of York. In his delightful exploration of naturalist accuracy in Beatrix Potter's work, he also investigates the development of Peter Rabbit's character through the three books that serve as sequels to the original story: *The Tale of Benjamin Bunny, The Tale of Mr. Tod,* and *The Tale of the Flopsy Bunnies.* In my own chapter, I look at the ever-burgeoning world of Peter Rabbit consumables and collectibles, up to and including the Peter Rabbit Barbie doll. And finally, Shin-ichi Yoshida, a translator of Potter and of many books about her, concludes this book with the story of how *The Tale of Peter Rabbit* arrived in Japan, first in pirate editions and then as a properly translated version of the original, an event which did not occur until 1971. For the past thirty years, he has been part of the worldwide campaign to bring Beatrix Potter to new readers, and it is fitting that his odyssey originated in the kind of bedtime reading with which I began this introduction.

NOTES

1. Irene Whalley, "The Beatrix Potter Society, 1980–2000," *The Beatrix Potter Society Newsletter* no. 77 (July 2000): 18–19.
2. David Rudd, *Enid Blyton and the Mystery of Children's Literature* (Basingstoke: Macmillan, 2000), 66–67.

1

TEXT

This opening section of the book explores two different contemporary readings of *The Tale of Peter Rabbit.* Lawrence Sipe presents the responses of a large number of urban American children to hearing the story read aloud to them. Their engaged and lively comments testify to the book's continuing and vivid power. In a very different approach, Carole Scott offers a scholarly interpretation of how words and pictures combine to tell this famous story. She investigates the subtle counterpoint of Potter's creation, in which words and pictures often send very different messages and the whole is indisputably greater than the sum of its parts. In the complexities of interaction between words and pictures, Potter performs subtleties that evoke sophisticated reading and viewing from even small children, as Sipe's chapter so eloquently illustrates.

1

Contemporary Urban Children Respond to *Peter Rabbit:* Making a Text Culturally Relevant

Lawrence R. Sipe

The one-hundredth anniversary of the first publication of *The Tale of Peter Rabbit*[1] is upon us. This little book, long considered a classic by experts in children's literature[2] is one of the handful of texts from that era still in print and still enjoyed by children. In what ways could this story, by a member of the British Edwardian upper-middle class and redolent of a rural culture, still function in a timeless way,[3] as a stimulating mirror for children today?[4] Missing from the many literary critical articles, essays, and books about this little tale is empirical research on the responses of *real children*. In one of the few studies, Landes described how seven year olds preferred Potter's original language and illustrations to that of an adaptation in which "it seemed as if the author had noted every literary aspect of Potter's language and illustrations and then set about to remove them";[5] the children were surprised and annoyed at the attempts at simplification. They much preferred Potter's language and illustrations to that of the adaptation, and could give good reasons for their preference. By so doing, they demonstrated their literary critical abilities. Landes' research thus suggests that young children can savor the literary qualities of Peter Rabbit, and encourages further research about the responses of contemporary children to this classic.

This chapter is based on a study of readaloud discussions of *Peter Rabbit* to a slightly younger population—five and six year olds. As well, the study focuses on a particular cultural context: urban classrooms with youngsters from low socioeconomic status backgrounds. The study sought to answer these questions: *What are the range and types of oral responses to readalouds of Peter Rabbit in several classrooms of young urban children? What responses are common across these groups of children?* In answering these questions, I discovered that the children were able to bridge the various cultural divides between their world and the world of the story, and that they were able to construct the story socially with cultural relevance for themselves. This chapter includes a summary of the study's theoretical framework (based on theories of reader response), a brief description of the methodological choices I made, and a discussion of the findings of the study.

THEORETICAL FRAME AND METHOD

The many forms of reader response theory,[6] though differing in several respects, all suggest that literary texts may evoke different responses on the part of individual readers. Social interaction during storybook readalouds, in the form of discussion among children, is therefore a sharing of different interpretations and perspectives on the story. In the classroom, the teacher and children together form an "interpretive community,"[7] collaboratively constructing a view of what constitutes "literary competence."[8] What "counts" as response may therefore vary across classroom interpretive communities. Given this amount of variation, the best way to understand a particular literary text's potential for evoking response is to examine the responses across a number of settings that involve numbers of children. Despite the emphasis of reader response on individual and contextual differences, however, there may be common features in response to one text across several situations and individuals. One of the claims about classic stories is that they appeal to just this range of situations (social, chronological, geographical, cultural) and individuals.[9] In other words, the question of wide appeal is empirically answerable. Reader response theory suggests that investigation of this appeal for modern, urban children will likely tell us as much about the children and their life situations as about the text of *Peter Rabbit*.

Wolfgang Iser's observation that understanding literature is heavily dependent on the reader's active filling in of the gaps of the text is another aspect of reader response theory that is relevant to this study.[10] Because *Peter Rabbit* is representative of a culture and time period far different from that of urban contemporary children, it would be expected that there would be many indeterminacies and gaps in this text for this set of listeners.

Because response is influenced by pedagogical, social, and cultural contexts, a large number of classrooms were sought as sites in order to maximize the potential range of children's responses. The sample of 15 classrooms was opportunistic, taking advantage of my connections to two professional development organizations in order to contact teachers who might be interested in participating in the study. Teachers who were members of these two organizations were also likely to read and discuss literature with their children on a regular basis. There were seven kindergarten classes, six first-grade classes, and two combined classes of kindergarten/first grade and pre-kindergarten/kindergarten. The choice of kindergarten and first-grade classes was based on the desire to include responses from young children who were of a likely age to respond appreciatively to the story. All classes were located in public schools within the city school district of a large eastern U.S. metropolitan area, and all had populations of over 85 percent African American children. One of the schools was an Afro-Centric charter school. Over ninety percent of the children were enrolled in the district's federally sponsored lunch subsidy program, an indication of low socioeconomic status. Thus the sample of classrooms was both diverse and homogeneous. It was diverse because there were fifteen classroom cultures with fifteen teachers; but it was homogeneous because most of the children shared similar cultural and social backgrounds. A total of 346 children were involved in the study, and the average class size was 23.

The Picture Puffin version of *The Tale of Peter Rabbit*[11] was used in all classrooms because it (1) contained all of Potter's original text and illustrations and (2) was large enough to be seen readily by a group of children (the original version is difficult to use with a whole class of children because of its small size). Teachers agreed to read the story to their classes and to audiotape the responses. Instructions to the teachers were minimal; they were asked to read and discuss the story with their children, and to encourage response during the reading of the story. The minimal instructions were intentional; it was desirable not to interfere unduly with the teachers' storybook readaloud styles because different styles may encourage different responses,[12] and a wide range of responses was a desideratum of the study. The teachers were requested to ask two specific questions: (1) Did you ever hear this story before? (2) Did anything like this ever happen to you? These questions were to be asked directly if, in the teacher's opinion, the children had not discussed these ideas spontaneously. Field notes were kept, primarily for the purpose of identifying the speakers, and audiotapes were transcribed completely. The transcripts were then analyzed on three levels. First, each conversational turn[13] by the children was assigned a conceptual label.[14] These conceptual labels were used to form conceptual categories of response by the constant comparative method of modifying, combining, and separating the conceptual labels iteratively and recursively as the analysis proceeded.[15] Second, stretches of conversational turns about the same topic were identified and analyzed (also by the constant comparative method) in order to discover important themes in the discussion.[16] Third, the transcripts were compared with each other to determine which themes were common across classrooms. To be considered "commonly occurring," the theme had to be present in over half (at least eight) of the transcripts.

CHILDREN'S RESPONSES

After I discuss the children's familiarity with the tale, I report on four aspects of the children's responses: discussion of the language of the story; discussion of the literary elements of the text; commonly occurring themes in the discussions; and children's own stories and personal experiences evoked by *Peter Rabbit*. All quotations are from the children, unless specifically labeled as teacher comments.

It was notable that over half the children said that they had heard the story before; when questioned, they often referred to versions of the story in other formats, for example video, Big Book versions, or anthologies of Potter's stories ("I got that same book, but it's got a lot of stories in it, Peter Rabbit and other animals"). Other children mentioned coloring books, posters, games, and toys associated with the story. The story, in its many avatars, appeared to be a common part of the experience of these urban children—it had entered both popular culture and their own lives.[17] Children reported having heard the book read in preschool, daycare, and the library; or (if they were six years old) in their previous classroom. Only a few children seemed familiar with the original format of the book ("I have this at home, but it's a lot smaller"). Similarly, few had heard the story read by a member of their family, but the various videos based on the story seemed to enjoy a considerable popularity at home.

Discussion of Story Language

In writing *The Tale of Peter Rabbit* and her other stories, Beatrix Potter did not use overly simplified language; indeed some of the phrases and individual words seem fairly sophisticated. As well, urban children might well be unfamiliar with vocabulary and concepts that refer to situations and objects more common to rural life. English phrasing at the beginning of the twentieth century might also be different from American usage at the beginning of the twenty-first century. For all these reasons, there was a considerable amount of attention paid to speculating about the language of the story by teachers and children, as they constructed meaning together.

Confusions over the homonyms *tale/tail* ("I think it's about his white little tail") and *fir/fur* ("maybe it's a bunny tree; it has fur like an animal") were explored and resolved. As well, children discussed words more common in rural contexts: *wheelbarrow* and *sieve*. In one classroom, which was studying dinosaurs, the children put their knowledge to work when speculating about the meaning of *sieve:* "Like when you're hunting dinosaur bones and you put the dirt in, like a sifter." *Cucumber frame* and *gooseberry net* also came in for a good deal of discussion; in these cases, Potter's illustrations were helpful in understanding these objects. Surprisingly, *fortnight* ("It was the second little jacket and pair of shoes that Peter had lost in a fortnight!") was mentioned in only one classroom discussion. Children speculated that it might mean a "full night" or "two nights," and were surprised at the teacher's explanation (two weeks): "I lose my clothes a lot more times than that!"

The phrase that elicited the most discussion was the friendly sparrows' exhortation to Peter, entangled in the gooseberry net: ". . . his sobs were overheard by some friendly sparrows, who flew to him in great excitement, and implored him to exert himself." In one first-grade class, the children offered several ideas:

- Stop crying!
- Be tough.
- Try to get yourself out.

- To get yourself together.
- And get yourself purpose. And give yourself some purpose.

The idea of *giving yourself a purpose* figured largely in this school, an Afro-Centric school that was very concerned with helping children develop feelings of self-worth and empowerment. In fact, the language of "having a purpose" was frequently used in this school by teachers, parents, and children. This is a powerful example of the ways in which specific cultural context shapes and enables response. In this case, the children had not only successfully interpreted Potter's text; they had also given the text a profound relevance and a particularly apt spin.

Discussion of Literary Elements

One first grader asked, "Is this a retelling? I'm just curious, because it could be a little bit the same as the original story or it could be a little different, too, like with different characters, and different things could happen." Children in this class were familiar with the concept of multiple variants of the same story because they had listened to many versions of traditional stories and had written their own variants. This child's use of "retelling" and his reference to the "original story" and to "characters" demonstrate that this class was learning the meta-language for talking about stories.

Children used the front cover (which shows Peter eating a radish in Mr. McGregor's garden) and frontispiece (showing Mrs. Rabbit giving Peter camomile tea in bed) to speculate on plot, characters, and setting:

- They [Mrs. Rabbit and Peter] must be the main characters.
- Teacher: Yes, we know that artists put main characters on the cover sometimes, and they also tell us about the setting sometimes.
- Yeah, this happens in a garden.

Structurally, children understood Flopsy, Mopsy, and Cotton-tail as foils for Peter, and Peter's father as a parallel character: "His dad was bad, and his sisters are good, so he *has* to be naughty." In terms of character motivation, Peter's intention in going into the garden was understood in several ways:

- Maybe he wanted to find out what happened to his dad, like see where his dad got killed.

- I think he was just curious.
- You know whenever you get told, like "Don't do that" you're gonna wanna do it.
- I just think he was hungry and he wanted some carrots.

Children also discussed the effect of the sparrows' exhortation, understanding it as an encouragement: "The birds help him. They don't help him, but they really *do* because they make him feel better, and it like gives him courage to get out."

Potter's handling of the ending of the story drew some critique in one class:

- That's a weird ending. The last thing is blackberries, and that's strange. I would have ended it when he went to bed or something.
- Yeah, it's not very happily ever after, is it?
- Maybe it should just end with that page [the next-to-last page] and the one tablespoon.
- Maybe if the last page was empty, I'd put *all* the characters in there. I'd make it bigger and show some clouds for the father, too.

This stance of suggesting alternatives to the plot was a common feature of the discussion in seven classrooms. For example, children had suggestions for resolving Peter's predicament of being caught in the gooseberry net:

- I'd take off the jacket and I'd start jettin' outta there!
- I might just eat the jacket! I might get sick, but at least you wouldn't die!
- I'd nibble off the buttons, 'cause bunnies got good teeth for that, and it's the buttons that's caught. Then his shirt would come off.
- Maybe he could just jump hard and tear the net.

Children's engagement in this literary experience was quite high. They reacted with predictive warning when Peter squeezed under the garden gate ("Uh-oh, he's gonna be in real trouble now!"); encouraged Peter along with the sparrows ("Don't give up, Peter! You can do it!"); echoed Peter's wariness about the cat ("I wouldn't trust him—some cats is mean"); and rejoiced at Peter's escape ("Thank *God* he didn't get killed!").

Commonly Occurring Themes

Although the children's responses varied across the fifteen transcripts, there were four topics that were common to over half of the classroom discussions.

Disobeying parents and consequences. Peter Rabbit made children think about times they were rebellious like Peter, and about the punishments that they received. They spoke of being forbidden to go outside, cross the street, visit a friend who lived far away, "be out of my mom's sight," and disobeying in other ways. Curiously, there was no discussion in any of the classrooms about the fact that Peter received no punishment for his actions, other than the natural consequence of not feeling well and missing his supper. Children seemed to relish talking about what punishments *they* had received for disobeying or doing something naughty. Common punishments included being barred from watching television, being grounded, getting sent to one's room, losing playtime, and getting a "whipping" or a spanking: " My dad gives me a spanking when he gets mad at me. He tells me that he is going to 'get into my world'! Sometimes he gets mad when I do my homework sloppy and makes me do the whole thing over again!"

Losing one's clothing. This was another common topic of discussion. Children spoke of losing mittens, sweaters, coats, scarves, jackets, shoes, and (in one case) a swimming suit! One child told of losing her shoes: "I lost my shoes one time and I never ever found them and they was my best shoes and I had got them the same day I lost them." Losing buttons and tearing one's clothing were also frequently discussed.

Discussion about food. Food figures largely in *Peter Rabbit*. Peter's sisters pick blackberries, and his mother goes to the baker's to buy bread and currant buns. Food is the primary temptation that lures Peter into Mr. McGregor's garden, and Peter's sisters enjoy a meal at the end of the story while Peter goes to bed with just a dose of camomile tea. As well, the threat of *becoming* food—for Mr. and Mrs. McGregor or the cat—is the source of most of the tension in the story. The transcripts contain many conversational stretches on the topic of food. Just after the teacher read that ". . . he ate some lettuces and some French beans; and then he ate some radishes," children commented,

- You're making me hungry!
- I hate radishes.
- You're making me hungry, too.
- What's radishes?

- They're vegetables.
- They're red.
- Yum, I love carrots.

Children also talked about the idea of a rabbit being made into a pie, at first questioning the concept ("A pie? A pie that you, like, eat? Real? Oh man!") and then discussing how, exactly, one would go about making a rabbit into a pie:

- They killed him. And then they chopped him up . . .
- And they cooked him, like a chicken.
- They split him through his body, and they took the skin off, and they cooked him.

Being chased. Children easily identified with the situation of being chased. Most of their comments related to being chased by dogs. For example, a kindergartener reported that "A dog was chasing me. We was playing 'What color is the egg?' and then I was running and a dog was chasing me. It was a pit bull." In a few instances, the chaser was human: "I got chased just last week. I was walking to my friend's house, and some old crazy man started after me, but I got away. My heart was beatin' so fast!"

In terms of the general tone of the discussions, I found that the story was taken very seriously by the children. It would be possible to find *Peter Rabbit* amusing or whimsical, and in one classroom, there was a great deal of laughter and light-hearted comments. In the other 14 classrooms, however, the tone was earnest, almost solemn. Peter's predicaments and dangers were approached with serious faces and thoughtful speculation. The commonly occurring themes discussed above are neither light-hearted nor unsubstantial; they deal with some of the daily anxieties and preoccupations of all children, and include concerns about issues facing young urban children in distinctive ways. For the children in this study, *Peter Rabbit* was an invitation to talk about these concerns.

Children's Own Stories

The stories children told combined elements of *Peter Rabbit* with their own experiences and inventions. This mix of reality and imagination, of story events, memories, and fantasies produced fascinating oral performances. In "storying" about the story, children also seemed to vie to "one up" each other, in telling longer and more complicated narratives that signified[18] on *Peter Rabbit* and on the other stories. For example, Peter's "trembling with fright" after almost being caught in the toolshed elicited this extended story:

Teacher: Have you ever been so frightened by something that you would start shaking and be nervous?
Child: (1) Well, one day, my Mom, she had told me not to go somewhere. (2) One day my Mom had told me not to go where my next door neighbor's bar is because she was going to put some more [unintelligible] through it, and I had went in there and I had grabbed a lot of carrots and I had gotten full. (3) So Mrs. Mc . . . um . . . so Mrs . . . um . . . whatever, she had caught me and I ran and I jumped in a pool. (4) And I went to my house and I jumped in a pool and she . . . and I sneezed and she caught me 'cause I was allergic to pool water and she had caught me. (5) I was allergic to the chlorine that they put in the water.
Teacher: The chlorine, mmm hmm.
Child: (6) Yeah, I was allergic to chlorine, and when I got in the pool I sneezed and swum out of the pool and I ran across the street and . . . and I ran across the street and I had got scared that she had tried to, um, catch me so she could kill me and eat me, and I was, like, You can't do that, because if you do that, God won't forgive you.
Teacher: God won't forgive you.
Child: (7) And then I had ran 'cause I wasn't going to get hurt, and my mother put me to bed without no food. And then . . . she, he . . .
Teacher: She put you to bed without what?
Child: Without my dinner. (8) And then the next morning I did it again.
Teacher: Oh, OK. Well, we're going to go on. But you were frightened. That's a good example, OK.
Child: (9) And then I got scared, and I had got the shivers.

In this fascinating little vignette, the child, a six year old, utilizes at least eight of the plot elements and details of *Peter Rabbit*. Situating herself as Peter, this little girl alternates between first- and third-person narration. Like Peter, she:

- is warned by mother not to go some place clearly off-limits: a bar (1)
- goes anyway (2)
- eats carrots and gets full (2)
- jumps in water [a pool is a fine substitute for a watering can!] (3)
- sneezes (4)

- reports that the next door neighbor was trying to kill her and eat her (6)
- is put to bed by her mother (7)
- is frightened and shivering (9)

Several features of this child's story are, of course, not in *The Tale of Peter Rabbit:* the allergy to chlorine as the cause of the sneeze; the admonition that "God won't forgive you"; being caught; going to bed without any food as a punishment (different from Peter's illness and inability to join in the supper); and doing "it" again the next morning. In these ways, the story is modified, extended, and injected with elements of the child's own experience and life. Altogether, it is an artful palimpsest of Potter's original tale.

Jane Yolen's observation that "stories lean on other stories" is exemplified in another child's story:

> One time my mommy told me not to go in somebody's garden, and her name was Mrs. DeVille. "Don't go in Mrs. DeVille's garden because she's very angry and she's very upset when people go in her garden." So I said, "Okay, I won't." Then I was playing with my friends Jasmine and Daniele and Jovana. They said, "Let's play tag in Mrs. DeVille's garden." Mrs. DeVille's garden, you know what's going to happen to her. Then she said, "Let's just be normal people." Normal people. We are normal people and I just went in her garden and they started eating. I was, like, "What are they eating?" They were, like [makes munching sounds]. I said, "What, are you eating tomatoes?" And then suddenly she said [low, grumbling voice], "Who's that eating tomatoes in my garden?" Not me, oh, no!—Mrs. DeVille![19]

In this narrative, the first-grade girl who tells the story appropriates a character from *One Hundred and One Dalmatians*—Mrs. DeVille sounds like the evil Cruella. This child also appropriates the formal structure of the troll's question in the *Three Billy Goats Gruff,* "Who's that tramping over my bridge?", or the witch in Hansel and Gretel, "Who's that nibbling at my house?" From *Peter Rabbit,* this child selects a similar cast of characters: her three friends correspond to Peter's three sisters; she assumes Peter's role; and there are two characters to both caution (mother) and threaten (Mrs. DeVille). This child's own life experiences are also reflected: tomatoes are much more likely to be present in an urban garden than carrots, and she uses the names of three of her friends. Thus, she weaves together the text of her own life and at least three other texts in constructing this little narrative.

Other life experiences were utilized in interpreting *Peter Rabbit*. In one class, children referred to a pet rabbit in another class at their school. In four classes, there was considerable discussion about how, exactly, one would make a pie out of a rabbit (Peter's father), and what it would taste like; a number of children had eaten rabbit, and liked it. The talk in three classrooms took the turn of discussing how Peter was a "chip off the old block" because his father had also gone into Mr. McGregor's garden; this led several children to confess that, even when they knew something was wrong, and were punished for it, they still "did it again." This also led to speculation about Peter's father as a ne'er-do-well whose actions had hurt his family:

> Well, his dad didn't care—he was bad and he got into trouble and got killed, and then Peter's mom had to take care of all of 'em.
>
> My dad's in jail, but my grandma takes care of us, too.

In this brief, poignant exchange, we see children thinking about Mrs. Rabbit as a single mother—burdened with sole responsibility for four offspring, one of whom is recalcitrant and headed for certain trouble like his absent father. In contrast to Mrs. Rabbit's isolated situation, however, children pointed out the strong extended family supports in their communities.

In one kindergarten classroom, rather than focusing on Peter's disobedience, children wanted to talk about their feelings during occasions when they were separated from their mothers. Thus, the focus was less on Peter's disobedience and punishment than on his feelings of fright and anxiety.

CONCLUSION

It is clear that this story still appeals to contemporary urban children; kindergartners and first graders in a number of classrooms responded to this classic tale with enthusiasm and a great variety of provocative responses. Despite some difficulties with the language and phrasing of the story, they socially constructed an interpretation of the story with each other and with their teachers. At the same time, they constructed many meaningful connections to their own lives. Their doing so suggests, that, in our concern to expose children to literature that is "culturally relevant," we should not conceptualize this phrase too narrowly.

Peter Rabbit became culturally relevant for these urban children; they *made* it relevant for themselves. As well, the experience of discussing and interpreting classic stories is a form of cultural capital for children, important for success in school; it is one of the cultural codes of power that is important for all children to learn.[20] It is equally important for children to experience stories that mirror their own lives and allow them easily to identify with characters and situations in stories. Thus, the most sound pedagogical practice may be to read a great variety of stories with urban children, including traditional and classic stories, as well as contemporary multicultural literature.

In a time when many curricula are emphasizing a deficit model of literacy for urban schools, with an emphasis on skill and drill approaches, the experience of talking about and interpreting stories is often considered a frill; this study shows children engaged in the process of understanding how a story works, and relating it to their own lives. These engagements are critical for children's literacy development, if they are to become more than mere decoders of text. Further research that might be done in this area could compare responses from the children in this study to the responses of children from suburban or rural areas in order to ascertain similarities and differences in the discussions. This study also suggests the importance of more research on the ways in which contemporary urban children make other classic and traditional stories relevant to their own lives.

Author's Note: I would like to express my sincere thanks to the teachers and doctoral students who assisted in this project: Michael Allen, Marta Bloy, Susan Browne, Isabell Cardonick, Deborah Cornatzer, Patricia Daley, Charles Haitz, Theresa Miller, Mary Beth Schaefer, Diana Schwinge, Caltropia Wilder, Angela Wiseman, Michael Wyncoop, and several others who elected not to be named.

NOTES

1. Beatrix Potter, *The Tale of Peter Rabbit* (1902; reprint, London: Penguin Books, 1991).

2. J. F. Eastman, "*The Tale of Peter Rabbit:* A Small Masterpiece," in *Touchstones: Reflections on the Best in Children's Literature,* vol. 3, ed. P. Nodelman (West Lafayette, Ind.: ChLA Publications, 1989), 100–107; M. Mackey, *The Case of Peter Rabbit: Changing Conditions of Literature for Children* (New York: Garland Publishing, 1998).

3. R. K. MacDonald, "Why This Is Still 1893: *The Tale of Peter Rabbit* and

Beatrix Potter's Manipulations of Time into Timelessness," *Children's Literature Association Quarterly* 10 (Winter 1986): 185–87.

4. L. Galda, "Mirrors and Window: Reading As Transformation," in *Literature-Based Instruction: Reshaping the Curriculum,* ed. T. E. Raphael and K. H. Au (Norwood, N.J.: Christopher Gordon Publishers), 1–11.

5. S. Landes, "Teaching Literary Criticism in the Elementary Grades: A Symposium," in *Children and Their Literature: A Readings Book,* ed. J. P. May (West Layfayette, Ind.: ChLA Publications, 1983), 163.

6. R. Beach, *A Teacher's Introduction to Reader-Response Theories* (Urbana, Ill.: National Council of Teachers of English, 1993); Louise Rosenblatt, *The Reader, the Text, and the Poem: The Transactional Theory of the Literary Work* (Carbondale: Southern Illinois University Press, 1978).

7. Stanley Fish, *Is There a Text in This Class? The Authority of Interpretive Communities* (Cambridge, Mass.: Harvard University Press, 1980).

8. J. Culler, *Structuralist Poetics: Structuralism, Linguistics, and the Study of Literature* (Ithaca, N.Y.: Cornell University Press, 1975).

9. Lawrence R. Sipe, "The Idea of a Classic," *Journal of Children's Literature* 22 (Spring 1996): 31–33.

10. Wolfgang Iser, *The Act of Reading: A Theory of Aesthetic Response* (Baltimore, Md.: Johns Hopkins University Press, 1978).

11. Potter, *The Tale of Peter Rabbit.*

12. M. Martinez and W. Teale, "Teacher Storybook Reading Style: A Comparison of Six Teachers," *Research in the Teaching of English* 27, no. 2 (May 1993): 175–99.

13. J. Sinclair and M. Coulthard, *Towards an Analysis of Discourse: The English Used by Teachers and Pupils* (London: Oxford University Press, 1975).

14. A. Strauss and J. Corbin, *Basics of Qualitative Research: Grounded Theory Procedures and Techniques* (Newbury Park, Calif.: Sage, 1990).

15. B. Glaser and A. Strauss, *The Discovery of Grounded Theory* (Chicago: Aldine, 1978); Y. S. Lincoln and E. G. Guba. *Naturalistic Inquiry* (Newbury Park, Calif.: Sage, 1985); R. Bogdan and S. Biklen, *Qualitative Research in Education* (Boston: Allyn and Bacon, 1992).

16. R. Beach and R. Philippot, "Framing Strategies in High School Students' Large-Group Literature Discussions," paper presented at the National Reading Conference 49th Annual Meeting, Orlando, Fla., December 1999.

17. Mackey, *The Case of Peter Rabbit: Changing Conditions of Literature for Children.*

18. H. L. Gates, *The Signifying Monkey: A Theory of African-American Literary Criticism* (New York: Oxford University Press, 1988).

19. J. Yolen, *Touch Magic: Fantasy, Faerie, and Folklore in the Literature of Children* (New York: Philomel, 1981).

20. J. C. Passeron and P. Bourdieu, *Reproduction in Education, Society, and Culture,* trans. R. Nice (London: Sage, 1977); L. Delpit, *Other People's Children: Cultural Conflict in the Classroom* (New York: New Press, 1995).

BIBLIOGRAPHY

Beach, R. *A Teacher's Introduction to Reader-Response Theories*. Urbana, Ill.: National Council of Teachers of English, 1993.

Beach, R., and R. Philippot. "Framing Strategies in High School Students' Large-Group Literature Discussions," paper presented at the National Reading Conference 49th Annual Meeting, Orlando, Fla., December 1999.

Culler, J. *Structuralist Poetics: Structuralism, Linguistics and the Study of Literature*. Ithaca, N.Y.: Cornell University Press, 1975.

Delpit, L. *Other People's Children: Cultural Conflict in the Classroom*. New York: New Press, 1995.

Eastman, J. F. "*The Tale of Peter Rabbit:* A Small Masterpiece." Pp. 100–107 in *Touchstones: Reflections on the Best in Children's Literature,* vol. 3, edited by P. Nodelman. West Lafayette, Ind.: ChLA Publications, 1989.

Fish, S. *Is There a Text in This Class? The Authority of Interpretive Communities*. Cambridge, Mass.: Harvard University Press, 1980.

Galda, L. "Mirrors and Windows: Reading As Transformation." Pp. 1–11 in *Literature-Based Instruction: Reshaping the Curriculum,* edited by T. E. Raphael and K. H. Au. Norwood, Mass.: Christopher-Gordon Publishers, 1998.

Gates, H. L. *The Signifying Monkey: A Theory of African-American Literary Criticism*. New York: Oxford University Press, 1988.

Glaser, B., and A. Strauss. *The Discovery of Grounded Theory.* Chicago: Aldine, 1978.

Iser, W. *The Act of Reading: A Theory of Aesthetic Response.* Baltimore, Md.: Johns Hopkins University Press, 1978.

Landes, S. "Teaching Literary Criticism in the Elementary Grades: A Symposium." Pp. 161–64 in *Children and Their Literature: A Readings Book,* edited by J. P. May. West Lafayette, Ind.: ChLA Publications, 1983.

Lincoln, Y. S., and E. G. Guba. *Naturalistic Inquiry.* Newbury Park, Calif.: Sage, 1985.

MacDonald, R. K. "Why This Is Still 1893: *The Tale of Peter Rabbit* and Beatrix Potter's Manipulations of Time into Timelessness." *Children's Literature Association Quarterly* 10 (1986): 185–87.

Mackey, M. *The Case of Peter Rabbit: Changing Conditions of Literature for Children.* New York: Garland Publishing, 1998.

Martinez, M., and W. Teale. "Teacher Storybook Reading Style: A Comparison of Six Teachers." *Research in the Teaching of English* 27, no. 2 (May 1993): 175–99.

Passeron, J. C., and P. Bourdieu. *Reproduction in Education, Society, and Culture,* translated by R. Nice. London: Sage, 1977.

Potter, B. *The Tale of Peter Rabbit* (1902; reprint London: Penguin, 1991).

Rosenblatt, L. *The Reader, the Text, the Poem: The Transactional Theory of the Literary Work.* Carbondale: Southern Illinois University Press, 1978.

Sinclair, J., and M. Coulthard. *Towards an Analysis of Discourse: The English Used by Teachers and Pupils*. London: Oxford University Press, 1975.

Sipe, L. R. "The Idea of a Classic." *Journal of Children's Literature* 22, no. 1 (Spring 1996): 31–33.

Strauss, A., and J. Corbin. *Basics of Qualitative Research: Grounded Theory Procedures and Techniques*. Newbury Park, Calif.: Sage, 1990.

Yolen, J. *Touch Magic: Fantasy, Faerie, and Folklore in the Literature of Children*. New York: Philomel, 1981.

2

An Unusual Hero: Perspective and Point of View in *The Tale of Peter Rabbit*

Carole Scott

Like the Victorian-Edwardian period itself, the apparently straightforward *Tale of Peter Rabbit*—the archetypical naughty-boy story with appropriate moral ending—readily reveals its intricate nature as soon as its surface is penetrated. While the story itself may be relatively simple, the complexity of the narrative perspective and point of view epitomizes the multiple levels of apparent and covert ideologies, values, attitudes, biases, and hypocrisies that the era sustained and toward which Potter's own ambivalences are apparent. Margaret Mackey, in *The Case of Peter Rabbit,* states that "On the surface, she is clearly on the side of law and order. . . . But the detached tone with which Potter describes Peter's disobedience actually functions to raise the question of just whose side she is on."[1] This important question deserves careful attention, and not only raises issues that involve the techniques and forms of communication that Potter employs to convey her ambivalent perspectives, but also leads us to examine the nature and role of her protagonist.

It is true that somewhat moralistic overtones pervade the book's verbal narrative and that only adults' words are recorded as spoken (we never hear directly from Peter or his sisters). However, I am not alone in my judgment that the sympathies of Potter, and thus the reader, are with Peter, despite, or perhaps even because of, his naughtiness, his flouting of the adults' received wisdom.[2] The inherent discord or disharmony between moral stance and affect gives energetic life to the plot. Although Peter disobeys his mother and causes her anxiety and grief, commits trespass and theft, and evades paternalistic authority symbolized by Mr. McGregor (who also represents the landed sector of society defending its borders from propertyless rabble), nonetheless he escapes all punishment for his misdeeds, except for a temporary stomachache resulting from his greediness. We cannot even applaud Peter's actions as revenge for his father's death, for it is his delight in breaking rules that motivates him.

While Potter as a young woman was a comfortable supporter of the class system and expresses in her diary her lack of sympathy with unemployed rioters to whose antisocial actions she was a witness,[3] there is little doubt that Peter, who stands for rebellion on all fronts, is the hero of the story. The techniques Potter uses to manipulate her reader to identify with Peter, and the characteristics of this unlikely hero will form the focus of this discussion.

THE ROLE OF WORD-IMAGE INTERACTION IN ESTABLISHING PERSPECTIVE AND POINT OF VIEW

Narratologists have made many attempts to grapple with the viewpoints from which a story is told, categorizing the relationship between the author and his or her narrative voice or voices, and the techniques involved in description, dialogue, and analysis that persuade the reader to see the characters and events as the author intends. We are all familiar with the range stretching from the omniscient third person to the single character's filtered analysis, with the variety of explicit and implicit values and world views of author and narrative voice(s), and with the tone and use of words that convince us with their honesty or, by means of delicate irony, subtly undermine the apparent statement.

The complexity of narrative perspective is multiplied in picturebooks, for pictures present characters and events in different ways and with different techniques from verbal texts, providing additional or alternative perspectives that add dimension to the reader's experience. The dynamic and sometimes unrecognized interaction between verbal and visual perspective and point of view deepens the reader's involvement in and comprehension of the story. In Potter's books, because she is both author and illustrator, the interplay between the two forms of communication is of special interest, since the two together express the creator's intention.[4]

In many of Beatrix Potter's books, *Peter Rabbit* included, the boundary between verbal text and illustration is absolute, in one sense at least, for words and pictures are on separate pages, divided by the gutter between them. In *Peter Rabbit,* except for the title page, cover and endpapers, no word of any kind appears in the pictures, and no hint of illustration creeps into the words. This format is totally consistent, with text and picture facing each other and printed with text back-to-back with text and picture back-to-back with picture, providing a sequence of doublespreads that read picture/text, text/picture, picture/text, etc.

This absolute division is softened, though, by the absence of a frame or border around the illustration, and by the irregular shape of the picture, which gives it a sense of freedom on the page rather than a feeling of being fixed in one place or form. This effect is reinforced by the variability in the illustrations' shape and the degree of contextual detail they provide. While the picture of Peter looking from the wheelbarrow toward the gate (48)[5] is in rough rectangle form with detailed foreground, middle, and distant views in perspective, the picture of Peter jumping into the watering can is completely without background or contextual setting (36). Between these two extremes is the picture of Mr. McGregor chasing Peter and waving a rake (27) in which the patch of ground on which Peter stands and the strip between them is featured, thus depicting the relationship between the two figures in spatial terms, but providing no further detail in the way of context.[6]

This continual shift in perspective, scope of vision, and setting creates a fluctuating rather than a fixed viewpoint. The variability of shape, detail, and degree of perspective finds echoes in the verbal text that involves changes in extent—from a few words to a full page—as well as in voice, diction, and approach. Thus the mutability of the two forms, especially the visual inconsistency, tends to subvert the formal separation between the picture page and the word page, as does the rhythmic reversal of picture-text order. We are alerted to the restless interaction that occurs between the facing pages with their different modes of expression, rather than to the gutter that divides them.

The narrative voice sometimes takes an adult judgmental tone: "Flopsy, Mopsy and Cottontail . . . were good little bunnies." "But Peter . . . was very naughty" (17–18). And certainly Mother Rabbit's perspective is focalized through her instructions and warnings to her children, and in her concern about Peter's irresponsibility: "It was the second little jacket and pair of shoes that Peter had lost in a fortnight!" (54). More often, the narrative voice is objective, even distanced in its presentation, and contrasts with the closeness and immediacy of the pictures. The full justification of the text adds to the formality of the tone. As we examine the interaction between the two more closely, the skillfully crafted dynamic becomes increasingly apparent. While the narrative voice of the verbal text may be ambiguous, the illustrations are clear.

The story opens with a picture of wild rabbits at the root of a tree, but the narrative voice of the accompanying text immediately challenges the veracity of the woodland scene, since the rabbits, though pictured as wild, are named and humanized. This naming is a foreshadowing of the next doublespread, where both image and words transform the rabbits into clothed creatures capable of human speech. This initial picture, though, establishes the perspective of the illustrations, for the rabbits are looking directly at the reader, at their own level, not upward to a large human being. This sense of closeness and immediacy is reinforced by the limits of the illustration, for the picture is all foreground, and the line of sight includes just a few feet of the tree trunk. While a hazy background of other trees provides an impressionistic context, the scene itself is quite limited, rather like looking through a peephole. This low-to-the-ground and close-up, limited view is repeated in most of the illustrations. Almost every picture features Peter close up and within touching distance, focusing on the small rabbit and helping us to identify with him. When Mr. McGregor appears, he is always on the far side of Peter; it is Peter's line of sight that we share. The illustrations rarely give us a long view or range of perspective: when they do, the reader takes Peter's point of view, or one close to it. Examples may be found in two consecutive pictures that feature Peter and the gate to freedom: the first shows Mr. McGregor interposed between Peter and the gate (48); the second features Mr. McGregor running toward it and us, but too far away to catch Peter (51).

Setting the viewpoint of the illustrations so low to the ground and with such a constricted vision continually reinforces the sense of peril and the reader's identification with Peter and his plight. This identification dramatically instills fear and tension in the reader, and interacts with the frequently distanced voice of the verbal narrative. An excellent example is the scene where Mr. McGregor attempts to trap Peter under a garden sieve (34–35). The voice of the verbal narrative is matter of fact, and the use of words cleverly chosen for their inappropriate affect: "Mr. McGregor came up with a sieve, which he intended to pop upon the top of

Peter; but Peter wriggled out just in time, leaving his jacket behind him." The words "came up with" are inadequate to express Mr. McGregor's motivation to hunt and trap the plaguey rabbit, whereas "pop upon the top of" is tea-party language, a casual and bland expression that masks and trivializes Mr. McGregor's murderous intention to capture, kill, and eat Peter. The choice of the third verb in the series, "wriggle out," is once again a gentle, restrained term to describe a fight for one's life.

While the narrative voice passes politely and distantly over the scene, the illustration offers a very different interpretation. Although the reader is not directly under the sieve with Peter, watching it descend, the reader's eye is extremely close, and the movement of the sieve is reinforced by the image of the three birds that fly away to left and right. Peter's crouching stance, with forepaws low and head and ears down and thrown back, his eyes blank and all energy centered in the hind legs that propel him forward, transmits the sense of desperate escape, while the very large hands that hold the sieve accentuate the sense of disparate power. At the same time, the phrase "leaving his jacket behind him" takes shape in the picture's image of Peter's nakedness, his transformation back into a simple nameless animal. And the jacket on the ground behind him still snared in the netting communicates his hairsbreadth deliverance.

These two pages not only express very different affective messages but also involve diverse and contradictory attitudes. While the verbal narrative, in its objective way, focalizes first Mr. McGregor and then Peter as it describes their actions, the choice of words for the narrative voice, which reduces the drama and intensity to an everyday occurrence, is clearly that of the powerful class and paternalistic authority of which Mr. McGregor is representative. The major conflict takes place between Mr. McGregor and Peter, between the fixed order of society and the forces that seek to undermine it, between those who have and those who want, between human civilization and animal nature. Mr. McGregor is clear about the rules, crying, "Stop thief!" as he chases the intruder. Rabbits reduce the output of Mr. McGregor's business, availing themselves of food, which is owned by another, and which, although there is plenty, is not for them. The land has been claimed, fenced, and gated, and they must stay outside. Although the forces of nature produce the food, the rabbits may not enter the garden, which belongs to human beings. Entering the garden leads to the loss of the clothes that mitigate the boundary between animals and human beings, and to possible loss of life. Eat and you will be eaten is the warning.

Meanwhile the pictures, which involve the reader in Peter's plight, are operating in a very different realm, one in which the have-nots see no reason why they should not help themselves to nature's bounty, and where gates and fences are boundaries to be challenged. Peter, it is true, does not enter the garden because he is hungry, for his mother feeds him well, but because he will not accept restraints to his freedom. For this he is willing to risk danger, and the loss of the clothes that may make him more human but that hamper his liberty of movement. This restriction is expressed not only in his narrow escape from the sieve but also in the early picture in which Mrs. Rabbit buttons a tight collar around his neck, while telling him, "don't get into mischief" (13). Thus the socio-political message of the verbal text is countered repeatedly by the individualistic stance of the pictures.

A comparable interaction between verbal and pictorial presentation may be found when Peter is first caught in the gooseberry net. "I think he might have got away altogether," says the narrator, using one of the "I"s that make her presence felt, "if he had not unfortunately run into a gooseberry net, and got caught by the large buttons on his jacket" (30). Once again the diction sets the action at a distance: "unfortunately" and "got caught" are unemotional, reserved words that accentuate the observer's remoteness and render the action low in drama and energy. And the tangential comment that follows, "It was a blue jacket with brass buttons, quite new," further detaches the narrator from the scene with its present danger. In contrast, the illustration shows Peter upside down, pinioned into immobility, enmeshed in the netting, with his feet poking through. The reader's viewpoint is right at ground level, the level of Peter's eye, a technique that thrusts the reader directly into the net. And because the netting forms the edge of the narrowly focused scene on all sides, with just a corner free, the sense of entrapment is accentuated.

Potter's balance of text and picture involves a variety of alternative functions, for example, disharmony in focalization between words and picture. The doublespread on pages 40–41 focalizes Mr. McGregor in the verbal text, but Peter in the illustration: "[Mr. McGregor] tried to put his foot upon Peter, who jumped out of a window, upsetting three plants. The window was too small for Mr. McGregor, and he was tired of running after Peter. He went back to his work" (41). The illustration, featuring Peter in mid-jump, once again puts us at Peter's eye-level, while Mr. McGregor's presence is represented by only a hob-nailed boot. But the identification with Peter is less intense than in some of the earlier pictures, for Peter is drawn as a veritable rabbit, with no hint of human posture or movement.

An interesting variant of this technique is found in a later double-spread where the verbal text describes Mr. McGregor's thought process and action: "Mr. McGregor hung up the little jacket and the shoes for a scare-crow to frighten the blackbirds" (52–53). The picture is one of the few that offer a longer perspective, and the angle of view is set quite high, so that the observer looks down on the scene from a raised position. While the words are simply descriptive, the illustration makes a clear comment. First of all, even though Peter himself isn't present, it is Peter's coat and shoes, placed upon a wooden cross, that dominate the picture, while Mr. McGregor is a faint figure in the background. Secondly, Mr. McGregor's action is humorously depicted as completely ineffective, for the robin perches on one of the scarecrow's arms, while three birds, at least two of them crows, stand at the base of the pole, looking inquisitively up. Two more large birds are sketched in a little further back. None is in the least afraid of the scarecrow, nor does Mr. McGregor's presence nearby cause any distress.

One rather different but very interesting technique shows a reversal of the more common picture-text combination in which the illustration carries the drama of the action in contrast to the verbal text's diffident or tangential discourse. In this case the words carry the action and the affect, while the illustration provides the diversion. "Peter was most dreadfully frightened," the text relates. "He rushed all over the garden, for he had forgotten the way back to the gate. He lost one of his shoes among the cabbages, and the other shoe amongst the potatoes" (29). The accompanying illustration focuses not on Peter's plight, his actions, or his feelings, but upon a robin peering curiously at one of his lost shoes. While the verbal text certainly gives the access to the picture, the illustration itself distracts from the action. Placed midway between the illustrations of Peter fleeing Mr. McGregor and Peter caught in the gooseberry net, this detailed, static image has an after-the-fact effect and distances the reader from the story. The little vignette features a small corner of the garden, and the perspective is not as close up nor as low to the ground as so many others. The large, almost square picture has a stillness and self-sufficiency about it, separate from the parallel action of Peter's desperate flight. This particular combination provides an anomaly to the more common pattern we have analyzed, and the verbal focus upon Peter's feelings permits the authorial voice to express in words the identification with Peter that had been repressed by the didactic voice but expressed through the images.

Potter does not always use contradictory effects in her word-picture interaction. The doublespread that features Peter standing by the locked door offers a harmony of the techniques and assumptions that guide the point of view (44–45). The verbal text is once again descriptive in a relatively objective manner, but, unlike the earlier passage cited, it states the facts without flippancy. Here the theme of disempowerment and inability to overcome obstacles is reinforced in both words and pictures: the door "was locked, and there was not room . . . to squeeze underneath"; the mouse "had such a large pea in her mouth that she could not answer. She only shook her head at him." The statement "Peter began to cry" is simply a reporting of fact, but the words are true and clear without irony or attitude, and set less distance between Peter's emotions and the reader.

The picture of Peter is a masterpiece. He is without clothes but, unlike his presentation in the earlier unclothed pictures, Peter is not just an animal, for his body, though anatomically accurate, as are all Potter's drawings, is posed in a human stance. He stands upright, one foot resting on the other as he leans against the door, and his left paw rests upon the door above his head, while his right is held against his face. A large tear runs from his eye. At least one critic has likened the illustration to Anna Lea Merritt's *Love Locked Out* (1889), with which Potter would have been familiar and which represents a spiritual union denied by death.[7] Whether or not the reader carries this somewhat spiritual reference into the illustration, the sense of identification with Peter is intense and the mood of entrapment and disillusion emphatic in both the picture and in the events described: the locked door, the too narrow space beneath, the only other living creature unable to speak to him. When Peter begins to cry, his human childlikeness speaks strongly to the reader because the illustration and the verbal text work in harmony to present his hopelessness and fearful exhaustion. The earlier vision of the garden as wealth and Peter as invader has given way to the sense of the garden as a place of fear and captivity and of Peter as its prisoner.

This analysis of the ways in which perspective and point of view operate in the interplay of verbal text and illustration reveals Potter's mastery of the picturebook form. Her manipulation of the reader's perception of and sympathy for her protagonist and his challenge of the sociopolitical boundaries she appears to defend is subtle and subversive, for the unmistakable perspective of the illustrations patently and intentionally undermines the studied ambiguous stance of her verbal message.

PETER AS UNLIKELY HERO

Potter's ambivalence, which raised Mackey's question of "just whose side she is on," is not simply a manifestation of Potter's own feelings about individual freedom and her experience of the constraints of the accepted paternalistic Victorian society that many of her works express.[8] It is also strongly tied to the accepted concept of an appropriate hero, and interrogates my earlier affirmation that "there is little doubt that Peter, who stands for rebellion on all fronts, is the hero of the story."

In considering the significance of Potter's perspective and her foregrounding of her protagonist, I have been repeatedly reminded of another rebellious figure challenging authority and established order, Milton's Lucifer in *Paradise Lost*. A number of readers, especially those with Romantic tendencies, have seen Lucifer-Satan rather than Christ as the "real" hero of the epic, for Satan displays any number of heroic traits with which readers may sympathize and identify: courage, leadership, intelligence, fortitude and resolve in the face of adversity, and a longing for freedom and self-determination. Thus, like Potter, Milton has provoked similar charges of ambivalence in his relationship to the established order, his choice of hero, and his covert heresies (though in Milton's case these were religious rather than sociopolitical).

While the supporter of Satan points to the heroism of the rebel who defies the power of the established order and sacrifices everything for individual autonomy, a study of the perspectives established by Milton reveals a different picture. Although *Paradise Lost* is a purely verbal text, Milton's verse is vivid in visual description and in image and, like Potter's work, displays a similarly fluctuating perspective. In Book I, Lucifer-Satan is foregrounded and presented through epic similes as larger than life, as he frees himself from the chains on the burning lake and presides over the construction of a great hall, where in Book II he addresses his followers in stately rhetoric from a lofty throne.

But this up-close viewpoint is juxtaposed to the longer view: first Milton's simile compares the massing hordes of hell to a swarm of bees, and is accompanied by a switch in perspective, in which "they who now seem'd / In bigness to surpass Earth's Giant Sons / Now less than smallest Dwarfs" (I, 777–9). And, shortly thereafter, when Satan's voyage from hell is described, the perspective of the piece is transformed when seen from God's panoramic viewpoint, and Satan is revealed as a small force in the magnitude of the universe, and compared to a vulture, a wolf, and a cormorant. Thereafter, when the reader is brought close to Satan's side, any sense of magnitude is lost, and Satan's manifestations as toad and snake further distance the reader.

In the case of *Paradise Lost,* the didactic approach of the author is reinforced by the perspective and by the images presented, in complete contrast to the situation in *Peter Rabbit.* Although faced with a degree of ambiguity in his challenge to "justify the ways of God to man," a highly complex task in view of the conflicting values of the time with regard to freedom and authority, the subtle distinctions of church theology and dangers of heresy, and the conventions of the epic genre, Milton manipulates his readers both rationally and emotionally to the conclusion he determines.

Margery Hourihan, in her work *Deconstructing the Hero,* adds an interesting dimension to this discussion of unlikely heroes in her analysis of the adventure story and her inclusion of *Peter Rabbit* as an example. She states that "*The Tale of Peter Rabbit* recognizes the division in our culture between the domestic sphere and the public world where power is situated, just as it recognizes the perceived division between humans and animals but, unlike most hero tales, it values the private world above the public and denies the imagined boundary between humanity and nature."[9] While I am in full agreement with her sense that this book undermines some of the dualities upon which the adventure story is set, I believe that Potter goes much further than Hourihan suggests.

In many ways Peter is the exact antithesis of the qualities that Hourihan identifies as necessary for the traditional hero, a difference that allows Potter to subvert rather than endorse the usual pattern of adventure. According to Hourihan's analysis, the traditional hero of the time is a young, white male; he leaves the civilized order of home to venture into the wilderness; he meets difficulties and dangerous opponents; he overcomes them because he is strong, brave, resourceful, rational, and determined to succeed; he achieves his goal; he returns home and is gratefully welcomed and rewarded. Furthermore, if we examine the good/evil dualism pairs that Hourihan selects from Val Plumwood's[10] list—reason/emotion; civilization/wilderness; reason/nature; male/female; order/chaos; mind-soul/body; human/nonhuman and master/slave—Peter embodies few of the positive aspects and most of the negative ones.

Potter is completely breaking the mold of the hero in this story, for Peter is a small, easily frightened, emotionally driven, and certainly not very rational animal. Although he is male—the one boundary Potter was unable to fracture—he is no heroic representative of the "innate superiority of civilized, rational, male order as against wild, emotional, female chaos" (Hourihan, 17). *The Tale of Peter Rabbit* is thus subversive not only of the period's premises and expectations of what it takes to be a good child—obedient, dutiful, respectful of authority, social mores, and conventions—but of the hero genre itself, together with its implicit values, whereby "the reader is required to admire courage, action, skill and determination, while qualities like creativity, sensitivity and self-questioning have no presence in the hero's world" (Hourihan, 41). Potter's polite, socially correct narrative voice is revealed as a façade, shielding the author from self-revelation.

In her seemingly gentle and her subtle way, Beatrix Potter has, like many other great children's literature authors, laid a depth charge beneath the calm surface of an innocent children's story. Her tale has been providing an explosive force for many generations of children, encouraging them to self-indulgence, disobedience, transgression of social boundaries and ethics, and assertion of their wild, unpredictable nature against the constrictions of civilized living. Potter also implies that this battle will be a constant, cyclical one, for there is no closure to the story, just a temporary hiatus. Mr. McGregor's spoils of victory—Peter's clothes—are hollow, and transient; they do not empower McGregor, as the scarecrow picture reveals, and, as we see in the Benjamin Bunny sequel, Peter has already outgrown them like a snake shedding its skin. The struggle for personal independence will include moments of panic and terror, and real danger. But the subliminal message is that this struggle is what life is all about, and that the price one must pay—a stomachache and no supper—is well worth the exhilaration and self-realization that results from the confrontation.

NOTES

1. Margaret Mackey, *The Case of Peter Rabbit* (New York: Garland, 1998), 5–6.
2. It is interesting that in designing her Peter Rabbit Game, Potter wrote the rules so that "the chances are strongly in favour of Peter." Cited in Judy Taylor's *That Naughty Rabbit* (London: Frederick Warne, 1987), 61.
3. Beatrix Potter, *The Journal of Beatrix Potter,* transcribed by Leslie Linder (London: Frederick Warne, 1966), 172–76. There are a number of other instances of similar sentiments expressed.
4. Maria Nikolajeva and Carole Scott's *How Picturebooks Work* (New York: Garland, 2001) delves into these matters in detail.
5. All page references are made to the original and authorized Warne edition of Beatrix Potter's *The Tale of Peter Rabbit,* this impression, 1993.

6. Mackey suggests that we take the rough ovals as frames and that frame-breaking occurs when an element of the picture (handle, ears, tail) protrudes beyond the background wash (9).

7. Anne Stevenson Hobbs, *Beatrix Potter's Art* (New York: Viking Penguin Inc., 1989), 22–23.

8. For further discussion of this conflict please see my article, "Clothed in Nature or Nature Clothed," *Children's Literature* 22 (New Haven & London: Yale University Press, 1994), 70–89.

9. Margery Hourihan, *Deconstructing the Hero* (London and New York: Routledge, 1997), 218.

10. Val Plumwood, *Feminism and the Mastery of Nature* (London and New York: Routledge, 1993).

BIBLIOGRAPHY

Hobbs, Anne Stevenson. *Beatrix Potter's Art*. New York: Viking Penguin, Inc., 1989.

Hourihan, Margery. *Deconstructing the Hero.* London and New York: Routledge, 1997.

Mackey, Margaret. *The Case of Peter Rabbit: Changing Conditions of Literature for Children.* New York: Garland Press, 1998.

Nikolajeva, Maria, and Carole Scott. *How Picturebooks Work*. New York: Garland Press, 2001.

Plumwood, Val. *Feminism and the Mastery of Nature.* London and New York: Routledge, 1993.

Potter, Beatrix. *The Journal of Beatrix Potter,* transcribed by Leslie Linder. London: F. Warne & Co., 1966.

———. *The Tale of Peter Rabbit.* London: F. Warne & Co., 1993.

Scott, Carole. "Clothed in Nature or Nature Clothed." *Children's Literature* 22 (1994): 70–89.

Taylor, Judy. *That Naughty Rabbit: Beatrix Potter and Peter Rabbit*. London: F. Warne, 1987.

2

PRE-TEXT

Three authors explore Beatrix Potter's background and the conditions that led to the creation of *The Tale of Peter Rabbit*. Out of the unlikely territory of a highly repressed Victorian nursery came an artistic energy that developed and manifested a shrewd understanding of children, animals, and society at large.

In this section, Judy Taylor draws on her extended expertise to look at Potter's life and at the history of the little story. Joyce Irene Whalley similarly mines a wealth of experience to describe Potter's artistic history and its impact on the book. Taking a strikingly different approach, Lissa Paul investigates Potter's grasp of market conditions and new technologies, and applies the contemporary concept of "coolhunting" to the story of how *Peter Rabbit* reached the marketplace.

3

The Story of *The Tale of Peter Rabbit*

Judy Taylor

The claim that *The Tale of Peter Rabbit*, by Beatrix Potter, is the most famous children's book in the world is well justified. The book has certainly stood the test of time: it was first written well over one hundred years ago, and first published exactly one hundred years ago. It has been translated into thirty-six languages, has been read and committed to memory by generation after generation of children, and has inspired ballet, film, and stage productions. Its hero, Peter Rabbit, has been the chosen symbol for countless merchandise campaigns—and has also been the victim of numerous imitations. *The Tale of Peter Rabbit* is indeed the most famous children's book, and it is a book that has a remarkable story of its own.

Now that so much is known about Beatrix Potter herself, it does not seem at all surprising that a rabbit was the hero of her first published work, for rabbits played an important part in her life from early childhood. Beatrix was the first child of wealthy, middle-class parents, who lived comfortably in Bolton Gardens, as fashionable a part of south-west London in the mid-1880s as it is today. The Potter family money was inherited from the Lancashire cotton trade, on Rupert Potter's side from the printing of calico and on Helen Leech Potter's side from the buying and selling of the same product.

The Potters' first child, Helen Beatrix, was born on July 28, 1866, and the baby was looked after in a well-appointed nursery at the top of the house, seeing her parents infrequently as was the custom in families of the Potters' status. An only child for nearly six years, Beatrix led a solitary life. She was also of delicate health and subject to frequent colds and headaches, which led her mother to be overprotective and to discourage outside friendships. When the Potters' second child, Walter Bertram, was born in 1872 and Beatrix was no longer the centre of her nurse's attention, the little girl found solace in the nursery's many books—and in her painting and drawing. Both her parents had sketched and painted, her father amusing himself by drawing while studying for the Bar.

Like many prosperous London families, the Potters went frequently to the country, for short holidays in April and May while the house was being thoroughly spring-cleaned, for longer, three-month holidays in the late summer, and for weekends as breaks from the noise and bustle of the city. Rupert Potter's father was the Liberal Member of Parliament for Carlisle and lived with his wife in a large house called Camfield Place, with a farm and an extensive garden, near Hatfield in Hertfordshire, some thirty miles from Bolton Gardens. Beatrix went to stay with her grandparents from an early age, her parents sometimes leaving her there with her nurse while they resumed their busy social lives in London. It was at Camfield that Beatrix's interest in nature and in the countryside was first nurtured, there that she learned the names of wildflowers and birds, and there that she first observed the ways of animals, both wild and domesticated.

When Beatrix was five years old, Rupert Potter took his family to Scotland for three months in the late summer, to a mansion he had rented in Perthshire. For the next eleven years Dalguise House, with its surrounding woods and fields and its spectacular views over the broad and winding River Tay, was the Potter summer home. When Bertram was old enough, he shared his sister's expeditions into the countryside, and together the two children drew and painted all they saw. Two of Beatrix's sketchbooks from her Dalguise visits of 1875 and 1876 have survived and are in the Potter Collection at the Victoria and Albert Museum in London. They are filled with carefully observed drawings of the life around her, together with copies of illustrations from the books she knew, meticulous records of birds' eggs and of the habits of caterpillars, and some half-human, half-rabbit fantasy figures at play.

There was nearly always a dog in the Potter household, and both the children kept pets, ranging from frogs and ring-snakes to hedgehogs and a blue jay, but Beatrix's favorites were always her rabbits. The first known to us by name was Tommy, with her at Dalguise in 1877 and the subject of a letter to the eleven-year-old girl from her father's friend, William Gaskell: "I hope [he] is taking his food properly and doing well. If you think he remembers me, please give him my kind regards."[1] Some years later Beatrix recorded in her *Journal* that she had surreptitiously brought a rabbit home to Bolton Gardens, bought "from a London bird shop in a paper bag. His existence was not observed by the nursery authorities for a week."[2]

Even when she was in her early twenties, Beatrix was still keeping rabbits. Her great favorite was Benjamin H. Bouncer, or Bounce for short. She covered the pages of her sketchbooks with drawings of Benjamin from every angle, when he was asleep or awake, while he was washing his ears or nibbling at the lettuces in the garden. And it was with Benjamin's help that Beatrix received her first commercial payment.

Every Christmas, Beatrix made greeting cards for the family, slipping them under their plates at breakfast on Christmas morning, and in 1889 her brother Bertram suggested that the cards were good enough for her to offer to a publisher, in the hope that they might bring enough money for the two of them to buy a small printing press. With additional encouragement from her uncle, Henry Roscoe, Beatrix prepared six new designs, using Benjamin Bouncer as her model. To everyone's delight the second publisher they approached, Hildesheimer & Faulkner, not only bought the pictures but asked the artist for more. They reproduced Beatrix's six original designs first as greetings cards and then used them as illustrations to a set of rhymes by the prolific versifier Frederic E. Weatherly in a booklet entitled *A Happy Pair*, which they published for Christmas 1890. Benjamin Bouncer was rewarded by Beatrix with a cup of hemp seeds, which made him "partially intoxicated and wholly unmanageable"[3] when he was required as a model again the following day.

Beatrix and Benjamin were seldom separated. In 1892 Beatrix took her beloved rabbit with her on the family holiday to Scotland, travelling overnight by train from London with Benjamin in a covered basket. Taking pets on journeys was not without its problems, for when Beatrix let Benjamin out on the way he "proved scared and bit the family,"[4] and when she exercised him on a leather dog-lead in the wall-less garden of Heath Park, their house that year in Birnam, she had to keep him on the lead "for fear he would run away."[5] It is not known exactly how long Benjamin Bouncer lived, but in 1892 Beatrix had a new rabbit "bought, at a very tender age, in the Uxbridge Road, Shepherds Bush, for the exorbitant sum of 4/6."[6] This new rabbit she called Peter Piper.

When she was away from London, Beatrix sent letters to the two older children of her last governess, Annie Moore. These letters to Noel and Eric Moore gave them news of the family's holiday activities, reports on the health of the Potter children's pets, and Beatrix's observations on the birds and animals wherever she was staying. Only rarely were there stories in her letters. Beatrix illustrated her newsy accounts with quick sketches and, occasionally, with more detailed and exquisite pen drawings. She would, in later years, send picture letters to Noel's and Eric's sisters, too, letters that the whole family treasured and kept safely wrapped from harm.

Noel Moore received his first picture letter in March 1892, when he was only four, and because he was the eldest child and frequently ill, he received more letters from Beatrix Potter than his siblings. But sometimes Beatrix ran out of news for him—and such a day was September 4, 1893, when the Potters were staying in Scotland in a house called Eastwood in Dunkeld, not far from their beloved Dalguise in Perthshire. Beatrix's letter that day began:

> My dear Noel,
>
> I don't know what to write to you, so I shall tell you a story about four little rabbits whose names were—Flopsy, Mopsy, Cottontail and Peter. They lived with their mother in a sand bank under the root of a big fir tree.[7]

Beatrix continued her story for another seven pages, telling Noel of the adventures of the disobedient Peter Rabbit and providing an illustration for every episode. At the end of the letter she added, "I am coming back to London next Thursday, so I hope I shall see you soon, and the new baby. I remain, dear Noel, yours affectionately Beatrix Potter." The following day she wrote a letter to Noel's brother Eric telling him about "a frog called Mr. Jeremy Fisher"[8]—but that is quite another story.

As Peter Piper grew and matured he gradually replaced Benjamin as Beatrix's drawing model and rabbits continued to appear frequently in many of Beatrix's pictures. Now she was amusing herself by featuring them in her own illustrations to a number of her favorite stories, among them *Uncle Remus, Alice's Adventures in Wonderland,* and the fairy tale of "Cinderella." Peter himself continued to make appearances in her letters to the Moores and to the children of her cousin, Edith Gaddum. To Noel Moore in February 1895 Beatrix wrote, "My rabbit Peter is so lazy, he lies before the fire in a box, with a little rug. His claws grew too long, quite uncomfortable, so I tried to cut them with scissors."[9] To Walter Gaddum in March 1897 she reported, "Peter Rabbit is very well and fat, generally asleep before the fire."[10]

It was the Moores' mother, Annie, who one day suggested to Beatrix that she try her hand at turning some of the stories from her letters into books. Because the children had kept their letters so carefully, Beatrix was able to borrow them back and to copy out those parts that she thought might be of use. For her first book she chose her letter to Noel about Peter Rabbit and, although it was already a complete and well-rounded story, when she came to set it out she saw that the text was too short for the book she had in mind. So she rewrote the story, doubling its length, and providing twenty-five new pictures. Among the new episodes were many of those that make the strongest impression on readers of today. They include Mrs. Rabbit warning the children about the fate of their father before she sets out with her basket to shop for currant buns, Peter weeping big tears while the sparrows plead with him to get free from the gooseberry net, Peter hiding in the watering can and then revealing his whereabouts by sneezing, the locked door in the wall against which Peter leans when making his vain request to the old mouse for help, and the white cat sitting "very, very still"[11] by the pond. It was at this stage, too, that Beatrix changed Mr. McGregor's basket, "which he intended to pop upon the top of Peter,"[12] into a garden sieve, a much harder and less comfortable trap for a young rabbit.

There were some parts of the new story that in later editions would be cut out again, most importantly the scene in which Peter is badly frightened by a peculiar scratching and the sinister singing of "Three Blind Mice," which "made him feel as though his own tail were going to be cut off . . . his fur stood on end."[13]

Beatrix copied her new story into a small exercise book, carefully placing the lines of text to balance the black-and-white drawing on each page. The only picture in color would be the frontispiece. *The Tale of Peter Rabbit and Mr McGregor's Garden,* by H. B. Potter, was ready. But how to find a publisher? For help Beatrix turned to an old friend she had met when she first visited the Lake District in 1882, Canon Hardwicke Rawnsley, himself a successful writer of children's rhymes. A number of publishers were approached, but they all rejected the little book, some saying that it was too small to compete with the much larger books that were thought appropriate for children, others asking for something with more color in it. But Beatrix was determined that her book should be just as she had planned it; that way it would be cheap enough for children to buy for themselves: "She [Miss Potter] would rather make 2 or 3 little books costing 1/- each, than one big book costing 6/- because she thinks little rabbits cannot afford to spend 6 shillings on one book."[14]

After at least six rejections and a certain amount of frustration, Beatrix decided that she would publish the book herself, exactly as she wanted it. She took the advice of another friend, Gertrude Woodward, on a suitable printer, and in 1901 she asked Strangeways & Sons of Tower Street in London to print two hundred and fifty copies of what she now called "*The Tale of Peter Rabbit* by Beatrix Potter." The zinc blocks for the forty-two line drawings, printed with the text in black, were made by the Art Reproduction Company in Fetter Lane; the three-color frontispiece was printed separately by Carl Hentschel of Fleet Street using the recently introduced half-tone process. Beatrix ordered five hundred copies of the frontispiece to be printed, in case she might need a quick reprint.

Even while the preparations for the printing of the private edition were well in hand, Canon Rawnsley was still trying to find a commercial publisher for *The Tale of Peter Rabbit*. Deciding that the story might attract more attention if it was in rhyming couplets, he rewrote it thus and submitted it again to Frederick Warne, together with Beatrix Potter's illustrations and the details of the blockmaking and frontispiece printing that had already been done. Rawnsley's version of the story was startlingly banal—and had hardly a hint of punctuation:

There were four little bunnies—no bunnies were sweeter
Mopsy and Cotton-tail Flopsy and Peter
They lived in a sand-bank as here you may see
At the foot of a fir—a magnificent tree

continuing for eighty-five pages until:

Enough now of Peter but what of the others
Those good little pattern obedient brothers
They sat down to tea too good mannered to cram
And ate bread and milk and sweet blackberry jam
And thought as we all think by far the best way
To do what we're told and our mother's [*sic*] obey[15]

To Frederick Warne's eternal credit they replied that they would prefer the text to be "simple narration . . . though there are many good ideas in your verses which might be introduced with advantage."[16] (Rawnsley had reintroduced the somewhat sinister singing of "Three Blind Mice.") Warne also thought that the book should be shorter and the illustrations should be in color throughout.

When Beatrix was shown their letter to Rawnsley, she wrote to Warne direct: "I did not colour the book for two reasons—the great expense of good colour printing—and also the rather uninteresting colour of a good many of the subjects which are most of them rabbit-brown and green."[17] She was, however, much encouraged by Warne's interest and the thought of commercial publication, and by mid-December she had agreed to cut her story to the length they required and to provide illustrations in color for what they called her "Bunny Book."[18] She was reluctant, though, to abandon her original concept of the book altogether and she continued with her plans for its private publication.

On December 16, 1901, two hundred and fifty copies of the first-ever edition of *The Tale of Peter Rabbit* were delivered to Bolton Gardens. It was a simple production, eighty-eight unnumbered pages, each spread with a few lines of text facing a black-and-white drawing. The endpapers were white, and the book, bound in greyish-green boards, had a picture of four rabbits, somewhat uncharacteristically beribboned, sitting between the title and the author's name. Beatrix was soon able to tell Warne, "It is going off very well amongst my friends and relations, 5 at a time."[19] In one copy of her little book she wrote, "In affectionate remembrance of poor old Peter Rabbit, who died on the 26th of January 1901 at the end of his 9th year . . . whatever the limitations of his intellect or outward shortcomings of his fur, and his ears and toes, his disposition was uniformly amiable and his temper unfailingly sweet. An affectionate companion and a quiet friend."[20]

Those copies of the book that she did not give away, Beatrix sold for 1/-, plus 2d for postage, and after only a week or so she realized that she was going to need more; her decision to have extra copies of the color frontispiece had been a wise one. For the second printing of the book, she made some changes. The board binding was of a slightly better quality, in olive-green instead of the original pale grey-green, and the book was also given a rounded back instead of a flat spine. As well as small punctuation alterations, there was an important change to the text. Beatrix made it clear that the sinister scratching heard by Peter was the sound of Mr. McGregor's hoe and that it was he who was singing "Three Blind Mice." She then omitted Peter's fear that his tail might be cut off. Unlike the first privately printed edition the reprint carries a date, February 1902, an important omission from the original.

Eight months later, in October 1902, the first trade edition of *The Tale of Peter Rabbit* was published by Frederick Warne. The text had indeed been shortened, with the "Three Blind Mice" episode cut out altogether, and eleven of the drawings had been dropped, a cost-saving decision to enable the book to be printed on a single sheet of paper. Beatrix had redrawn all the remaining illustrations in full color but not without some difficulty, for she had no model following the death of Peter Rabbit. Only after the pictures had been finished did she buy herself a new, young rabbit, and she confessed to her publisher that she felt "the drawings look wrong."[21] Frederick Warne, however, were pleased with her rabbits, but they were not so happy with her humans, and both Mr. and Mrs. McGregor had to be drawn again, Beatrix confessing that she had "never learnt to draw figures."[22]

The finished book was given pale grey-blue endpapers with a leaf pattern, and it was issued in two editions, one bound in paper boards (some in grey and some in brown) which cost 1/- each, and "a de-luxe" edition bound in the choice of three shades of green cloth, copies of which sold for 1/6d each. On the front cover of both editions the title and the author's name were stamped in white, and mounted within a blind panel was the picture of the prancing Peter that is still so familiar today.

The Tale of Peter Rabbit has been through countless editions since that first one over a hundred years ago, and in the early years the author made a number of small changes to the text. Four of the pictures were dropped in 1903, when the publishers needed four of the color pages on which to print the newly designed endpapers featuring the linked chain of animal characters from the new books, with a new character to be added as each new book was published. In 1907, when the printing plates had become so worn that new plates had to be made, Beatrix redrew two of the pictures altogether, keeping the content but adjusting the perspective. For reasons unknown the new pictures were used for only six or seven years before the originals were restored. There have been a number of different bindings of the book over the years, notably during the Second World War when light-brown covers with white dust wrappers were introduced. Beatrix wrote to her publisher, "I like the light coloured jackets. I like them much better than the sunk binding."[23] In 1987, when the original watercolors of the illustrations were newly photographed and new printing plates were made, a printed binding was introduced which closely resembled the original panelled version.

In November 1903, when Warne was reprinting for the sixth time and the total number of copies in print of *The Tale of Peter Rabbit* had reached 56,500, the author commented to her publisher, "The public must be fond of rabbits! What an appalling quantity of Peter."[24] In 1905 she wondered, "I suppose Peter will still be in print in 1907!"[25] And writing to a friend in 1938 she confided, "Peter never aspired to be high art—he was passable (except the covers which I had nothing to do with and always hated), but if not high art his moderate price has at least enabled him to reach many thousands of children, and has given them pleasure without ugliness."[26] And it was Beatrix herself who identified the appeal of *The Tale of Peter Rabbit* when, in 1905, she wrote, "I often think that that was the secret of the success of Peter Rabbit, it was written to a child—not made to order."[27]

NOTES

1. Unpublished letter from William Gaskell to "B" [Beatrix Potter], 23 August 1877 (Victoria and Albert Museum, Linder Bequest).

2. Letter from Beatrix Heelis [Potter] to Marian Frazer Harris Perry, 25 April 1929 (Private Collection).

3. Beatrix Potter, *The Journal of Beatrix Potter from 1881-1897,* transcribed from her code writings by Leslie Linder (London: Frederick Warne, 1966; revised edition 1989), 213.

4. Potter, *The Journal,* 246.

5. Unpublished letter from Beatrix Potter to Noel Moore, 21 August 1892 (Private Collection).

6. Leslie Linder, *A History of the Writings of Beatrix Potter* (London: Frederick Warne, 1971; revised edition, 1987), 110.

7. Letter from Beatrix Potter to Noel Moore, 4 September 1893 (Pearson plc, Victoria & Albert Museum, Linder Bequest).

8. Unpublished letter from Beatrix Potter to Eric Moore, 5 September 1893 (Private Collection).

9. Letter from Beatrix Potter to Noel Moore, 4 February 1895 (Pierpont Morgan Library).

10. Letter from Beatrix Potter to Walter Gaddum, 6 March 1897 (Victoria and Albert Museum, Linder Bequest).

11. Beatrix Potter, *The Tale of Peter Rabbit* (London: Frederick Warne, 1902, reoriginated edition, 1987), 46.

12. Potter, *The Tale of Peter Rabbit,* 34.

13. Beatrix Potter, *The Tale of Peter Rabbit* (Privately published, 1901), 58.

14. Letter from Beatrix Potter to Marjory [*sic*] Moore, 13 March 1900 (Pierpont Morgan Library).

15. Beatrix Potter and Canon Hardwicke Rawnsley, *Peter Rabbit's Other Tale* (The Beatrix Potter Society, 1989).

16. Letter from F. Warne & Co. to Rev. Canon Rawnsley, 11 September 1901 (Victoria and Albert Museum, Linder Bequest).

17. Letter from Beatrix Potter to Messrs. Warne & Co., 11 September 1901 (Frederick Warne Archive).

18. Letter from Frederick Warne & Co. to Beatrix Potter, 16 December 1901 (Frederick Warne Archive).

19. Letter from Beatrix Potter to F. Warne & Co., 18 December 1901 (Frederick Warne Archive).

20. Leslie Linder, *A History of the Writings of Beatrix Potter,* 110.

21. Letter from Beatrix Potter to N. D. Warne, 8 May 1902 (Frederick Warne Archive).

22. Letter from Beatrix Potter to Messrs. F. Warne & Co, 2 May 1902 (Frederick Warne Archive).

23. Letter from Beatrix Potter to Arthur Stephens, Frederick Warne, 7 February 1943 (Frederick Warne Archive).

24. Letter from Beatrix Potter to N. D. Warne, Esq., 9 November 1903 (Frederick Warne Archive).

25. Letter from Beatrix Potter to N. D. Warne, Esq., 4 March 1905 (Frederick Warne Archive).

26. Letter from Beatrix Heelis [Potter] to Josephine Banner, 28 February 1938 (Victoria and Albert Museum, Linder Bequest).

27. Letter from Beatrix Potter to Mrs. Fruing Warne, 26 September 1905 (Victoria and Albert Museum, Linder Bequest).

BIBLIOGRAPHY

Linder, Leslie. *A History of the Writings of Beatrix Potter*. Rev. ed. London: Frederick Warne, 1987.

Potter, Beatrix. *The Journal of Beatrix Potter from 1881–1897,* transcribed from her code writings by Leslie Linder. Rev. ed. London: Frederick Warne, 1989.

———. *The Tale of Peter Rabbit.* Reoriginated edition. London: Frederick Warne, 1902; 1987.

———. *The Tale of Peter Rabbit.* Privately published, 1901.

Potter, Beatrix, and Canon Hardwicke Rawnsley. *Peter Rabbit's Other Tale*. The Beatrix Potter Society, 1989.

4

Beatrix Potter's Art

Joyce Irene Whalley

I would like to begin by quoting a few comments made by Beatrix herself in her *Journal*. In 1883, when she was about seventeen, she wrote, "I can't settle to anything but my painting." In 1884 she revealed more about her attitude to her own art:

> It is all the same, drawing, painting, modelling, the irresistible desire to copy any beautiful object that strikes the eye. Why cannot one be content to look at it? I cannot rest, I must draw, however poor the result, and when I have a bad time come over me it is a stronger desire than ever, and settles on the queerest things. Last time, in the middle of September, I caught myself in the back yard making a careful and admiring copy of the swill bucket, and the laugh it gave me brought me round.

Later she stated, "I don't want lessons, I want practice." These three early quotations show immediately the seriousness with which Beatrix Potter regarded her art and also the emphasis she placed on accurate and practised *drawing*. As an adult, Beatrix became a fine artist in the English watercolor tradition, yet she never sold a painting for profit or exhibited any of her work during her lifetime. Moreover, her artistic fame today rests mainly on her book illustrations rather than her paintings.

In the light of these statements and facts, it is useful to consider Beatrix Potter's early years and the background influences that affected her development as an artist. It is probable that to some extent her talent was inherited from her parents—it was certainly encouraged by her father, Rupert Potter. A surviving sketchbook of Rupert's dating from

1853, when he was a young man, shows him copying contemporary illustrations and, probably, giving his own humorous touch to them. Later, we see him in the *Journal* as an indefatigable exhibition visitor around the London galleries—visits on which he was often accompanied by his daughter. As quite a young man he had taken up the new art of photography, and many examples of his work in this field survive to show him not just as a recordist but also as possessing an artistic eye in the selection and composition of his subjects. No doubt Beatrix herself learnt much from him on these topics, just as she must have done when discussing contemporary paintings with him.

In the nineteenth century it was usual for most middle- and upper-class girls in England to be educated at home, as was Beatrix Potter, and, no doubt, her mother before her. In addition to a certain amount of "book-learning," they were also expected to acquire "accomplishments." These consisted for the most part of music and watercolor painting. We know that Mrs. Potter had at least one of these accomplishments, since some of her watercolor paintings have survived. So we can be sure that she would have ensured that her daughter was also taught to paint—certainly well enough for a lady. Thus we can deduce that Beatrix Potter had encouragement from both parents when she showed some interest in painting and drawing. These are, moreover, occupations that can be pursued in solitude, and until her brother Bertram, nearly six years her junior, was old enough to be a companion, it seems that Beatrix Potter's life was a lonely one.

We are fortunate that some sketchbooks have been preserved from Beatrix's childhood, as well as some early drawings. As with most children, her first attempts were at copying, either from her own or her father's books—no bad thing in itself, since copying imposes a form of discipline. Later, she progressed to sketching things around her, especially flowers: *The Art of Flower Painting* was among her earliest books. But, as we can see from one of the quotations above, for the compulsive sketcher all is grist to the mill, even a pig-stye or a swill bucket.

Still-life can be found anywhere, even if flowers may not always be available, but it is helpful to have a subject of your own to hand, and here the two Potter children were fortunate. Though young companions were not encouraged in the nursery, animal pets seem to have been allowed, and both children took advantage of this. So, gradually, we have endless drawings of rabbits, mice, hedgehogs—or merely parts of them—as Beatrix strove to perfect her ability to catch the likeness and the movement of her own various pets and those of her brother.

But while she was learning and sketching, she was also looking. As she got older, she regularly accompanied her father to various exhibitions, from the grand Royal Academy ones to those in small private galleries. The pictures she saw, she analyzed in considerable detail in her *Journal,* laughing in later years at her own naïve criticism. Nevertheless, this detailed study of established painters, whether she approved of them or not, must have had an influence on her own work. She was also very aware of the major illustrators of the day, whom she mentions in her *Journal*. The middle of the nineteenth century had seen the rise of a number of illustrated journals, such as *Punch* and *The Illustrated London News*. Such magazines provided regular employment for illustrators whose work was of the highest quality. Artists such as John Tenniel, Richard Doyle, and Gustave Doré produced work for books as well as periodicals, and helped to raise the status of the "mere" illustrator. This high standard was carried on by the next generation of book artists, and whereas we know that the young Beatrix was familiar with the work of the older artists, no doubt from her father's library, it was the younger generation who were to have such an influence on her.

The two most important names in this field in the last quarter of the century were Walter Crane and Randolph Caldecott—the latter was especially important where Beatrix Potter was concerned. Walter Crane lived from 1845 until 1915, and he worked in many areas besides that of the book: he designed tiles, wallpaper, and other decorative items. But he is primarily remembered as an illustrator of children's books, producing a number of "toy books" in the last quarter of the nineteenth century. Not only did Beatrix know his work, but she certainly possessed one of his books at least. In her sketchbook of 1876, when she was ten years old, Beatrix copied a picture from Walter Crane's *The Baby's Opera,* and we can be sure that this was just the kind of up-to-the-minute book that the Potter parents would ensure that their children owned.

Randolph Caldecott was born in 1846 but died young, in 1886. However, his influence on Beatrix Potter's art was far more important than Crane's, because it was more in keeping with her own ideas. Whereas Crane was rather more of a book decorator, filling his pictures with a lot of detail, Caldecott was a true illustrator, in that he allowed his pictures to enhance or complement the text, and he was not afraid of blank spaces on the page. An appreciation of Caldecott's work was something Beatrix shared with her father: "Papa has become very extravagant. He went on the sly the other day and bought two little drawings of *The Frog*." This was Caldecott's toy book, *A Frog He Would A-Wooing Go*.

Anyone who looks at the pictures in this book cannot fail to recognize certain Potter figures—not only is there a foretaste of Mr. Jeremy Fisher, but surely also of Samuel Whiskers.

It was also Caldecott's style that influenced Beatrix Potter. The older artist's work had a simple clarity in the illustrations, and, like Beatrix, he used a palette of cool colors, often outlining his drawings in sepia, as did Beatrix in her earlier work. But, of course, there are differences. Randolph Caldecott's settings show an idealized world—they may look real, but you cannot find them on the map, as you can with so many of Beatrix Potter's backgrounds. Moreover, Caldecott chose to illustrate other people's writings, usually nursery rhymes or ballads, whereas Beatrix used her own creative imagination to produce characters and tales that perfectly complement one another in both text and picture. Where the British copyright law does not cover her work, there have been attempts by other artists to illustrate the little books—in America, in Poland, and in Russia, for example—but none of these reinterpretations has so perfectly matched the mood and the general *ensemble* of the original work.

One interesting contact of the Potter family who does *not* seem to have influenced Beatrix Potter—rather surprisingly perhaps—was her father's friend, the well-known painter Sir John Everett Millais. Few aspiring young artists can have had such an opportunity to see a famous painter at work, and to hear talk of his pictures. But Millais was painting in oils, and Beatrix, although she made some attempts to work in this medium, found it unsympathetic for what she wanted to do, preferring to work in the much more difficult medium of watercolor. But at least she knew firsthand what it was like to *be* an artist, and the work it involved. She also benefited to some extent from Millais's encouragement, even if, in her younger days, she had to endure his teasing.

Although Beatrix had drawn and painted from her earliest years, it was really during the 1890s that she was feeling her way to perfecting her art. Anxious to have some money of her own, she conceived the idea of selling some of her paintings as greetings cards, and was delighted when they were accepted by the firm of Hildesheimer and Faulkner. In 1892 she mentions in her *Journal* that she has just finished painting a Jackdaw for the firm of Nister—a watercolor that some people consider one of the finest of her early works. When she painted for the card market, she was not only constricted by the suitability of the subject matter, but also by technical consideration of the method by which her pictures would be reproduced. As a result, the cards that survive show the rather muddy muted colors of so much contemporary color printing. But when she was painting for her own pleasure, she made use of much brighter, fresher colors, often outlining her paintings in sepia ink, which gives them a very spontaneous appearance.

It was in this same last decade of the nineteenth century, too, that she began the series of letters to the Moore children that were to form such an important part of her later literary efforts. The letters were illustrated with pen-and-ink sketches as she went along, giving them a coherence and immediacy that would prove so valuable when she later borrowed back some of them to work up into the little tales.

By the beginning of the twentieth century, Beatrix was ready to start her career as a writer and illustrator of children's books. She had studied the various techniques required, she had practised her drawing, and she had experimented with various painting styles. She had also developed a literary style, which we know to have been based on Shakespeare and the Bible, but which had been refined to a personal one by her *Journal* writings and by her many letters to children. The latter aspect was particularly important, since not only was she, in the first place, usually writing to a specific child, but she would also have known how the accompanying pictures were received by the young recipient.

The story of *The Tale of Peter Rabbit* and the general history of the little books have been told many times. Here it is more important to consider the illustrations, though in every good illustrated book, text and pictures should form a coherent whole, as indeed Beatrix's do. The first thing to note about Beatrix's illustrations is the care taken over them. The animals are accurately drawn, and their background is also precisely portrayed. The pictures are not overcrowded, but at the same time there is room for small details that add to the text, even though they may not actually be mentioned in it—little "mini-scenes" of birds or insects, which delight the enquiring eye of the child. Moreover, the pictures are very carefully placed on the page, so that they relate to the relevant part of the text. For Beatrix's "art" involved more than just her drawings and paintings—she conceived her work as a complete artistic entity. The text, the page where the picture appeared, the position of both text and picture on the page, and shape and size of the book as a whole, all show Beatrix to have been a true book artist, in the fullest sense of the word.

It is hard for us at this distance to fully appreciate the impact the first of the little books must have had on the recipients. From the opening of the title-page, with its simple and clear type and with an equally simple frontispiece picture on a white background, through the various stages of the drama, the story and its illustration march hand-in-hand at the child's pace. Only a comparison with other children's books of the period, which sadly cannot be attempted here, reveals the true art of Beatrix Potter as a children's book writer and illustrator.

Fortunately for her child readers, *The Tale of Peter Rabbit* was not a one-off production. For the most part, Beatrix Potter continued to produce her little books along the same lines that had proved successful with the first. But this "sameness" was not comparable to that of Kate Greenaway, who, once she had found a successful style, stuck to it for the rest of her working life. Beatrix Potter continued to develop her art, though not always to her own liking, as is shown by the style of *The Tale of Mr. Tod,* where the pictures are all framed and far more elaborate than some of her earlier work. She did not repeat the woodcut effect of the black-and-white illustrations, reminiscent of Camille Pissaro's Eragny Press—perhaps she felt the style was too heavy in a children's book, though it certainly heightened the drama in this particular *Tale.* But she was prepared to continue with the framed "picture-style" colored illustrations when she felt these appropriate, although even in her later books, such as *The Tale of Johnny Town-Mouse,* she is still happy to revert to the vignetted style of *Peter Rabbit.* What made her choose the different types of colored illustration is difficult to say, since it is not a question of inside or outside scenes being regularly treated in one way or the other.

Beatrix Potter's backgrounds offer themselves as a study in their own right. It is interesting that, long after she had ceased to produce pictures for the little books, she continued to paint landscapes for her own pleasure, following up in her old age her own earlier statement about the compulsion she felt to draw whatever her eye fell upon. The art of the little books had benefited greatly from this attitude, as their settings vary from minutely observed interiors, some of which remain *in situ* today, to a broader sweep of countryside, which nearly always remains still recognizable. This continuing interest in landscape painting is to some extent typical of the first decades of the twentieth century. Beatrix Potter was a great reader—though how much time she had for this pastime in later years is doubtful. But the period when she was most involved with the little books was also that of the "Georgian" and "Weekend" poets and essayists, all evoking the same idyllic countryside which Beatrix offers us in her books, where the rain and mud she knew as a sheep farmer rarely, if ever, intrude.

The present book is concerned more especially with the first of the little books, *The Tale of Peter Rabbit.* But this chapter has a wider remit, in that it considers the art of Beatrix Potter as a whole, and not just the illustrations of one little book—or even a series of books. As the works by Leslie Linder and, more recently, Anne Hobbs have shown, Beatrix Potter's art embraced many subjects and a variety of media—a point further emphasized by the detailed catalogue of the Linder Bequest in the Victoria and Albert Museum. Moreover, we are fortunate in that so much of this variety has in fact been preserved, from the earliest childhood sketches to late impressionistic watercolors.

Beatrix Potter's earliest work, much of it done, no doubt, under the supervision of her governess, is typical of the sort of work most children produce if they have any interest in drawing and painting. It could have ended there, as most children's artwork does, but Beatrix went on. Her copies and her early flower paintings are no more than average, but it is extremely interesting to those of us who know her later years to see what she actually chose to copy—the paintings of caterpillars and the details about them are not every child's choice. But by the age of sixteen, she was producing work already fit to be judged on merit. Her highly finished paintings of fruit, or the Library at Wray Castle, show considerable talent, though still, naturally enough in a young person, influenced by contemporary styles. But outstanding among her *oeuvre* are the many detailed sketches produced from her earliest years until adulthood. These vary from frogs, or bits of frogs, hedgehogs, or parts of hedgehogs, to chairs and cupboards, often repeated again and again as the artist sought to perfect the form or catch the movement—whole sheets of ducks, of chairs, of cows and horses remain to testify to this determination to get it just right. Where Beatrix fails most noticeably is in her portrayal of the human species—not always even here, since her *sketches* are often good, as those done in Keswick market place show, but she failed lamentably when she tried to perfect them.

Her landscapes are particularly appealing, whether they form the background to an illustration or stand on their own. She had an eye for composition, no doubt trained by her father, from whom she learnt the art of photography. But here, too, she could produce the quick accurate sketch, or the atmospheric painting of Lingholm in *Rain,* or the late impressionistic series of snow scenes around Sawrey. And the joy of much of this work is that one can actually walk to the place or the building today—though not always! This writer remembers a warm September day amid prickly bracken, trying desperately to see from which viewpoint Beatrix had sketched a certain scene in the Newlands Valley. Only to realize that, yes, even she sometimes used artistic license, and that the objects seen in that particular painting could never have been as close together as she had painted them—but it was still a good picture and was later used in *The Tale of Mrs. Tiggy-Winkle*.

In the twenty years or so years of its existence, the Beatrix Potter Society has done its best through talks and publications to spread the knowledge of Beatrix Potter's wide range of interests and activities. The publication by Frederick Warne of her *Journal*, and selections of her art and letters, together with the promotion by the National Trust of her later Lakeland life as Mrs. William Heelis, have all tried to further this awareness. But still, to the world at large, she remains known first and foremost as the author/illustrator of *The Tale of Peter Rabbit*. Aided by the ever-increasing promotion of merchandise based on characters from the other *Tales*, no doubt the public must by now be aware that she did at least write other books! Rather sadly, she may eventually be best known as the creator of a series of videos based on these *Tales*. But artistically she was certainly more than just a children's book illustrator—it was the "more" which, in fact, made her work so outstanding in her chosen field. One of the meanings of the word "artist" given in my dictionary is "*a person who works with the dedication and attributes of an artist*"—and those words surely sum up the personality and art of Beatrix Potter.

FURTHER READING

Three books are devoted specifically to the art of Beatrix Potter:

Hobbs, Anne Stevenson. *Beatrix Potter's Art*. London: Frederick Warne, 1989. (A scholarly assessment of Beatrix Potter's art that is more selective than the Linder book below, though still wide-ranging.)

Linder, E. and L. *The Art of Beatrix Potter*. Rev. ed. London: Frederick Warne, 1972. (This book includes a wide range of artwork, but the color reproduction is poor, and there is little text.)

Taylor, Judy, Joyce Irene Whalley, Anne Stevenson Hobbs, and Elizabeth M. Battrick. *Beatrix Potter 1866–1943: The Artist and Her World*. London: Frederick Warne & The National Trust. Reissued 1995. (This volume was published as a companion to the exhibition at the Tate Gallery, London, in 1987–88. Chapters 2, 3, 4, and 6 by J. I. Whalley and A. S. Hobbs are particularly relevant to a study of Beatrix Potter's art in all its aspects.)

Other books of interest are:

Bartlett, W., and Joyce Irene Whalley. *Beatrix Potter's Derwentwater*. New ed. Leading Edge, 1995. (This work looks at the three *Tales* set around Derwentwater and considers the close link between the illustrations and the actual scenery.)

Hobbs, Anne Stevenson, and Joyce Irene Whalley. *Beatrix Potter: The V & A Collection. The Leslie Linder Bequest of Beatrix Potter Material.* London: Victoria & Albert Museum and Frederick Warne, 1985. (Primarily the catalogue of a collection, mostly of paintings and drawings, this book is, nevertheless, well illustrated and it also contains details of art work by Beatrix's father, mother, and brother.)

Potter, Beatrix. *The Journal of Beatrix Potter, 1881–1897*. Complete ed. Transcribed from her code writings by Leslie Linder. Rev. ed. London: Frederick Warne, 1989. (This transcription of her *Journal,* which she kept in code, sheds much light on Beatrix Potter's development as an artist.)

Taylor, Judy. *Beatrix Potter: Artist, Storyteller and Countrywoman*. Rev. ed. London: Frederick Warne, 1996. (The standard biography, this book admirably covers the place of her art in her life as a whole.)

Beatrix Potter, *The Tale of Peter Rabbit,* frontispiece (1902 edition).

5

Beatrix Potter and John Everett Millais: Reproductive Technologies and Coolhunting

Lissa Paul

Some scholarly essays, like growth rings on a tree, accumulate as layers of a life's work. Others have more haphazard origins: an idea glimpsed as it passes just out of sight across the mind, a chance observation, a casual remark. This essay belongs to the haphazard category. At the moment Margaret Mackey's request for a contribution to the *Peter Rabbit* anniversary collection appeared on my e-mail screen, I happened to be reading—in Joyce Irene Whalley's history of children's book illustration[1]—that Beatrix Potter (1866–1943) had known John Everett Millais (1829–1896). Prior to Margaret's request, I had given no thought to writing about Peter Rabbit or Beatrix Potter—let alone John Everett Millais.

As a children's literature specialist, I have, of course, taught works by Potter, and so read her biography, journals, some letters, and several critical texts. But I have no memory of knowing Potter's connection with Millais. I must have read about it, but not taken any conscious account. Because Margaret's request coincided with a chance encounter with a bit of unnoticed information, I found myself happily charting unexplored territory.

Initially, I assumed, vaguely, that I'd be looking for evidence of Millais's influence on Potter, but the futility of the exercise surfaced quickly. Instead, almost from the beginning of my formal research, I realized that the way to access the connection between Millais and Potter was not through influence but, rather, through something I took to calling "new reproductive technologies." Both artists engaged with the new photographic technologies of their time, and with the new technologies (of color lithography and photomechanical reproduction) used to reproduce unprecedented numbers of cheap color copies in picture books, greeting cards, and in the new, popular illustrated news magazines. Two magazines, *The Graphic* and *The Illustrated London News,* were particularly important in disseminating Millais's work and giving two of his pictures, *Bubbles* and *Cherry Ripe,* brand-name recognition throughout the empire. Beatrix Potter, with the savvy eye of what I would today call a "coolhunter," understood the market potential of those reproductions and the technologies that made their marketability possible. The evidence is in her letters, her journals and, of course, her books and their merchandise spin-offs. But I'm ahead of myself. Reproductive technologies and coolhunting are too far along in the story. They make sense only if the reader has access to the key codes—in much the same way that Potter's diaries make sense only once the code is revealed, or the way that chaotic shapes such as coastlines or mountain ranges make mathematical sense only if they are processed through fractal equations. Stories need key codes and beginnings.

It was Rupert Potter, Beatrix's father, who really had the connection with Sir John Everett Millais. This much of the story is well known. The Potters, with their two children, lived at 2 Bolton Gardens, about a mile away from the Millais family (there were eight children, one of whom, Carrie, was about the same age as Beatrix), who lived in an exquisite mansion at 2 Palace Gate in Kensington. Rupert, in the mode of a cultured Victorian gentleman with time and talent on his hands, occupied himself with the fashionable new high-tech toy of the period, the camera. He was apparently a good enough photographer to win election to the Photographic Society of London and, sometime in the 1880s, to begin supplying photographs for Millais: landscapes and reference pictures of people who were sitting for portraits. Millais and Rupert Potter also shared a passion for hunting and fishing. The two families spent long holidays together at Dalguise in Scotland, the holidays that Beatrix loved so much in her early childhood. Rupert took the holiday snapshots. Lots of them.

But adults and children, even when on vacation together, occupy separate landscapes. There is no evidence that the famous Sir John Everett Millais noticed Beatrix Potter as anything other than a child of a friend, a peripheral part of the family scene. Sir John did offer friendly advice on an art tutor for Beatrix and was encouraging in the disinterested way of a family friend, but never in the spirit of seeing Beatrix as anything other than a serious accomplished amateur. Because Millais died in 1896, eight years before the publication of *Peter Rabbit,* it is unlikely that he even suspected that her international popular fame would someday eclipse his or that her works would achieve the kind of widespread recognition and immortality he was just beginning to glimpse.

It is easy to see why he would not have thought of Beatrix as an artist in the way that he thought of himself as an artist, accomplished, even as a young child. She would not have fit his portrait of an artist as a young person: her amateur status was diametrically opposed to his own institutionally grounded formal art education.

John Everett, from his earliest childhood in Brittany and Jersey, was recognized for his precocious artistic ability. A brief, unhappy encounter with school prompted his mother to teach him herself, so he was spared the deadening effects of formal public schooling. At eight, when his talent was already outgrowing his provincial home, his parents moved to London to provide him with the necessary opportunities for artistic development. Once established in London, he learned to be an artist in the traditional manner: by copying masterpieces in the British Museum and the National Gallery. At ten, competing against adults, he won the Society of Arts open competition for 1839. At eleven he applied for admission to the Royal Academy. He was the youngest person ever accepted—and his record apparently stands. Once a student, John Everett moved through the school with dedicated, prodigious speed. Even as a child competing against adults, he swept up all the prizes as he shot through the curriculum. And in 1846, at the age of seventeen, he exhibited his first picture at the Royal Academy. As is often the case with prodigies, success is suspect once the cute stage is over. Though Millais apparently remained an attractive, commanding man all his life, there was a period in the late 1840s when the unstinting critical acclaim gave way to an episode of putting the young artist in his place. Millais weathered the criticism beautifully. In 1848, the Pre-Raphaelite Brotherhood was founded at his house. Millais, along with friends Holman Hunt, the Rossetti brothers, F. G. Stephens, and James Collinson (all hovering around age twenty), established a revolution in modern art. Even though the Brotherhood was short lived, it marked its members' transition into fully adult lives as artists.

Despite the fact that the young Beatrix, like the young John Everett (or the young Pablo Picasso or David Hockney), lived with hand welded to a pencil in constant motion, she had none of the institutional credibility that would have identified her as an artist. Beatrix was taught at home. She copied from nature rather than from classical sculptures in galleries, rejected (politely) the lessons of her tutor, and seemed destined to institutional rejection. Her meticulous, scholarly work on fungi, her accurate observations, paintings, and theories were scorned by the experts at Kew Gardens. The fact that Beatrix's thesis on fungi was later proved correct made little difference to her life or to her institutional acceptability. Beatrix Potter recognized, as her journals indicate, that she understood her artistic station relative to Millais. He was a famous painter; she was a talented amateur, the daughter of a friend.

Sir John Everett Millais was very much a high society painter, a star in his age. He had a wife, Effie (who remains historically interesting because she had been married to John Ruskin. The marriage was annulled after seven years because it had not been consummated). John Everett and Effie Millais had eight children. Millais produced many big oil paintings, often of famous people, paintings that hung on walls in big art galleries and received much critical attention. He had a long, almost constantly successful career (though he felt, as did Beatrix Potter, and critics generally, that his early work was his best work), lived in a big, fashionable house, had great society parties, enjoyed a high public profile, and was made a Baronet and the President of the Royal Academy.[2]

Beatrix Potter (almost forty years younger than Sir John) worked in watercolors and produced a small number (about twenty-three, though it depends on how you count) of small books for small children. When she felt she had no more to say, she stopped. She preferred small houses. She didn't marry until she was in her forties. She had no children. And she abandoned corseted, high-society Victorian life in London for sheep farming in the Lake District as soon as she could manage it. As an old woman, she wore a mob cap, as her grandmother had done. Beatrix Potter shunned publicity. After her marriage she was grumpy at being addressed as Beatrix Potter rather than as Mrs. Heelis. She also believed in sharing the wealth and making it public, as her legacy to the National Trust demonstrates to this day.[3]

The existing critical literature on the relationship between Potter and Millais confirms the futility of trying to demonstrate influence. The textual evidence is very thin, consisting mainly of Potter's references to Millais in her coded journal. The artistic evidence seems to present a kind of critical stumbling block. At one end of the spectrum, Michael Wilson, writing in *The Beatrix Potter Society Newsletter* 63, says emphatically that "Millais had no direct influence on Beatrix's art."[4] Notice, incidentally, the way the hierarchical ordering is inscribed in the names. Millais is addressed by his surname, suited to an adult male, a man of high station. But Beatrix is addressed by her first name, a low-status girl. That's an aside, but indicative of their relative positions. To return to the question of influence: at the opposite end of the spectrum is Joyce Irene Whalley. She says that "trying to assess the various influences on the work of an artist is rather like trying to unscramble an egg" (nice simile), and that "it is surprisingly difficult to decide how important this family friendship was."[5] I can see why.

Although there are about forty references to John Everett Millais in Beatrix Potter's journal, most (with some important exceptions to which I'll refer later) are criticisms of his paintings, made when she was viewing them in galleries. In the biography of Millais by his son John, there is only one reference to Rupert Potter (as being the host of the Dalguise fishing holidays), and Beatrix, as might be expected given the generational difference, does not figure at all. In the galaxy of who was who in Victorian society moving through the Millais family milieu, Rupert Potter was a very minor player. But for a critic looking for historical documentation to fill in what appears to be a gap, there is an intriguing possibility for the omission, one that surfaced in my research on the ambivalent role photographs and reproductions played in the work of Pre-Raphaelite artists. At the time, there were public debates about whether or not Pre-Raphaelite and other late Victorian artists were just trying to show that they could produce paintings that were as accurate as photographs. There were also public debates about another Pre-Raphaelite innovation, questions about whether or not they were just advertising their own fine art works when they produced engravings for illustrated texts. From the distance of one hundred years, it appears likely that John Guille Millais just didn't want to open the thorny discussion (about photographic naturalism and the use of graphic art in print texts) in the hagiography of his father's portraits—which were praised, after all, for their photographic realism and uniqueness as fine works of art.[6]

In the early days of photography in the mid-nineteenth century (really beginning with William Fox-Talbot's 1839 negative-positive developing process), there were warnings sounded that the photograph would mark the death of the portrait. As is often the case when new technologies are introduced, the announcement of the demise of the one it is supposed to supplant is often exaggerated. As we now know, movies, for example, did not ultimately replace live theatre, and television did not replace movies. But each technology does have an impact on the one it threatens. Although it was probably difficult to read at the time, in retrospect it appears that there was a symbiotic relationship between Pre-Raphaelite painting (technically dated from 1848 with the formation of the Brotherhood) and the emerging technological art form of photography. Both tended towards art that favored the close-up, the portrait, and minutely captured naturalistic detail. John Ruskin is the critic credited with defining the modern agenda of the Pre-Raphaelite Brotherhood, especially in his instruction to imitate nature perfectly: "rejecting nothing, selecting nothing and scorning nothing."[7]

As Beatrix Potter was growing up through the 1870s, the revolutionary edge of Pre-Raphaelite movement (which formally lasted for only five years after its inception) had faded into middle-aged respectability. But interest in photographic truth and the minute observation of the natural world endured. Beatrix Potter was privileged in that, as a child, she had intimate access to both photography (through her father) and the natural world (through their long summer holidays in the country). So she had a long acquaintance with the kind of close-up that a photograph could provide and admired the Pre-Raphaelites for their "somewhat niggling but absolutely genuine admiration for copying natural details."[8] Because Potter's milieu was typically a small restricted space, and because her own early models were small animals rather than large statues, small precise renderings were natural for her and, by happy coincidence, fashionable.

It is possible to say, clearly, that photography was so natural to Beatrix Potter that, when she was forbidden to go the Warne house to sketch, *in situ,* the doll house she wanted for *The Tale of Two Bad Mice,* she simply resorted easily to photographs, as she knew other artists, including Millais, did when they didn't have access to the subject that was to be painted. But the point, I think, is not that she knew how to access and use photographs when she needed them. Rather, the critical point is that with her artist's eye, she could isolate from the general pageant of everyday life the specific images that would make marketable art, consumer art. Through the filtered connections with Millais, through her intense analysis of fine art (as demonstrated in her journal critiques of the art exhibitions she saw), and through her experience of the illustrated newspapers of the time, she was learning to understand how works of art could be made and sold in multiple copies, and how this was a good way of producing an income. She also understood, again at least partly via Millais, that what was being sold was an image of England suitable for export: something rural, something innocent, something suggesting a time before or below a modern industrial time.

One of the most telling examples of the cumulative effect of Potter's exposure to photography and photographic reproduction is found in her prescient comments on the scenario that would produce Millais's *Bubbles* (fig. 5.1). The portrait was originally called *A Child's World.* Millais had caught his grandson, Willie James, in a wonderfully fragile, transient moment, blowing bubbles. The child literally became the poster boy for Pears soap. Although Millais originally sold the painting to William Ingram, the publisher of the *Illustrated London News,* Ingram sold it almost at once to the vice-president of Pears, T. J. Barratt.[9] It is a particularly interesting portrait because it was at the heart of an enormous controversy, both during Millais's life and long afterwards, about the relationship between art and commerce. *Bubbles* turned out to be a prototype of the kind of picture that could come off the wall and sell soap, art, and England, particularly English childhood, to the empire. Beatrix, at just nineteen, could not have predicted the future, but she certainly recognized a significant gesture, a gesture worth noting and recording, when she saw it:

> Mr. Millais came here the 15th, in the evening to get papa to photograph next morning. He seemed in good health and high spirits. "I just want you to photograph that little boy of Effie's [Willie, the child of Millais's daughter]. I've got him you know, he's (cocking up his chin at the ceiling), he's like this, with a bowl of soap suds and all that, a pipe, it's called *A Child's World,* he's looking up, and there's a beautiful soap bubble; I can't paint you know, not a bit (with his head on one side and his eyes twinkling) not a bit! I want just to compare it, I get this little thing (the photo of the picture) and I hold in my hand and compare it with the life, and I can see where the drawing's wrong."[10]

The passage is prescient because it focuses precisely on the salient feature of the image Millais caught, the cocked head looking up in wonder, a captured moment of transient childhood innocence. Because the young Beatrix Potter records the exchange so precisely, it also reveals her sharp eye for many of the same things.

When Potter describes Millais's imitation of his grandson "cocking his head up to the ceiling," she must have intuitively recognized the significance of gesture (as evidenced by the long, detailed account she

Figure 5.1. John Everett Millais, *Bubbles,* 1886.

gives), though she could not have imagined the resulting picture would ultimately be both praised and criticized (in wide public debate) for its ability to sell soap. It is exactly the sort of insight that would mark her now, at the turn of the twenty-first century, as a coolhunter, someone who can gaze at the undifferentiated screening of everyday events and spot the interesting moment, the trend that will translate it into a mass market commodity.

Coolhunters are employed by companies, like Nike and Reebok, to try to isolate something about a consumer item (such as running shoes) that distinguishes one from the pack, the thing that makes the item sell out at top price rather than sit forlornly on the deep discount table long after the season has gone. The difference between the two outcomes depends on a subtle ability to distinguish the cool detail from the conventional. Not an easy job. In "The Coolhunt," Malcolm Gladwell isolates the coolhunter's sharp eyes from the unfocused eyes the rest of us see with. He describes how a coolhunter works a crowd of teenagers in order to spot the hot seller. Gladwell wonders about the coolhunter: "how she made any sense of the two dozen shoes in her bag, most of which (to my [Gladwell's] eyes, anyway) looked pretty much the same, and how she knew which of the teens to really focus on was a mystery."[11] It was obvious to her. She understood how to distinguish the cool from a mass of ordinary stuff. So did Beatrix Potter.

Unlike the turn of the twenty-first century coolhunter, who knows that each hot seller has only a short shelf life in the mass market, Beatrix Potter, as a coolhunter at the turn of the twentieth century, was dealing with the infancy of mass marketing. The cool images she brought to market in her books and peripheral merchandise captured something enduring in the images of English childhood and English children, something that has continued as a marketable commodity. The images of childhood that were being reproduced were, as Anne Higonnet crystallizes it in her book of the same title, "pictures of innocence."[12] Those pictures were characteristically of innocent, Romantic children, often clothed in the costumes of a bygone era, and often portrayed with animals. These innocent children were more or less invented in the eighteenth century in child portraits by Gainsborough, Reynolds, and Lawrence. But the image could be consolidated and made to appear timeless in the nineteenth century only because of the large numbers of reproductions that flooded the market: lithographs and mezzotints sold relatively cheaply, and were often distributed through the Christmas supplements in the illustrated papers. The result, says Higonnet, is that "the modern child is always the sign of a bygone era, of a past which is necessarily the past of adults, yet which, being so distinct, so sheltered, so innocent, is also inevitably a lost past, and therefore, understood through the kind of memory we call nostalgia" (Higonnet, 27). The image of the Romantic, innocent child popularized through new reproductive technologies, is the link that connects Millais with Potter. But that's also why the link is hard to spot. And it is also why, when Joyce Whalley says of Potter's work, that "sometimes we can catch a glimpse of this influence or that, but for the most part the artist she became was the well-scrambled result of all she had seen and absorbed" (Taylor, Whalley, et al., 35), she is right, within the terms of reference she's using. She's looking for influence, not the kind of marketable trace recognizable to the coolhunter.

The influences of Millais (and other "fine" artists) on Beatrix Potter may be well scrambled, but they aren't unreadable. Judy Taylor, in fact, makes the point in "The Tale of Peter Rabbit" (Taylor, Whalley, et al, 100). Taylor, taking an observation by Margaret Lane, demonstrates that Potter's picture of "Peter by the locked door" echoes a painting that Potter is likely to have seen at an exhibition, and to have known: *Love Locked Out,* by Anna Lea Merritt. When the pictures are set side by side, the similarities in the pose are visible. Potter caught the endearing, enduring feature: the vulnerable body set against the unmoving solidity of the locked door. There are other examples, closer ones, I think, that demonstrate Potter's appropriation of the same kind of trace.

If I go back to Potter's verbal sketch of the marketable look that Millais caught on the face of his grandson, I can see that it is the gesture, the tilt of the cocked head to which she attends. So when I look at the cover of *The Story of Miss Moppet* (fig. 5.2), first published in 1906, with the cat tossing up the blue ball with the mouse in it, I see a reinterpretation, a trace of the characteristic gesture of childhood wonder and pleasure caught in *Bubbles*. Beside the cat's cocked head in Potter's picture a blue ball hangs suspended, as does the bubble (it was actually a crystal sphere) in Millais's painting. I've chosen the *Miss Moppet/Bubbles* example to begin my Millais/Potter comparisons because *Bubbles* was such a seminal image, enduring long after Millais's death in 1896.

In a controversial little exchange that occurred when the painting was first gaining public exposure as a soap ad, the popular novelist Marie Corelli had a character complain in one of her books about the

Figure 5.2. Beatrix Potter, *The Story of Miss Moppet,* p.33 (1906 edition).

way Millais "degraded" himself by "painting the little green boy" for Pears. Millais, who admired Corelli, was hurt initially, but was consoled, once Corelli apologized, after being told that Millais didn't paint it for Pears. She praises the picture because of its depiction of "the most exquisite and dainty child ever dreamed of, with the air of a baby poet as well as of a small angel" (Millais, *The Life,* 190). What is important for my argument, is that Beatrix Potter caught the gesture before the image even hit the marketplace, and adapted the image of childhood wonder when she needed it. The *Miss Moppet/Bubbles* connection is, however, not as significant as the others to which I will now turn, primarily because *Miss Moppet* isn't as famous as some of Potter's other characters and pictures. But it is a good place to start an explicit demonstration of Potter's ability to spot and translate the cool, marketable gesture that conveys the image of childhood innocence and childhood desire. Now I'll turn to the other famous Millais painting of childhood "innocence," *Cherry Ripe* (fig. 5.3), and its connection with the mob-capped mouse in *The Tailor of Gloucester* (fig. 5.4).

In Potter's neatly framed illustration for *The Tailor of Gloucester,* the mouse in the mob cap is admiring herself in the mirror. A self-assured mouse, she is conscious of her desirability. She is also being admired. Two mouse eyes are peeking out at her through a narrow gap in the elegant sequined and embroidered cloth (is it a cushion?) on which she sits. You have to look closely to see the eyes because they appear to be almost part of the pattern. The mouse sits primly in her eighteenth-century dress, her tiny, mouse toes just peeping out neatly in tiny white slippers from under the frills of her skirt. Opposite the illustration the Tailor of Gloucester is muttering: "No breadth at all, and cut on the cross; it is no breadth at all; tippets for mice and ribbons for mobs! for mice!" (13). The tailor is working on a table "all littered with cherry-colored snippets." This mouse in a mob cap, gazing at herself, and being gazed at admiringly, belongs to a genre of cherry-ripe (the sexual pun was apparently familiar by the early nineteenth century) girls with tiny toes peaking out from under full skirts and large mob caps on their heads. *Penelope Boothby,* painted in 1788 by Sir Joshua Reynolds, was the original, reinterpreted by Millais as *Cherry Ripe* in 1880, but also (as Laurel Bradley points out in "From Eden to Empire: John Everett Millais's *Cherry Ripe*") by Lewis Carroll in his photograph of Xie Kitchen, and by Kate Greenaway in her "1878 greeting card design."[13]

In Millais's late-nineteenth-century England, the portrait of *Penelope Boothby* was well known. It is, in fact, among the pictures that Beatrix

Figure 5.3. John Everett Millais, *Cherry Ripe,* 1880.

Figure 5.4. Beatrix Potter, *The Tailor of Gloucester.*

Potter records in her journal as seeing at an exhibition. She calls it "renowned," but finds it "pasty and faded" (*Journal,* 133). The child, just three, was apparently doted on by her parents. She died at nine. Anne Higonnet remarks that in the Reynolds painting, even though the child is in ordinary clothes for the time, she appears to be in costume, as if "nestled in an over-sized fluffy cocoon" (Higonnet, 28). The painting was shown several times in London through the 1870s. The actual occasion for Millais's *Cherry Ripe* seems to have been contrived almost as a publicity stunt. The *Penelope Boothby* costume was worn by Edie Ramage, the niece of *Graphic* editor William Thomas, to a fancy dress ball. John Guille Millais, in the biography of his father, says that "she was so charming that she was again dressed in character and carried off to the artist's studio" (Millais, *The Life,* vol. 2, 121). So when Millais made the portrait, he was evoking the costume and manner of the preindustrial age. It was part of a series of images designed to capture both innocence and the past. That's what sold, that was the cool image. Anne Higonnet talks about the way the image of the innocent child, invented in the eighteenth century "permeated popular consciousness" in the nineteenth "swept along by the proliferation of image technologies" (Higonnet, 9). *Cherry Ripe* literally became the pinup for the genre: a color lithograph of the picture was the centrefold in the Christmas 1880 issue of *The Graphic.*

Almost from its inception, *Cherry Ripe* was spotted by the publishers of *The Graphic* as a winner. Randolph Caldecott had been commissioned to do the cover art, as a tease for the picture inside. Laurel Bradley recognizes how Caldecott caught the spirit of the age and potential influence of the picture. He sets *Cherry Ripe* on an easel in the centre of the page, or, as Bradley puts it,

> the centre of the global theatre; vignettes of world events and exotic customs which inspire weekly editorial copy swirl around the peripheries of the page. Just as English readers relish weekly bits of news told by *Graphic* writers and illustrators, so, it seems, do naked savages, Turkish pashas, and Chinese gentlemen. From the *Graphic* they gain a sense of community and participation in Anglo-Saxon culture as represented by the image of *Cherry Ripe* and PEACE, the sensible English maiden in a straw hat. Pax Britannica ushers a queue of onlookers—including British soldiers and representatives of more exotic peoples—to the alter of *Cherry Ripe* (Bradley, *Cherry Ripe,* 179).

The immediate success of the picture was so great that the proprietors had to issue an explanation in the following issue to explain why they were having delivery problems. The reproduction of a color picture, they say, means that "each copy . . . has to be printed *fourteen* times,"[14] once through the press for each color.

Cherry Ripe turned out to be a picture that would go far. *The Graphic* sold a record breaking 500,000 copies of the centrefold, and it found its way into homes all over the world, to Canadian backwoodsmen, to South Africa, to all the far-flung corners of the empire. By 1881, a mezzotint was available too. John Guille Millais, describing the *Cherry Ripe* phenomenon in his biography of his father, reports that letters of thanks for the picture poured in from all over the world, including one from an "obscure backwoodsman" in Canada whose emotional response was so intense that he felt compelled to "break forth into poetry." From Hamilton Ontario, on January 1, 1882, Athole Bank wrote:

> An humble Cannok on the shores
> Of great Ontario's lake
> Who matchless 'Cherry Ripe' adores,
> The liberty would take
>
> To throw across the wintry sea
> A warm and grateful cheer
> To glorious Millais, and may he
> Enjoy a good New Year!
> (Millais, *The Life,* vol. 2, 122)

Beatrix Potter talks about the *Cherry Ripe* phenomenon in her journal, though the reference is a little difficult to interpret because she gets the historical details incorrect. In an entry for January 13, 1885, five years after the picture made its appearance in *The Graphic,* Potter mentions it in the context of her comments on a recently published article about Millais. Almost as an afterthought, she writes: "The *Illustrated* editors made £12,000 by *Cherry Ripe*. Mr. Millais did not think the picture a success and hesitated to ask £1,500 for it, which is on his mind" (*Journal*, 122).

What puzzles me is that the details are wrong. The picture appeared in the Christmas issue of *The Graphic,* not *The Illustrated London News* (to which I assume she is referring). And Millais, according to the biography by his son, charged £1,000 for it, not £1,500. It is impossible to ask exactly what she meant, where the error lies (Millais sold several of his pictures to both *The Graphic* and *The Illustrated London News*), but the important thing is that there must have been some discussion about the way copies of a single image generate profit and reach previously inaccessible audiences. It is in November of the same year, 1885, that Beatrix Potter records the conversation between Millais and her father about the pose that became *Bubbles.* That painting appeared in *The Illustrated London News* for the Christmas issue of 1887.

As Beatrix Potter indicates in her 1885 journal entry, she was cognizant of the impact, including the financial impact, of mass marketing, though I think it unlikely that she recognized consciously that the marketable thing was innocent, pastoral, something reassuringly hopeful. Laurel Bradley is able to articulate this quality almost one hundred years after the event. Bradley says that *Cherry Ripe,* as well as the other late-nineteenth-century mob-capped girls, embodied "an idealized past anchor[ing] the whirlwind present by offering hope for an Arcadian future" (Bradley, *Cherry Ripe*, 192).

Millais was on a financial roll with the portraits of children in antique costume. He sold others to *The Graphic* and *The Illustrated News* and those reproductions went out in unprecedented numbers to the colonies. In late-nineteenth-century England, the Romantic child, according to Anne Higonnet, was probably best signified by three top-selling images: Millais's *Cherry Ripe* and *Bubbles* and Gainsborough's *Blue Boy*. Higonnet argues that the green velvet "skeleton" suit (as it was called) worn by Willie James in *Bubbles* echoes the blue suit in Gainsborough, which is itself modelled on the suits worn by the Villiers children in a 1635 Van Dyck portrait. Beatrix Potter saw Gainsborough's *Blue Boy* at an exhibition in 1885. As she records in her journal, she loved the painting:

> There is one picture at the Grosvenor that puzzles me exceedingly, the *Blue Boy* is so exceedingly different and superior to all other pictures there of its class. The colour is rich and full, the manner careful and broad without the scratchiness and the figure stands with the grace and firmness of a Van Dyck—it was painted in 1770. Why did Gainsborough never paint any more to equal it? (*Journal,* 126–27)

In the context of her other criticism of both Old Masters and contemporary art, Potter's remarks on *Blue Boy* stand as high praise. *Blue Boy* was a much-copied picture, and appeared on playing cards and other pieces of merchandise. Anne Higonnet says that it was "the single most popular image of childhood" by the end of the nineteenth century because "it had been reproduced with such protean enthusiasm" (Higonnet, 46). Beatrix Potter comments on the "full and rich" color, the "firmness and grace" of the stance. In the way of the coolhunter, Potter does nothing as tacky as put *Blue Boy* on a chocolate box. She provides an image that is comfortingly familiar, but not obviously so.

If I set *Blue Boy* (fig. 5.5) next to the image of Peter Rabbit who graced the cover of *The Peter Rabbit Almanac* for 1929 (fig. 5.6), I see a figure whose blue jacket "full and rich" in color, sets off the "firmness and grace" of the rabbit. In that particular picture, Peter is posed exactly as Gainsborough's *Blue Boy*. Both have their feet firmly planted in a very stable "Y" position, one slightly in front of the other, their toes coming to neatly shod points. Their arms are positioned in similar ways: one down (*Blue Boy* holds his hat; Peter holds a trencher basket), the other angled (*Blue Boy* just with hands on hips, Peter with a shovel over his shoulder). Their heads both look purposefully at the viewer (though as rabbits have eyes at the sides of their head, Peter's head is tilted to show an eye). And both sport a triangle of belly (*Blue Boy* wears a white shirt; Peter has fur) peeking out under their respective, distinctive blue jackets—Peter shows a rather larger triangle of belly. When the pictures are placed side by side, the trace is visible.

In analysing the genre paintings that coded the innocent child in the nineteenth century—and that we've inherited—Anne Higonnet says that there are five basic types: children in costume (*Blue Boy, Cherry Ripe,* and *Bubbles* are prototypical), children with pets, the cupid/angel child, the mother and child, and the child prefiguring adult roles. By putting pets into costumes, Potter engages two of the elements that "sold" genre paintings in the nineteenth century.

It isn't the influence of the painters that marks her. It is the element that is being sold: the pastoral, the nostalgic. It is the detail, the detail that separates the conventional from the cool. So the blue jacket and pose are what link Peter Rabbit to *Blue Boy*. It is the reference to "cherry-coloured" silks, the mob cap, and the costume that link the mouse in the mob cap in *The Tailor of Gloucester* to *Cherry Ripe*. And it is the cocked head and the balloon/bubble that link *The Story of Miss Moppet* to *Bubbles*.

In the end, as I reflect on what made Beatrix Potter a successful coolhunter, I think it had to do with her ability to understand and value the way new reproductive technologies could circulate images widely. Because Beatrix Potter believed in public access, as her work with the National Trust demonstrated, she was able to let go of the definition of the artist as someone who produced originals for an elite, limited audience.

The Huntington Library, Art Collections and Botanical Gardens, San Marino, Calif.

Figure 5.5. Thomas Gainsborough, *Blue Boy*, 1770.

Figure 5.6. Beatrix Potter, *Peter Rabbit's Almanac* for 1929.

I think that's why her work is more successful than Kate Greenaway's, for example, Beatrix Potter's contemporary purveyor of nostalgia for a pastoral, innocent England. Greenaway always wanted to be a fine artist and was encouraged in her obsession by John Ruskin, so she was unhappy about not getting the kind of institutional recognition she imagined as success. Beatrix Potter, on the other hand, was able to articulate in her work something that marked a fundamental aspect of her age that has endured through ours: the image of the innocent, Romantic child mass-marketed in multiple images. Because she deflects the trace of that image through animals, the lingering tensions associated with children as objects of desire are deflected too. But, as I've tried to demonstrate, Beatrix Potter liked to play with the fine art images that were so much a part of her early life. I'd be willing to bet that it is possible to take her journal accounts of her criticism of pictures she saw in galleries through the 1880s and 1890s, or even to track the popular accounts of those exhibitions—and find the traces in her little books. Even the thought leaves me feeling like the happy possessor of a key code that will allow access to Beatrix Potter's images I couldn't understand before.

NOTES

1. Joyce Irene Whalley and Tessa Rose Chester, *A History of Children's Book Illustration* (London: John Murray with the Victoria and Albert Museum, 1988), 84.

2. The biographical sketch is synthesized from several sources, including J. G. Millais, *The Life and Letters of Sir John Everett Millais,* 2 vols. (Toronto: George N. Morang, 1900). Hereafter cited as Millais, *The Life*; A. L. Baldry, *Sir John Everett Millais: His Art and Influence:* (London: George Bell & Sons, 1899); G. H. Fleming, *John Everett Millais: A Biography* (London: Constable, 1998). Hereafter cited as Fleming.

3. The biographical sketch of Beatrix Potter is synthesized from several sources, including Margaret Lane, *The Tale of Beatrix Potter: A Biography* (London: Frederick Warne & Co, 1946). Hereafter cited as Lane; Judy Taylor, *Beatrix Potter: Artist, Storyteller and Countrywoman* (London: Frederick Warne, 1986). Hereafter cited as Taylor; Judy Taylor, Joyce Irene Whalley, Anne Stevenson Hobbs, Elizabeth M. Battrick, *Beatrix Potter: 1866–1943* (London: F. Warne and The National Trust, 1987). Hereafter cited as Taylor, Whalley et al.

4. Michael Wilson, "Beatrix Potter and John Everett Millais," *The Beatrix Potter Society Newsletter* 63 (January 1997), 9.

5. Joyce Irene Whalley, "The Young Artist and Early Influences," in Taylor, Whalley et al., 47.

6. Michael Bartram, *The Pre-Raphaelite Camera: Aspects of Victorian Photography* (Boston: Little Brown. A New York Graphic Society Book, 1985), 171. Bartram says that "[l]ike many painters, he [Millais] kept quiet on the subject of photography."

7. John Ruskin, *Modem Painters: Of General Principles and of Truth*. Vol. 1. 2nd ed. (London: George Allen, Sunnyside, Orpington, 1898), 448.

8. Beatrix Potter, *Beatrix Potter's Letters,* selected and introduced by Judy Taylor (London: Frederick Warne, 1989), 456. Hereafter cited as *Letters.*

9. Laurel Bradley, "Millais's *Bubbles* and the Problem of Artistic Advertising," in *Pre-Raphaelite Art in Its European Contex,* ed. Susan P. Castera and Alicia Craig Faxon. (Cranbury, N.J.: Associated University Presses, 1995), 193–94.

10. Beatrix Potter, *The Journal of Beatrix Potter from 1881–1897*, transcribed from her code writing by Leslie Linder, with an appreciation by H. L. Cox (London: Frederick Warne, 1966), 154. Hereafter cited as *Journal.*

11. Malcolm Gladwell, "The Coolhunt," *The New Yorker,* 17 March 1997, 81.

12. Anne Higonnet, *Pictures of Innocence: The History and Crisis of Ideal Childhood* (London: Thames and Hudson, 1998). Hereafter cited as Higonnet.

13. Laurel Bradley, "From Eden to Empire: John Everett Millais's *Cherry Ripe,*" *Victorian Studies* 32, no. 2 (Winter 1991): 187. Hereafter cited as Bradley, *Cherry Ripe.*

14. *The Graphic,* 25 December 1880 (no. 578, vol. 22), 642.

BIBLIOGRAPHY

Baldry, A. L. *Sir John Everett Millais: His Art and Influence.* London: George Bell & Sons, 1899.

Bartram, Michael. *The Pre-Raphaelite Camera: Aspects of Victorian Photography.* Boston: Little Brown. A New York Graphic Society Book, 1985.

Bradley, Laurel. "From Eden to Empire: John Everett Millais's *Cherry Ripe.*" *Victorian Studies* 32, no. 2 (Winter 1991): 181–203.

———. "Millais's *Bubbles* and the Problem of Artistic Advertising." Pp. 193–209 in *Pre-Raphaelite Art in Its European Context,* edited by Susan P. Castera and Alicia Craig Faxon. Cranbury, N.J.: Associated University Presses, 1995.

Engen, Rodney. *Pre-Raphaelite Prints: The Graphic Art of Millais, Holman Hunt, Rossetti and Their Followers.* London: Lund Humphries, 1995.

Fleming, G. H. *John Everett Millais: A Biography.* London: Constable, 1998.

The Graphic no. 578, vol. 22, Christmas (25 December 1880).

Harvey, Michael. "Rupert Potter and Millais: A Collaboration of Photographer and Painter." *Creative Camera, 1973.*

Higonnet, Anne. *Pictures of Innocence: The History and Crisis of Ideal Childhood.* London: Thames and Hudson, 1998.

Hobbs, Anne Stevenson. *Beatrix Potter's Art.* London: Frederick Warne, 1989.

Hobbs, Anne Stevenson, and Joyce Irene Whalley. *Beatrix Potter: The V & A Collection. The Leslie Linder Bequest of Beatrix Potter Material, Watercolours, Drawings, Manuscripts, Books, Photographs and Memorabilia.* Catalogue compiled by Anne Stevenson Hobbs and Joyce Irene Whalley with the assistance of Emma Stone and Cella O'Malley. London: Victoria and Albert Museum, 1985.

Jay, Eileen, Mary Noble, and Anne Stevenson Hobbs. *A Victorian Naturalist: Beatrix Potter's Drawings from the Armitt Collection*. London: Frederick Warne, 1992.

Lane, Margaret. The *Tale of Beatrix Potter: A Biography.* 1946. Rev. ed. London: Frederick Warne, 1968.

Linder, Leslie. *A History of the Writings of Beatrix Potter: Including Unpublished Work.* London: Frederick Warne, 1971.

Mackey, Margaret. *The Case of Peter Rabbit: Changing Conditions of Literature for Children.* New York: Garland, 1998.

Millais, John Guille. *The Life and Letters of Sir John Everett Millais.* 2 vols. Toronto: George N. Morang, 1900.

Potter, Beatrix. *The Art of Beatrix Potter.* 1955. London: Frederick Warne, 1972.

———. *The Tale of Peter Rabbit.* 1902. London: Frederick Warne, 1987.

———. *The Tailor of Gloucester.* 1903. London: Frederick Warne, 1987.

———. *The Tale of Mrs. Tiggy-Winkle.* 1905. London: Frederick Warne, 1987.

———. *The Tale of Miss Moppet.* 1906. London: Frederick Warne, 1987.

———. *Peter Rabbit's Almanac for 1929*. London: Frederick Warne, 1928.

———. *The Journal of Beatrix Potter from 1881–1897*. Transcribed from her code writing by Leslie Linder. London: Frederick Warne, 1966.

Riddle, Brian L. "Beatrix Potter and Sir John Everett Millais." *The Beatrix Potter Society Newsletter* (January 1985): 15.

———. "Rupert Potter and His Photography." *The Beatrix Potter Society Newsletter* (July 1992): 45.

Ruskin, John. *Modern Painters: Of the Imaginative and Theoretic Faculties.* vol. 2. London: George Allen, 1898.

Sinnema, Peter. *Dynamics of the Pictured Page: Representing the Nation in the Illustrated London News.* Aldershot: Ashgate, 1998.

Taylor, Judy. *Beatrix Potter: Artist, Storyteller and Countrywoman.* London: Frederick Warne, 1986.

———, ed. *Beatrix Potter's Letters.* London: Frederick Warne, 1989.

Taylor, Judy, Joyce Irene Whalley, Anne Stevenson Hobbs, and Elizabeth M. Battrick. *Beatrix Potter 1866–1943: The Artist and Her World.* London: Frederick Warne and the National Trust, reissued 1995.

Wark, Robert R. *Best-Loved Paintings: The Blue Boy and Pinkie.* San Marino, Calif.: The Huntington Library, 1963.

Whalley, Joyce Irene, and Tessa Rose Chester. *A History of Children's Book Illustration.* London: John Murray with the Victoria and Albert Museum, 1988.

3

CON-TEXT

In this section, six authors, in five very different ways, explore what it is that makes *The Tale of Peter Rabbit* so timeless, often looking at it alongside other books of lasting appeal to children. June Cummins draws a comparison between *The Tale of Peter Rabbit* and *Goblin Market* by Christina Rossetti. At first glance, these two books may seem an unlikely pairing but she investigates the revolutionary and redemptive qualities that they share. Eliza Dresang investigates the radical qualities of the book, qualities that allow contemporary readers to engage freshly with it from the perspective of readers raised in a very different environment. Scott Pollard and Kara Keeling look at the importance of food, both in *The Tale of Peter Rabbit* and in the lives of small children. A recipe for rabbit pie is their comparative text, as they explore both the survival and the socialization elements in young children's eating. Alice Byrnes draws on Jung and his archetypes to investigate what it is that makes *The Tale of Peter Rabbit* so perennially relevant to little children. Melissa Gross also addresses the issue of *Peter Rabbit*'s ongoing appeal, and compares it to a different story (but one in which eating remains important), *Where the Wild Things Are*.

6

"You Should Not Loiter Longer": Beatrix Potter, Christina Rossetti, and Progressive Intertextual Revision

June Cummins

Although they were English women who lived and wrote during the Victorian era, Christina Rossetti and Beatrix Potter may not seem to have much else in common. One is famous for writing poems for adults steeped in religious and sensual imagery; the other is celebrated for writing and illustrating tiny books for children about animal characters. While both authors have been compared extensively to Lewis Carroll and examined under the light of his overwhelming influence, there has not been inquiry into the relationship of influence between the two of them. The realization, however, that certain common patterns unite two of the most well-known of these author's works leads to an inquiry into the basis, origin, and ramifications of these commonalties. Rossetti's narrative poem *Goblin Market* and Potter's first published book, *The Tale of Peter Rabbit,* concern young, rebellious characters who ignore the advice of others to pursue luscious temptation in the forms of fruits or vegetables. Explained this way, it is obvious that both stories are indebted to the biblical tale of Adam and Eve. What is not quite as apparent, however, is the extent to which the authors not only *reflect* but *revise* the biblical story, as well as other literary predecessors, and what those revisions reveal not only about the connections between the two women but about the impact each had on the development of a progressive use of intertextuality. That is, as twentieth-century scholars have demonstrated, Christina Rossetti actively and consciously used the male-authored texts that came before hers in order to shape her material, but she altered those texts in ways that empowered her female characters (and perhaps her female readers, as well). I believe that Potter, perhaps unconsciously, patterned herself after Rossetti in this regard, revising archetypal narratives in order to give power to her *child* characters (and readers). Thus, I think it is more than coincidence that these authors' most well-known works are both deeply imbued with the story of Adam and Eve, and that Potter's use of this archetype follows directly in the footsteps of Rossetti's.

So many critics have discussed the feminist context of Christina Rossetti's works that Sandra Gilbert and Susan Gubar call *Goblin Market* "something of a textual crux for feminist critics."[1] Even when critics challenge some of the assumptions underpinning feminist analyses, as Gilbert and Gubar do, almost all note that Rossetti produced "meanings about and for women in particular."[2] Research into the status and condition of women in the late Victorian era, and their reflection in literature produced in that period, is prolific. Conversely, contextual studies of Potter during the time she wrote *Peter Rabbit* have not strayed far from the strictly biographical. While the biographical aspects of the authorship of that book are important and will be discussed below, it is also critical to note late Victorian attitudes toward children in order to discern how the tale reflects and perhaps influences the construction of childhood during that period.

The Victorian era saw sweeping changes in social attitudes toward children. On the most obvious level, the public consciousness of the exploitation of child workers grew, and throughout the century, laws were passed to improve conditions for these children. For example, the Factory Act of 1833 "restricted hours of work to eight between the ages of nine and twelve, and to twelve hours between thirteen and eighteen. Children were to receive two hours' education daily, and night work was forbidden under the age of eighteen."[3] As such laws gradually came into effect and people were made more aware of the egregious conditions under which children toiled in factories, in mines, and in sweatshops, public opinion about social welfare shifted toward more support and concern for these youngest members of the population. As a result, more people believed in mandatory education for children, and throughout the century, laws were passed that provided for and enforced school attendance for children.

Many children, of course, were not working class. But as conditions changed for that cohort, all children benefited from the increasing awareness of children's needs and rights. According to social historian Eric Hopkins:

> By the end of the nineteenth century . . . [f]ew children under the age of twelve were in full-time employment, and education up to that age had become compulsory and free. The general standard of health had greatly improved, together with the expectation of life, and there was much less physical chastisement; legislation now existed against cruelty to children. . . . The nature of childhood was better understood, both in respect of relationships with the adult world, and in its influence on learning processes in school.[4]

Another historian, Harry Hendrick, makes the broad and significant claim that "the new ideas also heralded the beginnings of what can be reasonably termed 'modern childhood' in so far as between circa 1880 and 1914 childhood was in very large measure legally, legislatively, socially, medically, psychologically, educationally, and politically institutionalized."[5] Hendrick focuses specifically on the years that Potter was first developing and then establishing herself as a writer. I will examine how her creation of her protagonist Peter reflects these new attitudes and institutions.

Keeping in mind that both women's and children's roles were changing, I will first compare Rossetti's poem to Potter's book. The protagonists of both *Goblin Market* and *The Tale of Peter Rabbit,* Laura and Peter respectively, slip away from the paths of obedience to pursue the oral pleasures that put them into grave danger. Although Laura at first is aware that Goblin Men are dangerous, she is "pricking up her golden head" even as she claims, "We must not look at goblin men, / We must not buy their fruits."[6] That she looks even while telling herself not to look suggests that she is mouthing someone else's rules, and it soon becomes clear that she will not follow these rules. Laura's righteous sister, Lizzie, must admonish Laura repeatedly as Laura not only looks but urges her sister to do the same. Rossetti contrasts several sets of lines to emphasize this point, for example:

> "Oh," cried Lizzie, "Laura, Laura,
> You should not peep at goblin men."

> Lizzie covered up her eyes,
> Covered close lest they should look;
> Laura reared her glossy head,
> And whispered like the glossy brook:
> "Look, Lizzie, look, Lizzie."
> . . .
> "No," said Lizzie, "no, no, no;
> Their offers should not charm us,
> Their evil gifts would harm us."
> She thrust a dimpled finger
> In each ear, shut eyes and ran:
> Curious Laura chose to linger. . . .[7]

Mrs. Rabbit's warning to her children is more direct and less poetic: " 'Now, my dears,' said old Mrs. Rabbit one morning, 'you may go into the fields or down the lane, but don't go into Mr. McGregor's garden; your Father had an accident there; he was put in a pie by Mrs. McGregor.' "[8] Mrs. Rabbit's use of the words "garden" and "don't" more quickly align her authoritative voice with that of God in Genesis. But temptation and the connection to Genesis are readily apparent in *Goblin Market* as well, because "Apples" are the first fruit mentioned, and this particular word is repeated several times throughout the poem, along with a plethora of other kinds of fruit.[9]

Both Laura's and Peter's reckless refusals to follow the rules align them with Eve, who succumbs to the entreaties of the serpent and to the sight of the tree itself, which is "good for eating and a delight to the eyes, and . . . a source of wisdom."[10] This description makes clear that Eve is first piqued sensually—through her desires to see and eat—and that wisdom is only a secondary goal. Similarly, in *Goblin Market,* Laura desperately wants to *eat* and once she does, her desire is to partake again: "I ate and ate my fill, / Yet my mouth waters still; / To-morrow night I will / Buy more."[11] Critics recognize that Laura gains more than sensual fulfillment when she eats. Catherine Maxwell claims that the goblins' fruits are "poems," and she quotes Gilbert and Gubar, who write that Laura is "metaphorically eating *words*."[12] Maxwell weaves in references to other literary works that mix fruit and knowledge, such as Keats' "La Belle Dame Sans Merci," Coleridge's "Kubla Khan," and of course, Milton's *Paradise Lost,* where fruit is described as "intellectual food."[13] However, Rod McGillis is correct to point out that Laura becomes silent after eating the fruit, and that "she buys from the Goblins a language without polysemy."[14] In other words, McGillis does not believe that she buys a powerful language. Rossetti wants readers to see that Laura seeks and experiences sensual gratification, and that this is perhaps a stand-in for sexual gratification. In Genesis, Eve's succumbing is linked to sexual gratification, as the first result of her deed is that she and Adam become aware of their nakedness, and Eve's specific female punishment is related directly to the results of sexual behavior.

Peter's search is for oral and gustatory satisfaction, as well as a quest for power. In the illustration depicting Peter triumphantly eating radishes, Peter's pleasure is exalting. The predominance of vertical lines conveys excitement and victory; the radishes in both his mouth and his hand suggest orgiastic gratification, his head is thrown back in ecstatic delight. Thus, he is visually aligned with Laura, who "sucked and sucked and sucked the more . . . / She sucked until her lips were sore."[15] While both protagonists gain sensual satisfaction, Peter also experiences triumph and victory—power—in addition to this oral gratification.

The repercussions of the two protagonists' pleasure come quickly and painfully. Both fall ill soon after their indulgence. Laura returns home and sleeps peacefully with her sister but awakens the next day "in an absent dream."[16] By evening, she seems to be losing her strength, and over the next few days, as she realizes she can no longer hear the goblins' cries although her sister can; "her tree of life drooped from the root."[17] Soon, "her hair grew thin and gray; / She dwindled, as the fair full moon doth turn / To swift decay and burn / Her fire away."[18] She becomes too weak to do her work and stops eating, which alarms her sister. Lizzie decides she must act when Laura seems "knocking at Death's door"[19] and goes off to find the goblin fruit that might revive her.

Peter's illness comes even more swiftly and has the opposite effect. Swelled and bloated from eating too much, Peter immediately feels "rather sick" and goes to look for some parsley—a mundane antidote compared to the one Lizzie seeks for Laura, but similar in being organically related to the cause of the illness. Then Peter must endure an agonizing episode that is also both similar to and different from Laura's. While she becomes less active and unable to work, Peter must run for his life from Mr. McGregor, who wants to kill him. In the remainder of the book, Peter breathlessly scurries around the garden to avoid Mr. McGregor and another predator, a cat. He must surmount obstacles, such as a locked door, and he must shed his clothes and return to his animal stature to free himself, finally, from that garden.

Both Laura and Peter are nursed back to health through the administration of food by maternal figures. Refusing to eat the goblin fruit,

Lizzie allows herself to be smeared with it in order to bring the juices and pulp to Laura. When she returns to her sister, Lizzie utters the famous lines:

> Laura . . .
> Did you miss me?
> Come and kiss me.
> Never mind my bruises,
> Hug me, kiss me, suck my juices
> Squeezed from goblin men for you,
> Goblin pulp and goblin dew.
> Eat me, drink me, love me;
> Laura, make much of me:
> For your sake I have braved the glen
> And had to do with goblin merchant men.[20]

Whether Rossetti intended the sexuality of these lines or not, it is quite apparent that Laura's cure is one gained through both food and love. Laura must cover Lizzie with kisses in order to lick up all the fruit that will eventually restore her health.

Peter's cure is tamer and more sedate. His mother sends him to bed, but she feeds him, as Lizzie feeds Laura. When he arrives home, spent, and collapses on the ground, his mother is shown in the forefront of an illustration that depicts her in the midst of cooking, with food heaped around her. The next illustration also shows her cooking; she is making camomile tea to give to Peter. Peter does not get to gorge on fruit as Laura does and as his sisters do, on the last page of the book ("[they] had bread and milk and blackberries for supper"[21]), but he is quite comfortable, in contrast to Laura who suffers agonizing physical pain as she eats the healing fruit. Despite these differences, Peter and Laura's stories are parallel: both are warned not to eat certain foods, yet both seek the foods anyway. Both gorge on these foods, satisfying themselves sensually and perhaps gaining other kinds of power in the process; both quickly fall ill from this consumption and are in a sense expelled from the "garden" where they ate it. Up to this point, one can see how the stories are like the Genesis story of Adam and Eve. But then an important change occurs. Whereas Adam and Eve are expelled and made to suffer, Laura and Peter experience something else: redemption.

Laura regains complete health and thrives. No permanent punishments are given to her, and she grows up to be a perfectly content mother. Peter does not get blackberries like his sisters, but he is put cozily to bed, and is not yelled at or hit. In fact, Beatrix Potter considered tea quite a treat, as she details in her *Journal* in 1890, when she recalls a place where she spent part of her childhood, Camfield Place: "The pleasantest association of that pleasant room for me is of our teas there in the twilight. . . . I remember always the first teas of the visit when we were thirsty and tired. . . . I seem to hear the chink of the crockery as the nurse-girl brought it out of the closet in the wall and laid the coarse clean table cloth."[22] In addition to being coddled, Peter will prove no lesson was learned in the sequel to *Peter Rabbit,* the book *The Tale of Benjamin Bunny,* when he returns to that garden.

Rossetti and Potter have revised the story of Adam and Eve in their versions of the old story. As many critics have noted from the time of the publication of her work, Rossetti often revised the poems and stories of her literary predecessors. More recently, scholars have seen a political agenda behind Rossetti's revisionary tactics. Antony Harrison claims that "her work's focus on broad cultural issues and traditions—religious, amatory, philosophical—draws attention to the inadequacies, hypocrisies, and false values of her society as well as the literary work that has preceded her and that proceeds all around her."[23] Maxwell sees this cultural critique as feminist and believes that Rossetti is consciously inserting herself in a male tradition of poetry in order to describe and possibly change conditions for women. Rossetti is "able to assess what can be taken and transformed to suit women's needs, turning her appropriations into new expressive forms for women."[24]

What works is Rossetti appropriating, and from whom? Clearly, the biblical influences on *Goblin Market* are strong and extend beyond Genesis. Many see that Rossetti borrows also from Christian scriptures in positioning Lizzie as a Christ figure who almost sacrifices herself for Laura and who urges Laura, in order to be saved, to eat and drink her like the eucharist. Following through with this religious iconography, others see *Goblin Market* as influenced by St. Augustine's *Confessions* because both texts focus on the plucking of fruit as the "free choice of the evil will."[25] The parallels between *Goblin Market* and *Paradise Lost* are obvious in this regard. Some critics focus on the Romantic poets, drawing connections between *Goblin Market* and Keats's "La Belle Dame Sans Merci" (where the imbibing of fruit is equated with sexual activity and results in enervation)[26] or "The Eve of St. Agnes," "where luscious fruits are an aid to seduction"[27] or various works by Tennyson, such as "The Lady of Shallott" or "Tithonius," where "the sexualized imaginative world is infinitely attractive but sterile and destructive, and those who commit themselves to longing for it waste away in gloom and frustration, cut off from natural human life."[28] One of the most interesting comparisons is between *Goblin Market* and Coleridge's *Rime of the Ancient Mariner,* which many have made. However, most of these comparisons connect the two poems in terms of fall and redemption without considering the differences in the kinds of redemption depicted. Coleridge's mariner survives his ordeal at sea, which comes about because he shot the albatross, but he is not completely redeemed. He is doomed to wander the earth and tell his tale repeatedly:

> Forthwith this frame of mine was wrenched
> With a woeful agony,
> Which forced me to begin my tale;
> And then it left me free.
>
> Since then, at an uncertain hour,
> That agony returns:
> And till my ghastly tale is told,
> This heart within me burns.[29]

These lines are a strong contrast to Rossetti's description of Laura's resurrection:

> Laura awoke as from a dream,
> Laughed in the innocent old way,
> Hugged Lizzie not but twice or thrice;
> Her gleaming locks showed not one thread of gray,
> Her breath was sweet as May
> And light danced in her eyes.[30]

No contemporary critic seems to have noticed the important ironic comment Rossetti makes: when Laura falls down in a stupor after sucking the fruit off her sister, as if dead, Lizzie watches as the night passes and Laura becomes "Life out of Death." This line surely was written in direct contradiction to Coleridge's description of the specter-woman who arrives by the demon ship; her name is "Life-In-Death" and she "winneth the ancient mariner." The small lexical change—"in" to "out of"—renders an enormous change in meaning not only in terms of redemption but also regarding women's roles. "Life-In-Death" is a demon "night-mare"; "Life *out of* Death" is a restored Laura.

This alteration typifies the major thrust of change Rossetti makes in all her revisions; she revives, redeems, and restores her women characters and female plots, in effect revising literature in favor of women. Rossetti's connections to earlier texts are not examples of unconscious reworkings of stories men tell, but intertextual revisions conscious of their predecessors, actively engaged with both honoring and challenging them.

The word "intertextuality" has become increasingly popular, but it is often used in a narrow sense of "allusion." In fact, "intertextuality" encompasses the very notion of textual production. As Julia Kristeva explains in "Word, Dialogue, Novel," "[A]ny text is constructed of a mosaic of quotations; any text is the absorption and transformation of another."[31] That is, all works of literature are connected to earlier works and arise out of an historical assortment of earlier and parallel texts. The concept of intertextuality holds that art always carries within it the echoes of art already made—no artist can escape the history behind what he or she creates. But Kristeva and other French theorists see intertextuality functioning on the level of discourse, not of influence. Kristeva's editor, Leon Roudiez, emphatically argues that intertextuality "has nothing to do with matters of influence by one writer upon another, or with the sources of a literary work; it does, on the other hand, involve the components of a *textual system*, such as the novel, for instance. It is defined . . . as the transposition of one or more *systems* of signs into another, accompanied by a new articulation of the enunciative and denotative position."[32] Despite this argument, American theorists, stemming from Harold Bloom in *The Anxiety of Influence,* have not denied the author's role in textual production, a stance Susan Stanford Friedman sees as reflective of differences in American and French history and culture. Friedman describes the work of feminist critics who view the erasure of the author, particularly the female author, as problematic. Nancy K. Miller, for example, develops a model she calls "arachnology" in which, as Friedman explains, she "examines the weaving of women's texts as they are interwoven with many other texts (female and male). The text as an intertextual weaving of other historical and cultural texts (the 'already read') is assumed, but Miller refuses to accept the concept of anonymity that Barthes, Foucault, and Kristeva promote in their versions of intertextuality."[33] If Barthes sees textual production as a "web," Friedman argues, "Miller insists on reintroducing the spider—as author, as subject, as agent, as gendered body, as producer of the text."[34] For feminist critics, female authors' use of intertextuality must be cognizant of the artists who wrote before them because their writing project is at some level always political. This author-centered definition of intertextuality is necessary in our attempt to understand what Rossetti and Potter were doing in their reworkings of the old stories. When texts are related in this way, not just echoing earlier versions of stories but revising them in corrective or empowering fashions, I call their interlinked connection "progressive intertextual revision." That is, these authors do not just continue in a traditional path, but both by paying homage to their predecessors and by suggesting new ways of telling and especially ending their stories, the authors make differences that are liberating, powerful, and inherently political.

Rossetti's *Goblin Market* unquestionably participates in intertextual "absorption and transformation," and we can see why her adjustments are progressive. Maxwell directly relates her tactics to feminist strategies, focusing on the trope of eating that Rossetti relies upon so heavily. Maxwell writes, "While the poem itself literally and figuratively demonstrates how each new text consumes other texts, is ceaselessly chewing over and redistributing the language of other texts, it also intimates that male-authored writings require extra-careful digestion by a woman's intertext. . . . Rossetti [is] banqueting, not on bitterness, as [other feminist critics suggest], but on the purloined spoils of her [literary] travels. . . ."[35]

Potter is also banqueting, in the same dangerous but ultimately successful way Peter does on Mr. McGregor's fruits, but on the texts not only of male authors but of a female author, too, namely Christina Rossetti. The influence of male-authored texts are apparent in *Peter Rabbit*. If one posits God to be male, as society generally does, then we can see not only the influence of Genesis, discussed above, but of the parable of the Prodigal Son, which relates the story of the son who leaves home and wastes his inheritance but is welcomed back into the family fold upon his return. Peter also does exactly what he should not be doing, abandoning his coat in the process, an economic loss his mother comments upon. Although his sisters behave appropriately, and he does not, he is not rejected when he returns. One can also observe strains of the David and Goliath story as well as the influence of Homer's *Odyssey,* with its story of an adventurous man who has extreme and exciting experiences but is determined to return home, even if he takes the long way round. Both Odysseus and Peter experience a *nostos,* a homecoming, that begins with each having to sleep on the floor, but each of them ends up back in the comfortable bed that is rightfully his.

Clearly, Potter engages male-authored texts. When she aligns Peter with characters who prevail, such as David or Odysseus, she does not greatly alter the contours of the archetypal story underlying her own.

But as discussed above, she definitely transforms the ending of the most closely linked story, that of Adam and Eve. We can wonder if she was influenced by Rossetti in this alteration. There is no evidence that Potter read *Goblin Market,* but her journals do reveal knowledge of the artist Dante Gabriel Rossetti, Christina's brother, and the Pre-Raphaelite group. In fact, Potter mentions Dante Rossetti several times in her journal. She also refers to Christina Rossetti once, when she wonders who should replace Alfred, Lord Tennyson as poet laureate. Potter makes several suggestions, including Rossetti, and thinks that her taking on the title would be "not altogether inappropriate at the end of our good Queen's reign."[36] Clearly, Potter was aware of Rossetti's work, so it seems quite likely that Potter would have known of *Goblin Market,* as it was widely disseminated. Whether or not she had Rossetti's retelling of the Genesis story in mind when she wrote *Peter Rabbit,* Potter reflects Rossetti because both authors tell stories with the same cycle set forth in Genesis, that of temptation, indulgence, and suffering, and both women also add the additional step of redemption.

Whether this reflection is conscious or not is less important than the parallels between the two women's work and how both of them do more than demonstrate their intertextual origins; remarkably, they both question and subvert those origins in ways that empower their protagonists. Scholars have noted this subversive element in Potter, as in the most well-known article on the subject, by Humphrey Carpenter, "Excessively Impertinent Bunnies: The Subversive Element in Beatrix Potter." Carpenter maintains that Potter's tales are "immoral" and that "the voice we hear again and again in her stories is not that of the late Victorian spinster decorously instructing her nieces and child-friends in acceptable social behavior, but of a rebel, albeit a covert one, demonstrating the rewards of nonconformity, and exhorting her young readers to question the social system into which they find themselves born."[37] In the same way that Rossetti scholar Harrison sees his author as writing "a critique of particular deficiencies and false values basic to the social reality of Victorian England,"[38] Carpenter argues that Potter "display[s] a vigorous contempt for most of the accepted Victorian values."[39]

Another Potter critic, W. Nikola-Lisa, focuses on the link between the social rebel Potter and her social rebel creation Peter. He believes Peter represents the conflicts Potter experienced as a woman, writing "Peter Rabbit *is* the projection of [the] inner state of tension indicative of women caught between the confines of the home and the lure of unrestricted freedom."[40] I would take Nikola-Lisa's argument a step further and claim that Peter stands in not just for the restrictions Potter felt because she was female, but also for the difficult limitations experienced by *children,* especially in Victorian England.

Although Potter married late in life and did not have children of her own, she would have had first-hand knowledge of Victorian childhood as she held a child's subject position for the majority of that era, a condition to be explored further below. Some argue that Potter was distant from children and therefore would not have understood their needs. At least one critic believes that Potter did not understand children well and was not comfortable with them. Ruth MacDonald opines "throughout her life Potter was both familiar with and aloof from children. . . . ."[41] But MacDonald's evidence that Potter felt estranged from children could be used to prove the opposite. MacDonald writes, "the opening line of [a] letter, which later developed into *The Tale of Peter Rabbit,* is indicative of the distance that Potter felt between herself and children, even though at the same time she was more at ease with children than adults: 'I don't know what to write to you, so I shall tell you the story of four little rabbits. . . .' "[42] Rather than seeing Potter's claim that she does not know what to say to children as indicative of uncomfortable and perhaps unbreachable difference, one could argue that her immediate discovery of just what she should say, namely the opening words of one the most successful children's stories ever written, in fact proves she understands children intimately and deeply. Potter continually observes children in detail throughout her *Journal*, revealing her conscious attention to this population.

Perhaps Potter was sympathetic because her own childhood was protracted, as it were, since she did not marry until she was 46 years old. In accordance with the custom of the times, she lived with her parents until her marriage. Thus, unlike most women, who acquire new identity markers fairly early in life when they marry or begin to work, Potter was first and foremost "daughter" for a very long time. The third-floor room in the Potter London home that served as Potter's nursery later became her "playroom, schoolroom and eventually her studio."[43] In effect, Potter inhabited her nursery for 46 years. More influential than her living arrangements, her parents' attitude toward Potter remained authoritative and controlling for as long as she lived in their household. They did not like to see their daughter developing independence and sought to preside over all her decisions. They also expected her to take care of them. MacDonald describes her parents' reaction when Norman Warne proposed to Potter. "That Beatrix Potter was gradually making enough money to become financially independent was threatening enough to her parents, who expected their daughter to remain always dependent and attentive. . . . That she would consider marriage to . . . a tradesman was, literally, beyond words. The young lady that the Potters *had kept so consistently stunted in the role of obedient child* was apparently growing up. . . ."[44] Potter was 39 years old.

Potter felt restricted and even oppressed by her parents, but it would not occur to her to take an activist stand against their control, on either the local level of staging protest within the household or on the global level of demonstrating for women's rights, as she was "opposed both by temperament and conviction to the idea of Woman Suffrage."[45] While she was very politically aware and wrote extensively and critically about the government in her journals, she was not a liberal and came to identify strongly with conservative policies when she found that the Liberal Government did not support the Tarriff Reform she believed was necessary for the foreign copyrights of her books and the production of the toys associated with them.[46] No one could claim that she demonstrated for women's rights or children's rights. But liberal, activist influences did have an effect on Potter. Her grandfather, Edmund Potter, of whom her father was very proud, was "a Dissenter . . . he campaigned for religious equality and toleration. He was a Radical, a free-trader, a humane magistrate, a delighted spectator of the progress of science, an amateur of the arts."[47] And Beatrix's own contemporary, her beautiful cousin Caroline Hutton, "held all sorts of radical and free-thinking views which Beatrix found stimulating, if rather outrageous."[48] Potter wrote in her diary that "Caroline talked of labourers, their miserable wages of eleven shillings a week, their unsanitary cottages, their appalling families and improvidence. All with feeling and sense, and a refreshing unconsciousness of the world's obstinacy and difficulties, always with common sense and courage."[49] Clearly admiring of her cousin, Potter may not have shared her views but learned that one could critique and try to change conditions. Accordingly, when Warne proposed to her and her parents vociferously objected to the idea of her marrying him, Potter did not accede to their demands. "Though her parents would not agree to it and there could be no public announcement, she quietly proclaimed herself engaged, and openly wore a ring."[50] Rebellion, even on a small scale, was an option for Beatrix Potter.

Close examination of the journals she kept for 15 years, from ages 15 to 30 (a crucial time in terms of the development of opinions and attitudes) reveals not only that Potter perceived injustices but that she also believed that she as an individual could make changes, even on a small scale. If Potter was an activist for any cause, it was for animals. Throughout her journals, she criticizes those who mistreat animals and she takes steps to aid animals when she can. An exemplary incident occurred when Potter was 26 years old and out walking her own pet rabbit, Benjamin:

> I saw Miss Hutton's black cat jumping on something up the wood. I thought it was too far off to interfere, but as [the cat] seemed leisurely I went up in time to rescue a poor little rabbit, fast in a snare. The cat had not hurt it, but I had great difficulty in slackening the noose round its neck. I warmed it at the fire, relieved it from a number of fleas, and it came round. It was such a poor little creature compared to mine. They are regular vermin, but one cannot stand by to see a thing mauled about from ones [sic] friendship for the race. Papa in his indignation pulled up the snare. I fancy our actions were much more illegal than Miss Hutton's.[51]

Potter's comments here are revealing in several ways. First, she does not romanticize a wild rabbit; she calls it "vermin" but does not see it as being less deserving of life and freedom from pain than her own well-fed pet. In addition, she acts swiftly and without heed to ownership when she sees an animal suffering, and she goes to great lengths to help heal a hurt animal. Finally, she is consciously aware that her father and she may have broken a law, but she believes that trapping an animal is wrong and thus her ethical sense permits this breach. This anecdote, a relatively small incident in the annals of fifteen years of keeping a diary, is critically important when one considers whose "side" Potter is on in her story of the naughty rabbit who must run for his life.

Can we assume that if Potter believed in animal rights she also believed in children's rights? Even if her conscious understanding of childhood and even of actual children themselves was limited, Potter was an acute observer of her society. While she herself spent her protracted childhood living in a Victorian regime, the world around her marched into the twentieth century. As discussed at the beginning of this article, conditions for children improved dramatically throughout the nineteenth century. It is important to note that historians consider these changes not just in terms of health and economics, but also in terms of the emotional lives of children. Hopkins claims, "there is no doubt in [my] mind that the state of childhood was transformed, not merely changed or modified, . . . in the second half of the [nineteenth] century; for the majority of children, life provided far greater opportunities for self-fulfillment and enjoyment in 1900 than in 1800."[52] Looking not only at educational improvements but also at the cultivation of the viewpoint that children pass through developmental stages with "different psychological characteristics and needs appropriate to each stage," and at the fact that the field of child psychology was gaining acceptance, and pointing out the legislation that protected children from abuse and ill-use, Hopkins concludes that these new perspectives demonstrate that "childhood in itself had gained a new status in the early twentieth century."[53]

Harry Hendrick looks closely at familial relationships, especially those between mothers and children. He notes that attitudes toward obedience, authority, and punishment were largely informed by economic class. Throughout most of the nineteenth century, working-class families enforced strict discipline and parents did not openly demonstrate love and affection, for, as Hendrick explains, "overcrowding and poverty encouraged rigid discipline."[54] However, as the twentieth century began, "there was a demographic background to the rise of 'progressive' child-rearing among sections of the middle class in the early 1900s, and . . . a parallel change occurred among the working class. Fewer children . . . made the home less overcrowded and easier to keep clean; there was more time for individual affection and less pressure to impose strict discipline."[55] Hendrick contends that smaller family size (from an average of six children in the 1860s to three in the 1900s) and the rising standard of living resulted in much improved relations between parents and children.[56] It is very interesting to note that Peter Rabbit's home situation does *not* reflect smaller family size or an increased standard of living. His mother is a single parent, the loss of his coat is an economic hardship, and there are all those *sisters,* yet Mrs. Rabbit's disciplinary measures are much more in line with parenting attitudes of the Edwardian era than of the Victorian era. That Peter is put to bed instead of being punished despite losing his coat, that he is not hit or given a talking-to or even scolded, all point to a patient tolerance and an enlightened approach to parenting. Potter seems aware of the social changes that led to such reforms in discipline techniques.

One could argue that Peter's misbehavior is accepted because he is a boy, but I believe that when child readers respond to him they are identifying with something else. Peter's appeal is that he bucks the system not because he is male (although his maleness is certainly valorized in the story), and not because he is an animal (although he must revert to his natural animal state in order to survive) but because he is a *child.*

While a definite contrast is set up between the "good bunnies" who are female and the "naughty" bunny, Peter, the text belies this distinction by aligning the reader's sympathy and interest with the naughty character (and by making the "good" bunnies look rather boring and dull, possibly even stupid). What is not challenged is that Peter survives Mr. McGregor when his own *father* did not. He refuses to heed his mother's reminder of why he should not go into the garden: by not only going there but by eating his fill *and* making it safely home, Peter undeniably bests his departed, eaten dad. Father is eaten; Peter is the eater. That Peter is not harshly punished for his misbehavior, that he is tucked into bed and taken care of, and that he will go out and do the same thing again, all put his children readers on his side, rooting for him and valorizing his activities. In effect, in the way Rossetti has written a feminist, pro-woman tale, Potter has written a *pro-child* story, and that may, in the end, explain its enduring popularity.

Comparing Rossetti and Potter this way helps us deepen our understanding of intertextuality and revision. In *Goblin Market* Lizzie tells Laura that she should keep away from the goblin men, that she "should not loiter longer" on the path near them. Male authors are not goblins, but "loitering" in their texts can be harmful, as such loitering is conservative and possibly reductive. Instead, some Victorian female authors moved in a progressive direction. Rossetti reworked older texts in order to write new stories that privileged and empowered women. Looking through the lens of intertextuality, we see that Potter walked in the footsteps Rossetti made, but broadened the path by focusing on the rights of children. Both women should be acknowledged as instigating a tradition of writing that would find fulfillment in the works of women and children's writers because both of these genres, women's literature and children's literature, would burgeon in the twentieth century. Neither woman denied the rich artistic tradition that lay behind her texts, but each enlarged literature as both art and history by refusing to loiter and instead traveling right through the garden, leaving it behind not because she was expelled but because she saw the intriguing landscape beyond.

NOTES

1. Sandra Gilbert and Susan Gubar, *The Madwoman in the Attic: The Woman Writer and the Nineteenth-Century Literary Imagination* (New Haven and London: Yale University Press, 1979), 566. For feminist analyses of Christina Rossetti in addition to studies discussed in the body of this article, see Elizabeth Russell

and Eileen Fauset, "Christina Rossetti: Contemporary Feminist," *Bells: Barcelona English Language & Literature Studies* 6 (1995):143–55; Frederick S. Roden, "Two 'Sisters in Wisdom': Hildegard of Bingen, Christina Rossetti, and Feminist Theology," in *Hildegard of Bingen: A Book of Essays*, ed. Maud Burnett (New York: Garland, 1998), 227–57; Virginia Sickbert, "Christina Rossetti and Victorian Children's Poetry: A Maternal Challenge to the Patriarchal Family," *Victorian Poetry* 31, no. 4 (1993): 385–410; Antony H. Harrison, "Christina Rossetti and the Sage Discourse of Feminist High Anglicanism," in *Victorian Sages and Cultural Discourse: Renegotiating Gender and Power*, ed. E. Thais (New Brunswick, N.J.: Rutgers University Press, 1990), 87–104; Isobel Armstrong, "Christina Rossetti: Diary of a Feminist Reading," *Women Reading Women's Writing*, ed. Sue Roe (Brighton: Harvester; 1987), 115–37.

2. Gilbert and Gubar, *Madwoman in the Attic*, 566.

3. Eric Hopkins, *Childhood Transformed: Working-Class Children in Nineteenth-Century England* (Manchester: Manchester University Press, 1994), 76.

4. Hopkins, *Childhood Tranformed*, 1.

5. Harry Hendrick, *Children, Childhood and English Society, 1880–1990* (Cambridge: Cambridge University Press, 1997), 14–15.

6. Christina Rossetti, *Goblin Market*, *The Norton Anthology of English Literature,* 6th ed., vol. 2 (New York: Norton, 1993), 1479, ll. 41–43.

7. Christina Rossetti, *Goblin Market*, 1480, ll. 48-54, 64–69.

8. Beatrix Potter, *The Tale of Peter Rabbit* (London: Frederick Warne, 1902), 10.

9. Neither the Hebrew Bible nor the Christian Bible refers to the fruit Eve eats as an apple. But contemporary audiences do equate the apple with Eve's temptation, based on a very long tradition cemented by John Milton in *Paradise Lost*. Cf. Book IX, line 584 of *Paradise Lost* (1674 edition).

10. Genesis 3.6.

11. Rossetti, *Goblin Market*, 1482, ll. 165-68.

12. Catherine Maxwell, "Tasting the 'Fruit Forbidden': Gender, Intertextuality, and Christina Rossetti's *Goblin Market*," in *The Culture of Christina Rossetti: Female Poetics and Victorian Contexts*, eds. Mary Arseneau, Antony H. Harrison, and Lorraine Janzen Kooistra (Athens, Ohio: Ohio University Press, 1999), 80.

13. Catherine Maxwell, "Tasting the 'Fruit Forbidden,' " 80–83.

14. Roderick McGillis, "Simple Surfaces: Christina Rossetti's Work for Children," in *The Achievement of Christina Rossetti*, ed. David A. Kent (Ithaca and London: Cornell University Press, 1987), 212, 218.

15. Rossetti, *Goblin Market*, 1481, ll. 134, 136.

16. Rossetti, *Goblin Market*, 1483, l. 211.

17. Rossetti, *Goblin Market*, 1484, l. 260.

18. Rossetti, *Goblin Market*, 1484, ll. 277–80.

19. Rossetti, *Goblin Market*, 1485, l. 321.

20. Rossetti, *Goblin Market*, 1488, ll. 464-74.

21. Potter, *The Tale of Peter Rabbit*, 59.

22. Beatrix Potter, *The Journal of Beatrix Potter* (London: Frederick Warne, 1966), 436.

23. Antony Harrison, *Christina Rossetti in Context* (Chapel Hill and London: University of North Carolina Press, 1988), 159.

24. Maxwell, "Tasting the 'Fruit Forbidden,' " 86.

25. Harrison, *Christina Rossetti in Context*, 99.

26. Cf. Mermin and Maxwell.

27. Maxwell, "Tasting the 'Fruit Forbidden,' " 82.

28. Dorothy Mermin, "Heroic Sisterhood in *Goblin Market*," *Victorian Poetry* 21, no. 2 (1982): 108.

29. Samuel Coleridge, *The Rime of the Ancient Mariner*, in *The Norton Anthology of English Literature*, 6th ed., vol. 2 (New York: Norton, 1993), 345, ll. 578–86.

30. Rossetti, *Goblin Market*, 1490, ll. 537–42.

31. Julia Kristeva, "Word, Dialogue, and Novel," in *Desire and Language: A Semiotic Approach to Literature and Art*, ed. Leon S. Roudiez, trans. Thomas Gora, et al. (New York: Columbia University Press, 1980), 66.

32. Leon Roudiez, "Introduction," in *Desire and Language: A Semiotic Approach to Literature and Art*, ed. Leon S. Roudiez, trans. Thomas Gora, et al. (New York: Columbia University Press, 1980), 15.

33. Susan Stanford Friedman, "Weavings: Intertextuality and the (Re)Birth of the Author," in *Influence and Intertextuality in Literary History*, eds. Jay Clayton and Eric Rothstein (Madison: University of Wisconsin Press, 1991), 158.

34. Friedman, "Weavings," 158.

35. Maxwell, "Tasting the 'Fruit Forbidden,' " 97.

36. Potter, *The Journal of Beatrix Potter*, 278.

37. Humphrey Carpenter, "Excessively Impertinent Bunnies: The Subversive Element in Beatrix Potter," in *Children and Their Books: A Celebration of the Work of Iona and Peter Opie*, eds. Gillian Avery and Julia Briggs (Oxford: Clarendon Press, 1989), 279.

38. Harrison, *Christina Rossetti in Context*, 149.

39. Carpenter, "Excessively Impertinent Bunnies," 279.

40. W. Nikola-Lisa, "The Cult of Peter Rabbit: A Barthesian Analysis," *Lion and the Unicorn* 15, no. 2 (1991): 65.

41. Ruth MacDonald, *Beatrix Potter* (Boston: Twayne Publishers, 1986), 12–13.

42. MacDonald, *Beatrix Potter*, 12.

43. Judy Taylor, *Beatrix Potter: Artist, Storyteller, and Countrywoman*. (London: Frederick Warne, 1986; reprint 1987), 17.

44. MacDonald, *Beatrix Potter*, 16 (italics added).

45. Margaret Lane, *The Tale of Beatrix Potter* (London: Frederick Warne, 1946; revised edition 1968), 105.

46. Potter was incensed when she realized other countries were manufac-

turing Peter Rabbit toys and that she could not get the toys made in England. Furthermore, because the United States had tariff laws, she could not get her books copyrighted there, and they were being pirated and reprinted with no payment to her. Potter became very involved with the Tariff Reform movement, hand-lettering and distributing signs for a cause that ultimately failed. This was Potter's one foray into politics and "the year of this memorable election was long distinguished in conversation by the Potter family as 'the year when Bee went into politics' (Lane, *Tale of Beatrix Potter*, 106).

47. Lane, *Tale of Beatrix Potter*, 18.
48. Lane, *Tale of Beatrix Potter*, 67.
49. Potter, *The Journal of Beatrix Potter*, 316.
50. Lane, *Tale of Beatrix Potter*, 84.
51. Potter, *The Journal of Beatrix Potter*, 300.
52. Hopkins, *Childhood Transformed*, 320.
53. Hopkins, *Childhood Transformed*, 321.
54. Hendrick, *Children, Childhood, and English Society*, 19.
55. Hendrick, *Children, Childhood, and English Society*, 18.
56. Hendrick, *Children, Childhood, and English Society*, 18.

BIBLIOGRAPHY

Carpenter, Humphrey. "Excessively Impertinent Bunnies: The Subversive Element in Beatrix Potter." Pp. 271–98 in *Children and Their Books: A Celebration of the Work of Iona and Peter Opie*, edited by Gillian Avery and Julia Briggs. Oxford: Clarendon Press, 1989.

Coleridge, Samuel. *The Rime of the Ancient Mariner*. Pp. 330–46 in *The Norton Anthology of English Literature*. 6th ed., vol. 2, edited by M. H. Abrams. New York: W.W. Norton and Co., 1993.

Friedman, Susan Stanford. "Weavings: Intertextuality and the (Re)Birth of the Author." Pp. 146–80 in *Influence and Intertextuality in Literary History*, edited by Jay Clayton and Eric Rothstein. Madison: University of Wisconsin Press, 1991.

Harrison, Antony. *Christina Rossetti in Context*. Chapel Hill and London: University of North Carolina Press, 1988.

Hendrick, Harry. *Children, Childhood and English Society, 1880–1990*. Cambridge: Cambridge University Press, 1997.

Hopkins, Eric. *Childhood Transformed: Working-Class Children in Nineteenth-Century England*. Manchester: Manchester University Press, 1994.

Kristeva, Julia. "Word, Dialogue, and Novel." Pp. 64–91 in *Desire and Language*, edited by Leon S. Roudiez, translated by Thomas Gora, et al. New York: Columbia University Press, 1980.

Lane, Margaret. *The Tale of Beatrix Potter*. London: Frederick Warne, 1946, revised edition, 1968.

MacDonald, Ruth K. *Beatrix Potter*. Boston: Twayne Publishers, 1986.

Maxwell, Catherine. "Tasting the 'Fruit Forbidden': Gender, Intertextuality, and Christina Rossetti's *Goblin Market*." Pp. 74–102 in *The Culture of Christina Rossetti: Female Poetics and Victorian Contexts*, edited by Mary Arseneau, Antony H. Harrison, and Lorraine Janzen Kooistra. Athens, Ohio: Ohio University Press, 1999.

McGillis, Roderick. "Simple Surfaces: Christina Rossetti's Work for Children." Pp. 208–30 in *The Achievement of Christina Rossetti*, edited by David A. Kent. Ithaca and London: Cornell University Press, 1987.

Mermin, Dorothy. "Heroic Sisterhood in *Goblin Market*." *Victorian Poetry* 21, no. 2 (1982): 107–18.

Nikola-Lisa. W. "The Cult of Peter Rabbit: A Barthesian Analysis." *Lion & the Unicorn*. 15, no. 2 (1991): 61–66.

Potter, Beatrix. *The Tale of Peter Rabbit*. London: Frederick Warne, 1902.

Potter, Beatrix. *The Journal of Beatrix Potter*. London: Frederick Warne, 1966.

Rossetti, Christina. *Goblin Market*. Pp. 1479–90 in *The Norton Anthology of English Literature*. 6th ed., vol. 2, edited by M. H. Abrams. New York: W.W. Norton, 1993.

Roudiez, Leon. "Introduction," Pp. 1–20 in *Desire and Language: A Semiotic Approach to Literature and Art*, edited by Leon S. Roudiez, translated by Thomas Gora et al. New York: Columbia University Press, 1980.

Taylor, Judy. *Beatrix Potter: Artist, Storyteller, and Countrywoman*. London: Frederick Warne, 1986. Reprint, 1987.

7

Radical Qualities of *The Tale of Peter Rabbit*

Eliza T. Dresang

Mr. McGregor, Gardener's Cottage
Dear Sir,
I write to ask whether your spring cabbages are ready?
Kindly reply by return & oblige.
Yrs truly,
Peter Rabbit[1]

"It's wonderful how Peter Rabbit keeps on selling,"[2] Beatrix Potter wrote to her publisher fourteen years after the Frederick Warne edition appeared in 1902. Peter Rabbit's popularity extends back to the first privately printed edition that Beatrix Potter produced for friends after being turned down by several publishers—and forward to the present day. The initial private "run" of 250 copies was immediately followed with 200 more due to substantial demand.[3] Prior to the appearance of the first commercial edition, the entire first printing of 8,000 had been spoken for,[4] and by the end of 1903, 50,000 copies had sold.[5] Year after year approximately 75,000 of the original version are purchased for libraries and homes.[6] Why this enduring popularity?

Numerous perspectives exist from which this question can be accurately addressed, among them the appeal of the archetypical home-away-home hero tale, the brilliance of Potter's artistic talent combined with her scientific knowledge, and the pull of her poetic prose. I propose in this essay another perspective from which to examine the instant and enduring popularity of *Peter Rabbit,* one of prime importance in the contemporary digital age, one that focuses on the radical qualities of Potter's deceptively simple story. These radical qualities, a departure from the norm both in Potter's time and throughout much of the twentieth century, are mentioned here and there in literary analyses, but only recently have they become noticeable and noticed in a large number of books for young readers. It was not until the late twentieth century that a literary theory, Radical Change, provided a holistic, explicative method for understanding the nontraditional traits found in numerous digital age books. Close examination reveals that many of the same radical characteristics appeared in a few precursors to these digital age books, creations of authors and illustrators like Potter, rebellious in their own way as the little rabbit himself.

A RADICAL THEORY

Radical Change[7] as a literary theory can be used to identify books with characteristics reflecting the interactivity, connectivity, and access associated with the digital world. It can be applied to books for youth published in any time period because these characteristics existed both in society and in literature long before they became as commonplace as they are in the twenty-first century. This interactivity, connectivity, and access in literature for youth can be identified through the presence of complex and unexpected forms and formats, perspectives, characters, topics, and themes that engage children's intellect and emotion, and show respect for and confidence in the sophistication of even the very young.

ADULTS, CHILDHOOD, AND LITERARY LINKS

Two ideologies about children and childhood have battled for preeminence throughout the past two centuries. One stems from the Augustine traditions of John Calvin, John Wesley, and later, Sigmund Freud who perceived an inborn sinfulness in children that had to be controlled and corrected. This ideology is children-as-depraved-and-in-need-of-redemption. A competing ideology that dominated much of nineteenth- and twentieth-century thought about children stemmed from the philosophy of Jean Jacques Rousseau, who idealized childhood and saw children as close to nature. The writings of Romantic poet William Wordsworth, who believed in the innate innocence of children that could be tarnished without proper care, also influenced the development of this ideology. It is best expressed as an ideology that sees children-as-innocent-and-needing-protection.

Perhaps this view developed, also, from the desire some adults had to right various wrongs that had been done children in forcing them into wretched work situations at very early ages. In a recent book, *Kids on Strike!* (1999), Susan Campbell Bartoletti presents historical evidence that while children *do* need a certain level of protection, this need neither signals innocence nor negates their capacity for leadership and collective power. Prior to the enactment of child labor laws in the United States, thousands of children were hired at low wages to work long hours in poor conditions. Such exploitation still happens today in many parts of the world. Ironically, although the many protests in which children were leaders brought attention, sympathy, and eventually managerial and legislative action, they also brought a backlash. An overly protective public did not recognize, or did not want to recognize, the ability and intelligence of the young people, particularly young women, who had participated in the protests.[8] These same adults did not appreciate that the protections put in place in reaction to harsh conditions were frequently overprotections that stifled creativity and productive independent thinking.

A third parallel strand of thought about children exists but was not widespread during the nineteenth and early twentieth centuries despite the visibility of accomplished, activist children apparent in labor disputes and elsewhere. It took perceptive philosophers and educators, such as John Dewey (late nineteenth century), or social critics, such as Marina Warner (late twentieth century),[9] to see behind the other ideologies to an alternative description of childhood. In the 1990s, other voices spoke up for the very apparent capabilities of children in the digital environment, among them MIT professor Seymour Papert, who refers to the remarkable affinity that youth have for the computer in *The Children's Machine* (1993), MIT professor Sherry Turkle, who says "it is our children who are leading the way,"[10] and Don Tapscott, author of *Growing Up Digital* (1998). Now, in the early years of the twenty-first century, suddenly a cacophony of voices is lauding the abilities of youth and noting that adults are learning from them, particularly in the area of technology. Finally, this third, and most respectful and productive, ideology of childhood has taken a prominent, though hardly uncontested, place in the public eye.

The theory of Radical Change is based upon the third ideology of children-as-capable-and-seeking-connection. The digital age with its interactivity, connectivity, and access provides children an opportunity to demonstrate their capabilities much sooner than most environments have done in the past. Children find their own access via computers and the Internet to arenas that were considered too complex for their understanding—yet they do understand, interact, and create world-wide connections.

It has long been accepted that what adult authors believe about children affects the literature that is written for them.[11] The "depraved" and the "innocent" ideologies have influenced the content of children's books, the former in producing moralistic tales for edification and the later in producing simple, straightforward, ultimately reassuring tales "with the appealing view of childhood as quaint, charming and unsullied"[12] such as those found in the works of Kate Greenaway, an influential illustrator whose works just preceded Potter's. Potter did not have a great deal of respect for Greenaway's artistic ability.

A few pre-digital age radical authors and illustrators ignored the children-as-depraved and the children-as-innocent paradigms and homed in on the children-as-capable point of view. The visual synergy of the text and illustrations in Wanda Gag's *Millions of Cats* (1928), the taboo topics of social class and race in Florence Crandall Mean's books of the 30s and 40s, the rebellious actions of Max in his wolf suit in Maurice Sendak's *Where the Wild Things Are* (1963), and the multilayered text in E. B. White's *Charlotte's Web* (1952) exemplify radical traits in pre-digital age books. Beatrix Potter's books can be numbered among these radical few, for her respect for the capabilities of children permeates *Peter Rabbit* and has led to its label as "the first English classic for very young children."[13]

A REBEL WITH A CAUSE

"More has been written about the life and works of Beatrix Potter than of any other purely children's writer except 'Lewis Carroll.' "[14] It is, therefore, not difficult to find evidence from which to draw parallels between aspects of Beatrix Potter's life that fall outside of late nineteenth- and early twentieth-century tradition and radical traits in the first and most famous of her writings for children, *The Tale of Peter Rabbit.*

At the time Potter wrote *Peter Rabbit* (and to some extent to this day), both women and children were marginalized members of society. Even in upper-class British society, Beatrix Potter led a lonely life as a child and young woman, unable to realize her ambition to become a recognized scientist or artist. The most radical quality about Beatrix Potter's picture books is that they liberated her own pent-up creative spirit while liberating the children to whom her stories were addressed. She was a rebel with a cause, using her picture books and the profits from them to move from the marginalized position in which society had placed her to a place of centrality, and providing a vehicle for the children for whom she wrote and generations after to travel with her.

INTERACTIVITY, CONNECTIVITY, AND ACCESS

The digital age qualities identified by Radical Change have appeared, thus far, to fall into three types of change—changing forms and formats, changing perspectives, and changing boundaries—all of which become apparent in an analysis of *Peter Rabbit* looking back over the twentieth century from the radical change perspective.

Changing Forms and Formats

The changing forms and formats identified by Radical Change occur in books that convey information in a bold, graphic manner and in exciting new forms and formats. They incorporate one or more of the following characteristics: graphics and text in new forms and formats; words and pictures reaching new levels of synergy; nonlinear organization and format, nonsequential organization and format, multiple layers of meaning; interactive formats. A case can be made that each of these characteristics is incorporated into the original *Peter Rabbit,* a startling assertion about a book written and illustrated nearly 100 years prior to the digital age.

A Child-Centered Format

Beatrix Potter made it plain that she wanted *Peter Rabbit* to be small enough for young children to hold conveniently. Evolving from the sixteenth-century horn book, typically 2 1/2 × 3 1/2 inches, books for children had usually been small. However, by the time Potter's books were produced, Randolph Caldecott, Walter Crane, and Kate Greenaway, the "fathers and mothers" of the modern picture book, had brought the larger, now-familiar, horizontally laid-out format into vogue. Some of the publishers who rejected her book urged Potter to make it bigger. In 1969 Rumer Godden wrote an amusing "imaginary correspondence" between the ghost of Miss Beatrix Potter and Mr. V. Andal, editor of the De Base Publishing Company, Inc., who was suggesting the inclusion of *Peter Rabbit* in a series called "masterpieces for mini-minds."[15] Mr. Andal says, "I hasten to thank you for 'Peter Rabbit', a most charming tale, and am sure that, when made larger (it must be enlarged—people like to get their money's worth) and given good illustrations, it will make a magnificent book for our series."[16] In Godden's fantasy, the ghost of Potter, like her real life predecessor, maintained her respect for her readers and refused to agree to any changes. Although small-sized picture books have appeared throughout the 100 years since *Peter Rabbit*'s publication, they have never been the preferred format and continue to be somewhat radical, except in board books for babies.

Hypertextual Reading

Nonlinear refers to reading that does not march forward in lock-step, straight-line fashion. The reader may meander along the way. *Nonsequential* indicates that what comes next is not clearly the next logical progression from what comes before. Hypertext formats in the digital age provide nonlinear, nonsequential reading experiences. Randolph Caldecott (whose original drawings were collected by Potter's father and studied by Potter as she drew) and Beatrix Potter established "rules" for the picture book that made it the first hypertext-like reading experience for children. The pronounced ongoing development of this tradition started by Caldecott and Potter perhaps paved the way for the facility with which twenty-first century children adapt to hypertextual reading.

The first picture the reader encounters in *Peter Rabbit* is Mrs. Rabbit presumably trying to give Peter the "one table-spoon full" of his camomile tea "to be taken at bed-time" while Peter, in non-compliance, is hiding his head under the covers. This picture precedes the title page yet is the last event in the story that involves Peter, and the matching text is not at the beginning, but rather, on the next to last page of the book. Immediately as the book begins, the reader, therefore, is introduced to a nonlinear, nonsequential event that sharp young readers will discern. This picture also presents a sophisticated, "radical" concept in a picture book, i.e., foreshadowing. Peter is obviously not a "good little bunny." The reader knows that before a word is read.

Perhaps the most obvious example of the nonlinear storytelling that Potter employs, showing faith that her young readers will follow, is in the structure of her sentences. "But round the end of a cucumber frame, whom should he meet but Mr. McGregor!" surely is more pleasing than "Mr. McGregor came round the end of the cucumber frame." And, "It was a blue jacket with brass buttons, quite new" is more pleasing to the ear and folkoric in quality than "It was a quite new blue jacket with brass buttons." In a critique of a retelling of *Peter Rabbit,* one that rephrases the sentences into a more conventional order, Margaret Mackey comments, "Perhaps she [the author of the adaptation] thinks that young readers need to have their sentences composed always in standard order. . . . What results, however, is a sentence whose distinctive rhythm has become broken-backed and counterproductive."[17]

The irony that Potter brings to some of her word/picture combinations produces the need to read the pictures in relation to the words in a nonlinear manner. A truly amusing post-mortem to Peter's episode is the text that says, "Mr. McGregor hung up the little jacket and the shoes for a scare-crow to frighten the blackbirds." Glancing back to the illustration, the reader finds the blackbirds peering curiously up at the jacket. They are, after all, friends of Peter's and are probably wondering why his jacket and shoes are hanging on a pole. The robin is perched on the scarecrow itself, and the sparrows are hopping around nonchalantly in the background. Mr. McGregor is pictured faintly in the background, never noticing that his device is ineffectual—a symbolic representation, perhaps, of his failure to capture the mischievous bunny. A picture *is* perhaps worth a thousand words.

Half of the pictures, because they are printed back-to-back precede the text in yet another nonlinear way. The position of the scarecrow illustration adds to the irony of the situation because it tells the reader that the scarecrow is not scary even before, out of sequence, we find out why Mr. McGregor has placed it there.

Synergy of Words and Pictures

Perry Nodelman describes many of the relationships that exist between words and pictures: they can be in agreement with the text (the most traditional form of illustration), they can extend the text (as the pictures of the sparrows do), or they can contradict the text (as in the scarecrow example above.)[18] Radical Change adds to this another concept: that of synergy: "Words become pictures and pictures become words. In the most radical form of synergy, words and pictures are so much a part of one another that it is almost impossible to say which is which."[19] *Alice's Adventures in Wonderland* is an early radical example of this kind of synergy. Carroll, read by Potter as a child, experiments with text as picture. Readers encounter nonlinear, pictorial text on the very first text page of *Peter Rabbit.* "Once upon a time there were four little Rabbits and their names were—

Flopsy,
Mopsy,
Cotton-tail,
and Peter.

By drawing a unique picture of their names with her words, Potter tells readers that "these bunnies are not all alike," but we see the focus is on Peter where the stair-step words stop.

Potter's most radical, most akin-to-hypertext, word-picture synergy appeared, however, in her first writing of *Peter Rabbit* in a picture-letter on September 4, 1983, to young Noel Moore, the son of her former governess and friend, Annie Carter Moore. This synergistic, nonlinear, nonsequential form of *Peter Rabbit* became accessible to children only in 1999 and only on the endpapers of a more traditionally-illustrated picture book about her letter, *My Dear Noel: The Story of a Letter from Beatrix Potter.*[20] Interestingly, the publisher laid out a facsimile of the original picture-letter on the front endpapers, but placed it "cleaned for greater legibility and laid out in the correct [read sequential] reading order" on the back endpapers. Did children need this assistance? In this picture-letter Flopsy, Mopsy, and Cotton-tail are drawn and named in a linear manner, all shown on the same level, whereas Peter is pictured and named slightly below and to the right side, making the word-picture emphasis even more dramatic. A comparison of Kevin Henkes' *Lily's Purple Plastic Purse* published in 1996 with the picture-letter of *Peter Rabbit* written in 1893 shows striking similarities of word-text synergy.[21] Perhaps it has been explained, but nowhere have I seen the explanation of why *Peter Rabbit* was not published in its original, picture-letter form, but I suspect it was at least partially because of the inadequacy of the printing technology of the day—and perhaps also it was just too radical to conceive.

White Space

The digital era has brought a realization that white space is not empty space. Every space in the digital world is coded with some combination of "1s" and "0s." So when something appears on a computer screen as "white space" or "nothing," it has been created as surely as if "something" was there. A radical quality of Potter's *Peter Rabbit* is the amount of white space left surrounding the illustrations. Gradually as the digital world has emerged, we have more often begun to think of white space as room to reflect rather than wasted paper. In *Peter Rabbit,* Potter respects the child's need for time to pause, to make the connections and understand the interactions between picture and text. A digital-age example of this use of white space is Jon Scieszka's and Lane Smith's *The Stinky Cheeseman and Other Fairly Stupid Tales* in which an entire blank page appears right in the middle of an otherwise dramatically busy story.[22]

Multilayered Meaning

The complexity of Potter's seemingly simple book lies not only in the relationship of words and pictures, but also in the multilayered meanings that are conveyed in her tiny text and illustrations. A topic that has generated much discussion, and the "gist" of which I will not go into here, is the animal/human nature of Potter's animals. To put it simply, which are they: animals or humans acting like animals? Peter Hollindale responds to these queries by stating that he will identify "three broad lines of descent for the modern animal story, all originating in the 1890s and the Edwardian decade, and try to establish Potter's special place among them."[23] Hollindale concludes that "no one is better than Potter at having her cake and eating it. As a mix of fantasist and realist she is inimitable. . . . The truth, surely, is that in Potter the gap between humans and animals is so narrow that we scarcely notice it."[24] Gillian Avery, according to Hollindale, states that "Beatrix Potter's astringent observation of human society, adroitly transferred to animals so as to engage the child's interest, is something unique in children's books. She could give her sardonic humour full play because ostensibly it was not being directed at human characters."[25] The author who accurately understands children knows that they can grasp large concepts but that the concepts must be communicated in a manner consistent with their own understanding of the world. Potter's ability to do this was radical then and remains radical 100 years later.

"The classics" may bring to mind lengthy books full of words that push the child reader to sophisticated thinking. But in Peter Rabbit, Potter has done the same with parsimony. The underlying "meaning" of her Peter Rabbit story is far more complex than immediately meets the eye, but Potter's belief that the first child for whom she wrote it and all subsequent children could appreciate it is quite correct. Many contemporary writers, with their newfound view of childhood, are realizing that the simple can be complex and that children can and want to understand complexity—and that multilayered stories in which everything is *not* immediately evident, done properly, are superbly suited to satisfy children's often insatiable desire to explore.

Changing Perspectives

The second way in which radical change digital-age characteristics are manifest in books for youth is through changing perspectives. This type of change incorporates one or more of the following traits: new perspectives, visual and verbal; previously unheard voices; youth who speak for themselves.[26] Potter's *Peter Rabbit* pictures are drawn from the close-up point of view of a small child, giving to children their own perspective. In some pictures, for example, when Peter is eating radishes, he seems even taller than the very young reader looking on. (Only in the scarecrow picture is the perspective obviously that of the narrator rather than the child-participant in the story.) Potter was not afraid to connect young children emotionally to the action and to allow them to be lured by their own interests into the story drama just as Peter was lured into Mr. McGregor's garden.

Well into the second half of the twentieth century, the norm for illustrations in a picture book for children was a protective mid-range, straight-on view. Chris Van Allsburg set off a contemporary exploration of varied perspectives in 1979 with a picture book, *The Garden of Abdul Gasazi,* in which he illustrates the story from many angles; a dramatic use of perspective is carried forward in his subsequent books. Since Van Allsburg entered the scene, the traditional mid-range point-of-view has not been so prevalent, but it still persists. Potter ignored this traditional approach, showing respect for her young audience by presenting Peter (who is almost always the center of attention) to them not through the perspective of an adult but through their own eyes, the eyes of a child.

Changing Boundaries

The third way in which interactivity, connectivity, and access show up in *Peter Rabbit* and other books is through changing boundaries. This way could be translated into a contemporary colloquialism: pushing the envelope. Evidence of this phenomenon includes qualities such as the introduction of subjects previously forbidden in children's books; settings previously overlooked; characters portrayed in new, complex ways; new types of communities; and ambiguous or unresolved endings to stories. Like many of her digital-age successors, Potter broke through numerous barriers with her Peter Rabbit tale.

Death on the Doorstep

The Tale of Peter Rabbit starts with a death—not just any death, but Peter's father's death. Moreover, he is made into rabbit pie. Mrs. Rabbit is left a single parent. Death and single parenthood are two topics that are avoided by many authors and illustrators (and/or publishers) of books for young children even a century after Peter Rabbit's publication. In 1998, Chris Raschka, who wrote and illustrated three pictures books that have appeared on the ALA Notable Books for Children list and one that was a Caldecott Honor book, dared to create a picture book about a fish named Arlene Sardine who dies relatively early in the book. One reviewer lamented that this story about "Arlene's life cycle, the high point of which is dying and being stuffed into a can, seems a dubious topic upon which to write a book for preschoolers."[27] No matter that Arlene celebrates becoming a sardine! Like Raschka's account, Potter's book minces neither words, nor ideas. Perhaps she led a sheltered life, but she does not wish to avoid reality in her books.

Crossing another forbidden boundary, Potter is ambiguous on the subject of "being good." While Mrs. Rabbit sternly warns Peter not to go to Mr. McGregor's garden, Peter disobeys and still he is clearly the hero of the tale, the most appealing character. His punishment (from which he hides his head anyway) is far from severe. Says Nicholas Tucker, who identifies Potter's books as real stories for real children, "few children's authors have straddled this Puritan-carnivalesque duality as successfully as she managed to do. . . . a profligacy not uncommon in stories written at the time for older children. But in the more protected world of picture books, Beatrix Potter offered something new and fresh."[28] She entertains while ever so lightly seeming to instruct. In Peter Rabbit and Potter's other books real children have access to far more reality than in many of the books that have followed.

A Rebellious Rabbit

The first words in this essay are quoted from a letter from Peter Rabbit to Mr. McGregor. In addition to her picture-letters, Potter sent many miniature letters, written from one of her book characters to another, to the Moore children and others, illuminating her opinion of her characters. Peter's personality shines in this little missive. He is a provocative character adored by the very young, a rupture of tradition that reverberated throughout the twentieth century and into the twenty-first. An appealing but rebellious rabbit, he not only plans to return to Mr. McGregor's garden, but also taunts him by writing ahead to inquire about the cabbages, politely demanding an immediate answer.

Potter's Community

Potter subtly, almost without notice, created a community with her array of animal tales. This innovative community-building is an important precursor to the connectivity of the digital world. Peter Rabbit's world is not an obvious community like that of the Uncle Remus animals or of the animals in the Milne's Half-Acre Woods. Nevertheless, a close reading of Potter's books reveals that *The Tale of Peter Rabbit* introduces an ongoing story of a community in the making with purposefully inserted cementing symbols woven into picture and text.

Like the robber who appears and reappears in each of the stories that may or may not be connected in David Macaulay's ground-breaking 1990 picture book, *Black and White,* the robin who first appears in *The Tale of Peter Rabbit* provides continuity as he reappears throughout the book and in subsequent books. The robin is not mentioned in the text until *The Tale of Mrs. Tiggy-Winkle,* where we learn his name is Cock-Robin when Mrs. Tiggy-Winkle washes and irons Cock-Robin's red waist-coast, Peter Rabbit's shrunken blue jacket (another symbolic link from book to book), and Squirrel Nutkin's red tailcoat. The robin appears five times in *Peter Rabbit*, twice again in *The Tale of Benjamin Bunny,* and again at the end of *The Tale of the Flopsy Bunnies*. His largely visual-only role is as open-ended as that of Macaulay's robber.[29]

Numerous other connective, community-building features are worked into *Peter Rabbit* and its companions. Such features include the detailed settings of most of her books near Sawry, which has been identified and catalogued by Potter devotees. (This catalogue does not include the setting of *Peter Rabbit,* written before Potter's move to the Lake District.) One of the most amusing examples occurs in *Ginger and Pickles* when the reader sees various characters from previous books, including Peter Rabbit, appearing in the illustrations, unmentioned in the text.

The Wonder of Words

One of the most radical, boundary-pushing elements of Potter's *Peter Rabbit* is her exquisite use of language and her assumption that young children can make the connections to interpret narrative even when they do not know the exact meaning of individual words. Perry Nodelman makes this case in point when he has the students in his children's literature classes read and discuss Edward Lear's "The Owl and the Pussy Cat." He reports that these adults often decide that the poem is unsuitable for children who would not understand words such as "runcible" and "bong-tree." After awhile, he queries them on exactly what these words do mean—pointing out that they themselves enjoyed the poem without knowing, yet they were unwilling to assume children could do the same.[30] Potter knew intuitively that children would understand her un-watered-down text. Likely she would have been horrified at the fact that her Peter Rabbit book is "graded" as fourth grade reading level in Advantage Learning's *Accelerated Reader Program*. This program takes the words and sentences in a book, figures the length and complexity of each, and assigns a reading level to it. The implication of this assessment is that Potter's *Peter Rabbit* is among the "grade-level" books that fourth graders may read and be examined on for points or prizes.

TWO RADICAL POTTERS: A CENTURY APART

Beatrix Potter, born in 1866, author of *Peter Rabbit,* first publicly published in 1902, and another British author, Joanne Rowling, born in 1966, author of the Harry Potter books, first publicly published in 1997, share a legacy—both are innovative authors of ground-breaking books with radical qualities. The first book in a series of seven, *Harry Potter and the Philosopher's Stone* (1997), like *Peter,* was turned down by several publishers, but was finally picked up by a small publisher, Bloomsbury. Subsequently both books became enormously (and probably enduringly) popular, once readers seized upon them. Both authors have sold their books in the millions, both have their books translated into numerous languages. Had Beatrix Potter lived in the digital age, perhaps her sales records would have more quickly reached the million mark, as word of Peter, like Harry, might have sped via the Internet rather than crept around the globe by word of mouth.

I suspect that some of the enduring popularity of *Peter Rabbit* explains the immediate popularity of *Harry Potter*. Both authors show profound respect for the ability of children—there is no watering down, no avoidance of difficult concepts or tough topics. Both create a hero who is neither saint nor sinner—a hero who must struggle to achieve his goals. Both choose vocabulary, subjects, and settings that break barriers but communicate their complexities in a context that children can understand. Both write with layers of meaning that can be teased out by the reader—or not. Both have lively imaginations; both record their imagings with great attention to detail that is imprinted permanently upon the minds of their readers. Both appeal to readers of all ages. Both are gifted authors who tell a good story with memorable characters, specific settings, and universal themes that provide multilayered meanings, create subtle connectivity among individual books, produce a sense of community among readers, and provide intellectual and emotional access for which children long.

The only surprise, perhaps, is that the respect both these women show for young readers remains suspect to so many adults even today, that treating children-as-capable-and-seeking-connection is not preferable for some to treating children-as-innocent-and-in-need-of-protection. The folly of this is, of course, that the greatest protection of all comes from helping children connect with their emotions and with the information they need. It is only as adults regard children as capable can they recognize the outstanding milestones of children's literature as sophisticated and meritorious. As Gregory Maguire, children's literature author and critic, mused in a review of one of the Harry Potter books, "Maybe . . . J. K. Rowling will have achieved what people who love the best children's books have long labored after: breaking the spell of adult condescension that brands as merely cute, insignificant, second-rate the heartiest and best of children's literature."[31] Both Potters who have cast an alternative spell with their expertly executed radical qualities deserve this break.

NOTES

1. Beatrix Potter, "Letter to Moore Children, undated" in *Letters to Children from Beatrix Potter,* collected and introduced by Judy Taylor (New York: Frederick Warne, 1992), 91.

2. Beatrix Potter, "Letter to Harold Warner, July 6, 1916," in *Beatrix Potter's Letters,* selected and introduced by Judy Taylor (New York: Frederick Warne, 1989), 226.

3. Judy Taylor, *Beatrix Potter: Artist, Storyteller, and Countrywoman,* rev. ed. (New York: Frederick Warne, 1996), 72.

4. Taylor, *Beatrix Potter: Artist* (1996), 76.

5. Elizabeth Buchan, *Beatrix Potter: The Story of the Creator of Peter Rabbit* (New York: Frederick Warne, 1998), 26.

6. "Potter, Beatrix," in *Children's Books and Their Creators,* ed. Anita Silvey (Boston: Houghton Mifflin, 1995), 534.

7. A full explication and application of the theory is found in Eliza T. Dresang, *Radical Change: Books for Youth in a Digital Age* (New York: H.W. Wilson, 1999).

8. Bartoletti suggests that some decided that young women should not work for the same reasons they believed that women should not vote or own property or manage their own money or study subjects like law, mathematics, or biology. They worried about the independent spirit as well as the health of working girls. *Kids on Strike!* (Boston: Houghton Mifflin, 1999), 33.

9. See Marina Warner, "Little Angels, Little Monsters" in *Six Myths of Our Times* (New York: Vintage, 1994), 43–62.

10. Sherry Turkle, *Life on the Screen* (New York: Simon & Schuster, 1995), 10.

11. See Dresang, "Appendix B: Ideas about Children and Literary Links, A Selective Overview: Middle Ages—1990s (Western Europe and the United States)," *Radical Change* (1999), 316–17.

12. "Picture Books," in Silvey, ed., *Children's Books and Their Creators* (1995), 523.

13. Humphrey Carpenter and Mari Prichard, *The Oxford Companion to Children's Literature* (New York: Oxford University Press, 1985), 423.

14. Carpenter and Prichard, *The Oxford Companion* (1985), 424. This statement was written almost two decades ago before several other substantial books on Potter appeared, including additional biographies, a selected collection from among her 1,400 letters, a collection of her letters to children, and a picture book for children recounting the writing of the most famous of her letters to young Noel Moore in 1893. This letter was the initial version of *The Tale of Peter Rabbit.*

15. See Rumer Godden, "An Imaginary Correspondence," in *Only Connect* (New York: Oxford University Press, 1969), 62–69. Although the context is invented, some of Potter's remarks come from her letters.

16. Godden, "An Imaginary Correspondence," 64.

17. Margaret Mackey, *The Case of Peter Rabbit: Changing Conditions of Literature for Children* (New York: Garland, 1998), 37.

18. See Perry Nodelman, *Words about Pictures: The Narrative Art of Children's Picture Books* (Athens, Ga: University of Georgia Press, 1988).

19. Dresang, *Radical Change* (1999), 88.

20. Jane Johnson, *My Dear Noel: The Story of a Letter from Beatrix Potter* (New York: Dial, 1999).

21. A discussion of Henkes' work in Dresang, *Radical Change* (1999), 111–14, reveals the evolution of this synergy in his own work, not pronounced until the mid-1990s.

22. Jon Scieszka, *The Stinky Cheeseman and Other Fairly Stupid Tales*, illustrated by Lane Smith (New York: Viking, 1992), np.

23. Peter Hollindale, "Animal Stories since Beatrix Potter and Her Influence on the Genre," in *Beatrix Potter Studies VIII: Beatrix Potter As Writer and Illustrator* (Trowbridge, England: Redwood Books, 1999), 28.

24. Hollindale. "Animal Stories" (1999), 30.

25. Hollindale, "Animal Stories" (1999), 31.

26. Potter exhibited in her personal life a "radical" perspective that has now been incorporated into many books for children—that of speaking, writing, and drawing for oneself. She was a prolific letter writer and journalist. Potter's letters, many of which were picture-letters and many of which were addressed to children, brought her in touch with the community of youth, a community she never experienced as a young person herself for her education was through governesses and her parents did not allow her to socialize with other children. Her diaries, written between ages fifteen and thirty-one, and detailed drawings gave her her own voice and possibly helped her realize the importance to all children of having their voices heard.

27. Irene Cooper, "Review of *Arlene Sardine* by Chris Raschka," *Booklist* 94 (September 1, 1998).

28. Nicholas Tucker, "Beatrix Potter's Fiction: Real Stories for Real Children," in *Beatrix Potter Studies VIII: Beatrix Potter As Writer and Illustrator* (1999), 9–23.

29. Critics examining the robin in Potter's *Peter Rabbit* disagree on his role. Hollindale in his "Animal Stories" notes that Maurice Sendak sees the robin as representing "the helplessness and concern we feel for Peter. He seems ancient and philosophical in doomlike observation of Peter's shoe under the cabbage" (25). Hollindale disagrees, "We must forgive Sendak, who is after all an American, for not knowing English robins. But those on the inside of English ornithological social psychology will know that Potter's robin is not mournfully concerned for Peter's welfare: he is snootily indignant on behalf of Mr. McGregor. The robin is the gardener's friend" (25). Catherine Golden posits a third and opposing opinion, providing a detailed analysis of the robin as conscience in "Natural Companions: Text and Illustration in the Work of Beatrix Potter," in *Beatrix Potter Studies VIII: Beatrix Potter As Writer and Illustrator* (1999), 58–62.

30. Perry Nodelman, *The Pleasures of Children's Literature,* 2nd ed., (New York: Longman, 1996), 15–17.

31. Gregory Maguire, "Lord of the Golden Snitch," *New York Times*, 5 September 1999, http://www.nytimes.com/books/99/09/05/reviews/990905.05maguirt. html.

BIBLIOGRAPHY

Advantage Learning Systems. "The Tale of Peter Rabbit Reading Practice Quiz." *Accelerated Reader Program, 2000.* http://www.advlearn.com/apps1. Accessed 9 November 2000.

Beatrix Potter Studies VIII: Beatrix Potter As Writer and Illustrator. (1998 Conference, Ambleside). Trowbridge, England: Redwood Books, 1999.

Bartoletti, Susan Campbell. *Kids On Strike!* Boston: Houghton Mifflin, 1999.

Buchan, Elizabeth. *Beatrix Potter: The Story of the Creator of Peter Rabbit.* New York: Frederick Warne, 1998.

Carpenter, Humphrey, and Mari Prichard. *The Oxford Companion to Children's Literature.* New York: Oxford University Press, 1985.

Carroll, Lewis. *Alice in Wonderland.* London: P.R. Gawthorn, 1900.

Cooper, Irene. "Review of Arlene Sardine by Chris Raschka." *Booklist* 94 (September 1, 1998).

Dresang, Eliza T. *Radical Change: Books for Youth in a Digital Age.* New York: H.W. Wilson, 1999.

Gag, Wanda. *Millions of Cats.* New York: Coward-McCann, 1928.

Golden, Catherine. "Natural Companions: Text and Illustration in the Work of Beatrix Potter," Pp. 58–62 in *Beatrix Potter Studies VIII: Beatrix Potter As Writer and Illustrator,* Trowbridge, England: Redwood Books, 1999.

Godden, Rumer. *Only Connect.* New York: Oxford University Press, 1969.

Harris, Joel Chandler. *The Complete Tales of Uncle Remus.* Boston: Houghton Mifflin, 1995.

Henkes, Kevin. *Lily's Purple Plastic Purse.* New York: Greenwillow Books, 1996.

Hollindale, Peter. "Animal Stories since Beatrix Potter and Her Influence on the Genre," Pp. 24–35 in *Beatrix Potter Studies VIII: Beatrix Potter As Writer and Illustrator.* Trowbridge, England: Redwood Books, 1999.

Johnson, Jane. *My Dear Noel: The Story of a Letter from Beatrix Potter.* New York: Dial, 1999.

Macaulay, David. *Black and White.* Boston: Houghton Mifflin, 1990.

Mackey, Margaret. *The Case of Peter Rabbit: Changing Conditions of Literature for Children.* New York: Garland, 1998.

Maguire, Gregory. "Lord of the Golden Snitch," *New York Times,* (5 September 1999). http://www.nytimes.com/books/99/09/05/reviews/990905.05maguirt.html. Accessed 4 April 2001.

Milne, A. A. *The World of Pooh: The Complete Winnie-the-Pooh and the House at Pooh Corner*. New York: Dutton, 1957.

Nodelman, Perry. *The Pleasures of Children's Literature,* 2nd ed. New York: Longman, 1996.

———. *Words about Pictures: The Narrative Art of Children's Picture Books.* Athens, Ga.: University of Georgia Press, 1998.

Papert, Seymour. *The Children's Machine*. New York: BasicBooks, 1993.

Potter, Beatrix. *The Tale of Benjamin Bunny*. New York: Frederick Warne, 1965.

———. *The Tale of the Flopsy Bunnies*. New York: Frederick Warne, 1962

———. *The Tale of Ginger and Pickles*. New York: Frederick Warne, 1965.

———. *The Tale of Mrs. Tiggy-Winkle*. New York: Frederick Warne, 1963.

———. *The Tale of Peter Rabbit*. New York: Frederick Warne, 1958, 1902.

Rowling, J. K. *Harry Potter and the Philosopher's Stone*. London: Bloomsbury Press, 1997.

Scieszka, Jon, and Lane Smith. *The Stinky Cheeseman and Other Fairly Stupid Tales*. New York: Viking, 1992.

Sendak, Maurice. *Where the Wild Things Are*. New York: Harper & Row, 1963.

Silvey, Anita, ed. *Children's Books and Their Creators*. Boston: Houghton Mifflin, 1995.

Tapscott, Don. *Growing Up Digital: The Rise of the Net Generation*. New York: McGraw-Hill, 1998.

Taylor, Judy. *Beatrix Potter: Artist, Storyteller and Countrywoman*. New York: Frederick Warne, 1996.

———. *Beatrix Potter's Letters.* New York: Frederick Warne, 1989.

———. *Letters to Children from Beatrix Potter*. New York: Frederick Warne, 1992.

Tucker, Nicholas. "Beatrix Potter's Fiction: Real Stories for Real Children," Pp.9–23 in *Beatrix Potter Studies VIII: Beatrix Potter As Writer and Illustrator.* Trowbridge, England: Redwood Books, 1999.

Turkle, Sherry. *Life on the Screen*. New York: Simon & Schuster, 1995.

Van Allsburg, Chris. *The Garden of Abdul Gasazi.* New York: Houghton Mifflin, 1979.

Warner, Marina. *Six Myths of Our Times*. New York: Vintage, 1994.

White, E. B. *Charlotte's Web.* New York: Harper, 1952.

8

In Search of His Father's Garden

Scott Pollard and Kara Keeling

Rabbit Pie
981. Ingredients.—1 rabbit, a few slices of ham, salt and white pepper to taste, 2 blades of pounded mace, 1/2 teaspoonful of grated nutmeg, a few forcemeat balls, 3 hard-boiled eggs, 1/2 pint of gravy, puff crust.
Mode.—Cut up the rabbit (which should be young), remove the breastbone, and bone the legs. Put the rabbit, slices of ham, forcemeat balls, and hard eggs, by turns, in layers, and season each layer with pepper, salt, pounded mace, and grated nutmeg. Pour in about 1/2 pint of water, cover with crust, and bake in a well-heated oven for about 1 1/2 hour. Should the crust acquire too much colour, place a piece of paper over it to prevent its burning. When done, pour in at the top, by means of the hole in the middle of the crust, a little good gravy, which may be made of the breast- and leg-bones of the rabbit and 2 or 3 shank-bones, flavoured with onion, herbs, and spices.
Time.—1 1/2 hour. *Average cost,* 1*s.* to 1*s.* 6d. each.
Sufficient for 5 or 6 persons.
Seasonable from September to February
Note.—The liver of the rabbit may be boiled, minced, and mixed with the forcemeat balls, when the flavour is liked.
—*Beeton's Book of Household Management* (1861)

There are eight recipes for rabbit in the Poultry section of *Beeton's,* sandwiched between the four recipes for pigeon and six recipes for turkey. The pages of rabbit recipes also include informational paragraphs subtitled The Rabbit, The Common or Wild Rabbit ("The common wild rabbit is of a grey color, and is esteemed the best for the purposes of food."[1]), Varieties of Rabbit, Fecundity of the Rabbit, The Rabbit-House, The Hutch, Fancy Rabbits, The Hare-Rabbit, The Angora Rabbit, The Himalaya Rabbit, as well as attractive pen-and-ink drawings of the five featured species and a boiled rabbit and a roast rabbit. At 1,112 pages long and as a symbol of a fastidious culture, *Beeton's* is an encyclopedic volume dedicated to the efficient and complete exploitation of resources available to the average Victorian household, written so that no available resources need ever be wasted.

Rabbit Pie, then, is standard Victorian fare, and it would not have been a stretch of the imagination at all for Beatrix Potter to imagine Peter's father prepared as a pie by Mrs. McGregor, for one would not just kill the garden pest when one could—and should—eat him as well. To extend such neat logic, one perhaps should imagine—at least in 1901, when Beatrix Potter published *The Tale of Peter Rabbit,* at the very end of the Victorian era—that Peter (or his mother or his sisters, for that matter) might come to a similar end one day, roasted, boiled, curried, or baked in a pie.

Whatever psychological drama one might see Peter working through in *The Tale of Peter Rabbit*—for example, an adolescent male rebelling against maternal authority, an adolescent male following the path of an absent father in the hope that that path might confer meaning and purpose to the son's life (a telemachiad)—that drama unfolds in an explicitly culinary world whose sign systems are clearly divided by the gate of Mr. McGregor's garden. Outside the garden gate, the book focuses on Peter's family and the day's efforts to prepare a meal. As the story is written, the meal that culminates the book organizes and directs the actions of Peter's mother and sisters throughout the day. This meal should give meaning and form to the whole family, but, of course, it does not, because Peter is on the path to another kind of food, another kind of meaning. Under the authority of the mother, the members of the family act as civilized beings, for they are subjects enacting the rituals that give their collective lives meaning. As Roland Barthes says about French society in "Toward a Psychosociology of Contemporary Food Production," "food has a constant tendency to form itself into a situation,"[2] where situation signifies a particular way of life with food giving symbolic shape to that life. Just as the French act to construct food as a symbol of the French past, so do Peter's mother and sisters dedicate themselves to using the food they gather, prepare, and eat as the signifying center of the family's civilizing culture. Mrs. Rabbit is a model of maternal propriety, sensibly dressed in layers and with "a basket and her umbrella," going "through the wood to the baker's," where she buys "a loaf of brown bread and five currant buns."[3] The sisters, "who were good little bunnies, went down the lane to gather blackberries."[4] The sisters take this free time—their mother has given them no tasks to complete while she is off to the baker—and use it constructively to provide for the family meal. Their foraging is not meant to sate their own hunger. In contrast to Potter's illustration of Peter eating in the garden, she pictures his sisters only picking berries, not eating them. Only a thieving sparrow, analog to Peter in the McGregors' garden, takes advantage of the sisters' labors and eats their berries.

The deferral of eating—that is, the deferral of pleasure—on the part of Peter's mother and sisters indicates what Stephen Mennell calls the civilizing of the appetite: "The sense of delicacy and pressures toward self-control are . . . closely interwoven. In eating, it is the developing sense of delicacy which first becomes apparent, but that eventually becomes entangled with restraint."[5] At the end of *The Tale of Peter Rabbit*, "Flopsy, Mopsy and Cotton-tail had bread and milk and blackberries for supper,"[6] and in the accompanying illustration they sup their milk from a bowl with small spoons, napkins tied around the necks of two sisters. In *Sociology on the Menu*, Alan Beardsworth and Teresa Keil note that as a child is socialized into the foodways of a culture, "the child will be taught, and will learn by experience, how to distinguish between foods and non-foods," and that "a crucial feature of nutritional socialization involves learning how to reduce the risk of introducing hazardous substances into the body."[7] Beardsworth and Keil focus solely on the quality of what is or is not to be ingested—the food or non-food in and of itself—but they do not take into account how *place* functions as fundamental to food socialization. As is clear in *Peter Rabbit*, the foods that Peter and his sisters eat—although distinctly different—are, in and of themselves, in no way hazardous: whether a bowl of milk or carrots out of the garden, the food is nutritious. Rather, place is the key to proper food socialization in *Peter Rabbit*. At home, food is nutritious, but its value is also delimited by the rituals and activities that shape the food into a symbol of the home as a safe haven, a place of comfort and sustenance.

By contrast, in the garden—a place outside the civilizing sphere of family and home—the food is, for Peter, hazardous to his health and well-being, because the food is *in the garden*, a place where Peter is no longer in control of his identity. As he searches for his father's food, Peter embarks on a very dangerous game: he dares to have his subjectivity taken from him, dares to become an object of another. And as Peter's subjectivity is reworked into the object of Mr. McGregor's wrath, Peter dares becoming food for someone else's table. The garden is an ambivalent space where the line between subject and object, eater and eaten, becomes blurred. One obvious antecedent for the garden is the gingerbread house in *Hansel and Gretel.* In "Edible Architecture, Cannibal Architecture," Allen S. Weiss notes, "The pleasure of eating dissimulates its opposite, the threat of being devoured, for the confectionery house hides its origin, the very oven that is to be the site of the childrens' [*sic*] destiny. A single location, where the edible dissimulates the cannibal, is simultaneously utopic and dystopic, revealing the antithetical sense of primal gustatory emotions."[8] As the starving children approach the house, the desire for food—that is, their bodily need—guides their actions. Their rational minds, which might have signalled caution—a strange house in a harsh environment—do not function, and, as a result, both children surrender their subjectivity to become, momentarily, the objects of the old woman's hunger. Like Peter Rabbit with Mr. McGregor, Hansel and Gretel become identified as food, and only when they fight against this objectification, turning the table on the old woman and tricking her into the oven—that is, once they have become cooks and transformed the old woman into food—do they assert their subjectivity again and act rationally to plan their return home. At this point, they do not eat the old woman, do not become cannibals, and refrain from eating the house, thus deferring the pleasures of the body and demonstrating a civilized appetite.

An important antecedent text for such tension between mind and body is Plato's *Phaedo.* There, Socrates states that the philosopher should not "concern himself with the so-called pleasures connected with food and drink," and that in general "a man of this kind . . . keeps his attention directed as much as he can away from [the body] and toward the soul."[9] For Deane W. Curtin, Plato establishes a logic of identity "primarily through his determination to represent the world in terms of exclusive dualisms."[10] When Hansel and Gretel come upon the gingerbread house, their minds are confused by hunger. For the two children the distance between mind and body has been lost: their bodies thus dominate their minds, and their identities become confused. As a result, they are ripe for objectification and likely to become the old woman's food. Only once they begin to think and to scheme, and then cook and kill the old woman, do they return the world to dualistic purity.

As Grimms' fairy tale reinforces the Platonic ideal of the mind/body split, teaching us to prefer the mind and deny the body, so too does Beatrix Potter with Peter Rabbit. Peter's desire for food puts him in danger of becoming food, thus "the pleasure of eating dissimulates its opposite."[11] Just as Hansel and Gretel would eat the gingerbread house, and would be eaten by the old woman, so too would Peter eat the vegetables in the garden and be eaten by Mr. McGregor, who ate Peter's father before him. In the garden, Peter first eats "some lettuces and some French beans; and then he ate some radishes; And then, feeling rather sick, he went to look for some parsley."[12] Carolyn Korsmeyer notes that Aristotle in the *Nicomachean Ethics* defines gluttony as "indulgence not only in the pleasures of taste but in the sheer quantity of food,"[13] which corrupts one's humanity—that is, one's identity as human—and lowers the glutton to the level of a brute. M. F. K. Fisher does not speak of gluttony with such disapproval, however. For her, gluttony is just a simple fact of our humanity: "I cannot believe that there exists a single coherent human being who will not confess, at least to himself, that once or twice he has stuffed himself to the bursting point . . . for no other reason than the beastlike satisfaction of the belly."[14] Fisher is a twentieth-century romantic: for her, being true to one's emotions is being true to one's self, and "beastlike" desires are as human as the enlightened mind. If M. F. K. Fisher had written *The Tale of Peter Rabbit,* Peter would have been a devoted food enthusiast who would have sneaked into Mr. McGregor's garden regularly to eat his fill and would never have had to pay a price for his pleasure, because, for Peter, eating would have been an act of self-affirmation. But Beatrix Potter wrote *Peter Rabbit,* and for her, a repressed Victorian, all pleasures have their price, because the virtuous self is not defined by pleasure but by self-control, restraint, routine, and denial: the very traits that define Peter's family.

It is not only that Peter is following his desires unabated that gets him in trouble; it is also the fact he is eating alone, outside his community. According to Mary Lukanuski, in "A Place at the Counter: The Onus of Oneness," "for the solitary eater there is no sense of proper eating behavior. There is no etiquette or societal expectation on how to eat alone. Some solo eaters may still behave as though they're being watched. Others find themselves freed from the responsibilities usually incurred when eating: responsibilities like a 'balanced' meal, etiquette, a table, napkins."[15] Peter clearly desires to separate himself from his mother and sisters in order to eat differently, like his father. Through the solitude and the gorging, Peter liberates himself from the restrictive behavioral routines of family life. While his mother and sisters automatically choose structured activities that provide food for the family table, only by separating himself from the company of his sisters and daring to get into the mischief that his mother warned them all against can Peter pursue the unfettered freedom to satisfy his appetite for raw, unwashed vegetables. Alone in the garden, Peter does not have to follow any rules—neither in terms of how to behave nor how much or what to eat. But this desire for freedom is socially suspect, because eating is normally a shared activity that regulates the eating behavior of the diners. Lukanuski notes that, "Those participating in an activity that should be shared are obviously unwanted and unconnected. The solitary diner is either a social misfit or the victim of some tragedy. He or she all too easily reminds us of the precariousness of our own situation: but for the grace of God, there go I."[16] Because Peter chooses to go to the garden alone, he appears to be a solitary, unconnected being with neither family nor loved ones. Peter's father, because he also visited the garden alone to pursue his own desire for solitary eating, died tragically; now his son tempts the same fate. Again, for Beatrix Potter, solitary, wild, uncontrolled eating is unacceptable, and a price must be paid for such excessive and abnormal behavior.

We know that Peter is a naughty rabbit because his gluttony makes him sick, and when he looks for the cure for his aching stomach, he runs into Mr. McGregor. Potter insists that Peter suffer more than a simple tummyache for the abnormal satisfaction of his appetite. Up to this point, Peter has not yet surrendered his subjectivity. He is nauseous, but he knows the cure—parsley. Peter still has control over his body because he knows how to mitigate the effects of his gluttony. Only with Mr. McGregor is Peter's subjectivity sufficiently threatened because, for Mr. McGregor, Peter is only his body, only his appetite (as a consumer of food), and only his carcass (as a food source itself). It is only when Peter's life as an autonomous subject is threatened by Mr. McGregor, who chases him determinedly with hoe and sieve and boot, that Peter pays a sufficient price for his pleasure. For the rest of the time that he remains in the garden, Peter must figure out how to get out of it, and to that end he uses his intelligence, not his stomach.

When Peter enters the garden and eats, he does not follow the guidance of his head but that of his taste buds. In *Making Sense of Taste,* Carolyn Korsmeyer notes that taste has been considered the lowest of the five senses because "Taste requires perhaps the most intimate congress with the object of perception, which must enter the mouth, and which delivers sensations experienced in the mouth and throat on its way down and through the digestive track."[17] Again, we see that it is the blurring of the boundary between subject and object that creates the problem, because the subject—the mind—is in danger of corruption, dissolution, losing itself or the path to truth. Whether Plato or Beatrix Potter, their aim is to keep subject and object, mind and body, separate. So, in trouble and needing to exit the garden without losing his life, Peter must now do what Lisa Hedke calls "head work."[18] He must deny his stomach—deny his body—and think. Korsmeyer notes that for Plato, "the ability to transcend the body, to govern the senses, to gain knowledge, is a masculine ability that when exercised well will keep one embodied as male," whereas "the lower, proximal senses with the appetites and the dangerous pleasures . . . are in one way or another associated with femininity."[19] Unfortunately, Peter's father did not transcend his body soon enough; fortunately, Peter does.

Of course, this metaphysical argument works only because, as readers, we personify Peter, seeing him as human, at least in part. In *The Pleasures of Children's Literature,* Perry Nodelman succinctly describes the relation between animals and children: "Apparently, we tend to think of "kids" as basically animal-like savages who must be taught to act like civilized humans. Not surprisingly, then, many characters in children's literature are animals—animals who represent the animal-like conditions of children." Nodelman says of Peter Rabbit that he "is torn between the opposing forces of his natural instincts and the societal conventions represented by his mother." As long as Peter remains clothed, he is marked as civilized, but once he loses his jacket and shoes, he loses those items that signifed him as civilized, and he is reduced to animal-like barbarity: that is, he is no longer a reasoning animal. Nodelman notes that for animal characters, clothing is "often a source of discomfort, something that prevents them from behaving like their natural selves. . . . Peter and his jacket buttons nearly lead to his death."[20] In "Clothed in Nature or Nature Clothed: Dress As Metaphor in the Illustrations of Beatrix Potter and C. M. Baker," Carole Scott makes a similar point:

> The sense of being trapped and suffocated inside the wrong coverings makes an ironic comment on his [Tom Kitten's] earlier experience. Another example may be found when Peter Rabbit escapes from Mr. McGregor and certain death by casting off his shoes, which impede his running, and by wriggling out of his blue coat with brass buttons, which entraps him in a gooseberry net. As he sheds his shoes and coat, Peter becomes increasingly rabbitlike, running on all fours instead of just his hind legs, thus evading Mr. McGregor's sieve.[21]

Both Nodelman and Scott speak of Peter's unclothed state as somehow "natural" and right, but part of his natural state is that he is a rabbit paralyzed by fear, that he is prey to Mr. McGregor as predator. Only once Peter is exhorted to act by the sparrows—only once a community of animals is established in the garden—does he run and save his life. Moreover, Potter does not leave Peter in his "natural" state. Peter is like a child, after all, and in Potter's moral schema he needs to return to the civilizing sphere of his family. From his "natural" state, then, Peter embarks upon a path of redemption that restores at least a portion of his civilized existence.

When Peter goes in search of parsley, he has begun to transcend his body again, yet the purpose of the parsley is to make Peter's body feel better, so, perhaps, that he can go back to eating. Potter thus uses Mr. McGregor to deliver a shock strong enough to force Peter to transcend his bodily needs more quickly and absolutely. In the presence of Mr. McGregor, Peter is no longer concerned with either food or his stomach because Peter recognizes that if he does not escape he shall himself become food. Initially, Peter just runs; he is not thinking yet, but is merely trying to avoid the mortal peril that Mr. McGregor represents. Children, like Peter, rebel against parental authority, give into excess, and, when they get in trouble, run away. Yet simply running away does not solve the problem; the child, again like Peter, must learn to stop and think. Peter has reached the nadir of his experience, nearly repeating his father's death, when Mr. McGregor almost catches him with the sieve.

But once Peter has space to consider his options, once he stops simply reacting to Mr. McGregor's threats and begins to act proactively to rescue himself from the garden, he begins to recover his subjectivity. He does so physically when Potter depicts him as standing upright when he finds the first possible solution to his problem: a door in the garden wall. Though he has lost his clothes, his posture nonetheless suggests that he is a lost little boy, emphasized by the positions of his feet (one foot tentatively resting on top of the other) and of his front paws, which act as arms, one supporting his weight against the door and the other cradling a trembling lip. Unfortunately, the door "was locked, and there was no room for a fat little rabbit to squeeze underneath."[22] This sentence simultaneously suggests the ambiguity inherent in Peter's double identity as child and animal: as child he might be able to open the gate were it not locked; as animal he might be able to go beneath it to escape. Peter's subjectivity is strengthened also at this point when he forgoes his solitude and begins to reconnect with other members of the animal community. He takes the advice of the three friendly sparrows, who "[implore] him to exert himself,"[23] and then, after more chasing by Mr. McGregor, he seeks help from a mouse: "An old mouse was running in and out over the stone doorstep, carrying peas and beans to her family in the wood. Peter asked her the way to the gate, but she had such a large pea in her mouth that she could not answer. She only shook her head at him. Peter began to cry."[24] Like Peter, the mouse steals from the garden, but unlike him, she does not indulge her own appetite despite the excessive size of the pea. Instead, she carries home the results of her foraging for her own family, thus modeling appropriate familial behaviors. At this point the mouse substitutes for the rejected mother of the beginning of the story: even though she says nothing to him, her maternal role as food-gatherer reconnects him to his own family. In the next scene, when he encounters the predatory cat—a solitary hunter—he remembers and acts upon his cousin Benjamin Bunny's advice, reinforcing the family connection.

As Peter wanders the garden looking for a way out, he is frightened by the noise of Mr. McGregor's hoe and hides in the bushes. Yet the autonomic response of fear fades quickly, and Peter's reason asserts itself again: "But presently, as nothing happened, he came out, and climbed upon a wheelbarrow and peeped over."[25] Seeing that Mr. McGregor's back is turned to him, Peter then takes a calculated risk and makes a daring and successful dash to the gate. Like Hansel and Gretel, Peter reasons his way out of his predicament. In both tales, final escape, survival, and triumph are contingent upon the characters' ability to be quick on their feet and to take advantage of the opportunities that present themselves.

If *Peter Rabbit* were an epic tale, Peter would end the story as a hero. He has dared to traverse a hazardous, barbaric world that is the polar opposite of his family's civility. He has eaten of the forbidden food associated with his father. He puts his subjectivity on the line and dares to be objectified as food, and he escapes his objectifier in the end. He successfully navigates an alien realm that his father could not. The garden is Peter's wine dark sea, and Mr. McGregor his Poseidon. Likewise, Peter returns to civilization just as Odysseus washes up on the shore of the land of the Nausicaans, exhausted and naked. Yet, if the Nausicaan episode demonstrates how Odysseus has begun to integrate the experiences of his twenty-year ordeal to become an even greater leader of men than he was when he left Ithaca, Peter's return is marked by his abject surrender to his mother's authority. He does not step into his father's shoes to become the man of the house. He is not a boy who has become a man. In spite of the "character-building" experiences in the garden that taught him to think for himself and to scheme for his own survival, Peter is a boy who returns home still a boy. And unlike Hansel and Gretel, who return to their father with riches that ensure the family's future comfort, Peter returns with nothing, not even his shoes and jacket. Beatrix Potter has not written a *bildungsroman* in *Peter Rabbit*. Rather, in a tradition of children's works of which Maurice Sendak's *Where the Wild Things Are* is a part, she tells a story in which a child's adventure functions not as a maturation experience but as a release valve, allowing the child to expend the disruptive energy that has kept him outside the civilizing sphere of the family and to reintegrate himself properly into that family as subordinate, as child.

And it is food that, perhaps, in the end best symbolizes Peter's humble return. His mother puts him to bed without dinner and with only a little soothing camomile tea. In the garden, Peter eats too much, sates his body too fully. By forcing Peter to fast, his mother would purify him of all that wild food he ingested and repress the wild times he experienced. His mother would diminish Peter's focus on the body and reinstate the mind/body split. Pictorially, Beatrix Potter emphasizes the dominance of prepared (ergo, civilized) food in the final three illustrations of the book, which offer an orderly progression of cooking, serving, and eating. In the first illustration, with the naked and exhausted Peter—still beastlike—lying on the ground in the left background, Mrs. Rabbit prepares dinner in the kitchen in the right foreground. She stirs food in a pot that she holds, other pots and pans hang on the wall over a counter, and raw vegetables lie on the floor for her to cook. In the second illustration, Mrs. Rabbit stands over the kettle in the fire pouring camomile tea into a china cup for Peter, who watches from his bed in the darkened corner in the back of the burrow, while his sisters, in the foreground, illuminated by the light of the fire, sit observing their mother pour the tea. The final illustration features Flopsy, Mopsy, and Cotton-tail delicately sipping their "bread and milk and blackberries for supper,"[26] models of a restrained, decorous appetite.

Yet the thematic arc of these last three illustrations can be disrupted if the frontispiece is interpolated in its narrative place as the third figure of a set of four. In the frontispiece, Peter's mother leans over a bed, trying to nurse Peter with a "table-spoonful" of camomile tea, but he hides his head under the covers, rejecting her ministrations. Obviously, the wild food, the wild day, and the desires that initiated Peter's garden adventure have not yet been purged from him, and perhaps never will be. In contrast, at the end of *Where the Wild Things Are,* Max is exhausted and repentant and ready to accept his mother's food. Max is really a "good" bad boy, whereas Peter remains naughty, a "bad" bad boy, all the way through the story. Although the final illustration of the three good sisters eating would seem to offer a clear resolution to the story, a clear triumph of mind over body, of decorous self-control over gorging, of obedience over rebellion, the frontispiece problematizes such a resolution. If we look at only the three final illustrations, it is clear that Beatrix Potter is subtly and smoothly repressing Peter, literally forcing him into the background and making him disappear between the final two pictures. But the frontispiece makes visible Potter's attempt to make Peter invisible and thereby to allow propriety an unproblematic triumph. If she had wanted such a triumph, she would not have included the picture at all, but by placing it at the beginning—no matter that it is separate from the final three illustrations—simply by including it as part of the book, Potter seems to admit that an unproblematic solution to the triumph of mind over body is not to be achieved easily, even if the final arrangement of illustrations makes exactly that suggestion.

In *The Tale of Peter Rabbit,* Beatrix Potter describes two realms of civilization, the human and the animal, each marked by a particular set of foodways. Mr. McGregor cultivates a garden for the sake of the produce he can harvest from it, and he polices the garden to rid it of the pests (e.g., rabbits) that would wreak havoc on the orderly life he has created within the garden walls. Correlatively, as we have already said, outside the garden walls Peter's mother and sisters also use food preparation to create a familial order. The garden walls, gate, and door function most obviously as the physical boundary between these two discrete worlds, and as long as that boundary is not breached, they can exist happily side by side. And both social worlds, as constructed by Mr. McGregor and Mrs. Rabbit, are meant to reinforce such an idyllic and mutually exclusive co-existence, yet neither the physical nor social boundaries act as barriers, because of the split in gender roles in the Rabbit household. The women create the social structure—marked clearly by particular habits of food gathering, meal preparation, and eating—that should organize family life, but neither Peter nor his father feels bound by their efforts, nor do they feel bound by the Rabbit family foodways. In search of other, wilder foods that offer a greater visceral satisfaction, Peter and his father cross a cultural barrier, putting themselves as well as the family at risk. The Rabbits are already a single-parent household, and given the fact that Peter is still disobedient in the end, there is a chance that at some point in the future the family may become all female. What point is Beatrix Potter trying to make? Is *The*

Tale of Peter Rabbit a lesson in obedience, particularly for boys, which means to teach responsibility for the maintenance of the traditional nuclear family? Or does the book offer a more sobering lesson concerning the evanescence of the traditional nuclear family, particular in the light of male resistance to the civilizing influence of family? Beatrix Potter seems to be walking a thin line here, preferring obedience but admitting in a subtle and backhanded way that the idyllic existence that obedience might make possible is not possible at all. Given such balance and tension, a meal of blackberries, currant buns, and milk must stand on equal footing with rabbit pie.

NOTES

1. Isabella Beeton, *Beeton's Book of Household Management: A First Edition Facsimile* (New York: Farrar, Straus and Giroux, 1969), 487.
2. Roland Barthes, "Toward a Psychosociology of Contemporary Food Production," in *Food and Culture: A Reader,* eds. Carole Counihan and Penny van Esterik (New York: Routledge, 1997), 26.
3. Beatrix Potter, *The Tale of Peter Rabbit* (London: Frederick Warne, 1902), 14.
4. Ibid., 17.
5. Stephen Mennell, "On the Civilizing of Appetite," in *Food and Culture: A Reader,* eds. Carole Counihan and Penny van Esterik (New York: Routledge, 1997), 328.
6. Potter, *The Tale of Peter Rabbit,* 54.
7. Alan Beardworth and Teresa Keil, *Sociology on the Menu: An Invitation to the Study of Food and Society* (London: Routledge, 1997), 54.
8. Allen S. Weiss, "Edible Architecture, Cannibal Architecture," in *Eating Culture,* eds. Ron Scapp and Brian Seitz (New York: State University of New York Press, 1998), 161.
9. Plato, "Phaedo," in *Cooking, Eating, Thinking: Transformative Philosophies of Food,* eds. Deane W. Curtin and Lisa M. Heldke (Bloomington: Indiana University Press, 1992), 24.
10. Deane W. Curtin, "Food/Body/Person," in *Cooking, Eating, Thinking: Transformative Philosophies of Food,* eds. Deane W. Curtin and Lisa M. Heldke (Bloomington: Indiana University Press, 1992), 5.
11. Weiss, 161.
12. Potter, *The Tale of Peter Rabbit,* 21–22.
13. Carolyn Korsmeyer, *Making Sense of Taste* (Ithaca: Cornell University Press, 1999), 23.
14. M. F. K. Fisher, *The Art of Eating* (New York: MacMillan, 1990), 613.
15. Mary Lukanuski, "A Place at the Counter: The Onus of Oneness," in *Eat-*

ing Culture, eds. Ron Scapp and Brian Seitz (New York: State University of New York Press, 1998), 115.

16. Ibid., 116.

17. Korsemeyer, *Making Sense of Taste,* 3.

18. Lisa M. Heldke, "Foodmaking As a Thoughtful Practice," in *Cooking, Eating, Thinking: Transformative Philosophies of Food,* eds. Deane W. Curtin and Lisa M. Heldke (Bloomington: Indiana University Press, 1992), 204.

19. Korsemeyer, *Making Sense of Taste,* 31.

20. Perry Nodelman, *The Pleasures of Children's Literature* (New York: Longman Publishers USA, 1996), 151.

21. Carole Scott, "Clothed in Nature or Nature Clothed: Dress As Metaphor in the Illustrations of Beatrix Potter and C. M. Baker," *Children's Literature* 22 (1994): 78.

22. Potter, *The Tale of Peter Rabbit,* 45.

23. Ibid., 33.

24. Ibid., 45.

25. Ibid., 48.

26. Ibid., 59.

BIBLIOGRAPHY

Barthes, Roland. "Toward a Psychosociology of Contemporary Food Production." Pp.20–27 in *Food and Culture: A Reader,* edited by Carole Counihan and Penny van Esterik. New York: Routledge, 1997.

Beardworth, Alan, and Teresa Keil. *Sociology on the Menu: An Invitation to the Study of Food and Society*. London: Routledge, 1997.

Beeton, Isabella. *Beeton's Book of Household Management: A First Edition Facsimile.* New York: Farrar, Straus and Giroux, 1969.

Curtin, Deane W. "Food/Body/Person." Pp.3–22 in *Cooking, Eating, Thinking: Transformative Philosophies of Food,* edited by Deane W. Curtin and Lisa M. Heldke. Bloomington: Indiana University Press, 1992.

Fisher, M. F. K. *The Art of Eating*. New York: MacMillan, 1990.

Heldke, Lisa M. "Foodmaking As a Thoughtful Practice." Pp.203–25 in *Cooking, Eating, Thinking: Transformative Philosophies of Food,* edited by Deane W. Curtin and Lisa M. Heldke. Bloomington: Indiana University Press, 1992.

Korsmeyer, Carolyn. *Making Sense of Taste*. Ithaca: Cornell University Press, 1999.

Lukanuski, Mary. "A Place at the Counter: The Onus of Oneness." Pp.112–20 in *Eating Culture,* edited by Ron Scapp and Brian Seitz. New York: State University of New York Press, 1998.

Mennell, Stephen. "On the Civilizing of Appetite." Pp.315–37 in *Food and Culture: A Reader,* edited by Carole Counihan and Penny van Esterik. New York: Routledge, 1997.

Nodelman, Perry. *The Pleasures of Children's Literature.* New York: Longman, 1996.

Plato. "Phaedo." Pp.24–27 in *Cooking, Eating, Thinking: Transformative Philosophies of Food,* edited by Deane W. Curtin and Lisa M. Heldke. Bloomington: Indiana University Press, 1992.

Potter, Beatrix. *The Tale of Peter Rabbit.* London: Frederick Warne, 1902.

Scott, Carole. "Clothed in Nature or Nature Clothed: Dress As Metaphor in the Illustrations of Beatrix Potter and C. M. Baker." *Children's Literature* 22 (1994): 70–89.

Weiss, Allen S. "Edible Architecture, Cannibal Architecture." Pp. 161–68 in *Eating Culture,* edited by Ron Scapp and Brian Seitz. Albany: State University of New York Press, 1998.

9

A Jungian Perspective on the Enduring Appeal of *Peter Rabbit*

Alice Byrnes

When anyone reaches a hundredth birthday, people invariably wonder about the secret of that person's longevity. As we commemorate the hundredth anniversary of *Peter Rabbit's* publication, people might also speculate about the phenomenon of *Peter Rabbit's* enduring appeal. Since its initial publication, *The Tale of Peter Rabbit* has enjoyed a sustained degree of popularity. For generations, the "little book" has appealed to children throughout the world. In fact, *Peter Rabbit* has been translated into at least thirty-six languages including French, German, Dutch, Italian, and Japanese.

One explanation for *Peter Rabbit's* pervasive appeal may be found in Carl Jung's theory of the archetypes. Jung believed that there are basic, psychic instincts shared by all humans. He attributed each of those instincts to an individual archetype. Among the varying archetypes defined by Jung is that of the child. We can explore how the archetypal symbol of the child seems to have influenced Beatrix Potter in her life and in her creation of *The Tale of Peter Rabbit,* and we might conjecture how the archetypal quality of *Peter Rabbit* holds a universal appeal for readers of all ages.

JUNG'S ARCHETYPE OF THE CHILD

Carl Jung introduced the concept that archetypes emanate from the unconscious. He claimed that each human being functions out of a personal unconscious, while humanity as a whole operates from a collective unconscious. There is a parallel in the processes of the personal and collective unconscious that might explain the paradox that what is most personal is invariably most universal. Jung believed that each person is a microcosm within a macrocosm and that "the psyche of the individual contains *reflections* of that larger universe."[1] Jung claimed that, "We shall probably get nearest to the truth if we think of the conscious and personal psyche as resting upon the broad basis of an inherited and universal psychic disposition which is as such unconscious, and that our personal psyche bears the same relation to the collective psyche as the individual to society."[2]

Because archetypes are embedded in the realm of the unconscious, they cannot be known directly. Therefore, archetypes are represented indirectly in the form of symbols. It might be said that symbols are the language of the unconscious. Because symbols are an integral feature of literary expression, archetypes frequently appear in literature. Stories containing archetypal symbols might arise from unconscious stirrings within the author's psyche. Also, archetypal literature resonates with a quality, so mysterious and powerful, that readers of all ages and cultures are drawn to it.

The child is one of the archetypes identified by Jung, and it frequently appears in children's literature. What is key to an understanding of the archetypal child is that it be regarded as a symbol and not as a child per se. Jung cautioned that one should not mistake the literal meaning of the child for the psychological reality that the archetype represents. Jung believed that "all we can do is to circumscribe and give an approximate description of an *unconscious core of meaning*."[3] References to the archetype of the child are made in a positive context of child-like, as opposed to a negative connotation of childish. In discussing the child archetype, Jung described qualities of abandonment, wholeness, invincibility, and immortality.[4] In this chapter, I consider how these distinguishing characteristics are reflected in the life of Beatrix Potter and in her *Tale of Peter Rabbit.*

THE CHILD ARCHETYPE AND BEATRIX POTTER

Abandonment and Beatrix Potter

Beatrix Potter did not experience physical abandonment in the sense of being orphaned, as frequently occurs in stories of the archetypal child.

Nevertheless, she did suffer a rather solitary existence in an environment that was not especially friendly to children. Biographer Margaret Lane said that Beatrix Potter was "born into a period and a class which seemed to have had little understanding of childhood."[5] Beatrix's loneliness was exacerbated by the fact that she did not enjoy the friendship of other children. Her Victorian parents did not permit her to go to school for fear that she would contract illness. Her only childhood companion was her younger brother, who was born when Beatrix was six years old. Beatrix was fond of Bertram and was heartbroken when he was sent away to boarding school.

Wholeness and Beatrix Potter

Although the feeling of abandonment typically experienced by the archetypal child is painful, there might be a positive aspect to it. That sense of isolation could offer a child like Beatrix Potter an opportunity to move beyond the limits of childish dependency into a healthier spirit of self-reliance. Jung described the archetypal child as maturing into adulthood and achieving a sense of wholeness. Wholeness is achieved when there is a healthy balance of opposites.

A well-integrated personality is a composite of corresponding traits such as male and female, consciousness and unconsciousness, freedom and responsibility, as well as imagination and practical intelligence. The archetypal child integrates the positive traits of both the child and adult. While Beatrix Potter grew up in the society of adults, she enjoyed the inner life of a child. She entertained a vivid sense of imagination, and she loved to draw. That sense of wonder remained with Beatrix into adulthood. Margaret Lane asserted that when Beatrix Potter began to compose *The Tale of Peter Rabbit,* "The child in her had not been superseded or outgrown, and the bright areas of first discovery and experience were still real to her."[6] Fifty years after the publication of *Peter Rabbit,* Beatrix Potter acknowledged, "I have just made stories to please myself, because I never grew up."[7] In response, Margaret Lane commented that "there is truth, of a limited kind, in this assertion. But it would have been truer still to say, 'because the child in me lived on.' "[8] This idea seems validated by one of the last entries that Beatrix Potter recorded in her journal: "What heaven can be more real than to retain the spirit-world of childhood, tempered and balanced by knowledge and common-sense."[9]

Beatrix Potter's childlike spirit of reverie was kindled in the country. That is where Beatrix was at home. During family vacations, she and her younger brother would romp freely through the countryside exploring nature. Invariably, she would try to keep her country vacation alive by bringing pets back to her nursery in London.

The adult side of Beatrix Potter was cultivated in her city home in London. Life at 2 Bolton Gardens was restricted, and her human interactions were limited mostly to her governesses. Her superior intelligence was cultivated by the tutoring she received in subjects such as literature, foreign language, mathematics, science, and art. She inherited a natural talent for art that was encouraged by her father and tutors. She would visit science displays at the nearby Victoria and Albert Museum and sketch pictures of plants and animals. Even today, her sketches of fungi are regarded as scientifically accurate. Beatrix took pains to make drawings of her pets that accurately depict the natural characteristics of their species. At the same time, she endowed their portraits with human personalities.

Her artistic leanings gave way to her literary expression. Her striking watercolors seem to drive the story. Few authors possess the artistic and literary talent both to illustrate and narrate a story. Beatrix Potter "knew exactly what interested children, and was able to do magic things with paint-brush and pencil."[10] Consequently, there is an organic unity that singularly distinguishes Potter's work. In contemporary psychology, one might hypothesize that Beatrix Potter, the artist and storyteller, was able to exercise both the right and left sides of her brain in a unified act of creation. Such a fullness of expression has a powerful impact on the reader. In Beatrix Potter, the child-adult, all aspects of her experience seemed to coalesce—city and country life, animal and human interactions, science and drawing, as well as art and storytelling.

Invincibility and Beatrix Potter

Beatrix Potter's creation of her picture books was a manifestation of her personal development. The sickly child, who had been isolated in the nursery of her parents' house, not only survived, but developed into a vibrant and independent adult who created a life for herself as an internationally acclaimed author of children's books. As Beatrix Potter matured, she was transformed from a vulnerable girl into an invincible woman.

In Jungian psychology, the process of personal growth and transformation is often symbolized by a journey. Physical movement represents psychological progression from the conscious world into the unconscious realm. While the device of the journey is a familiar literary device, it is also a common activity in everyday life. People frequently move when they want to initiate a new life. People travel on vacation in order to relax. People go on retreat in order to renew themselves. Going to another location not only represents a change in one's life; it actually engenders such a revitalization.

The frequent vacations that the Potter family enjoyed in Scotland and northwest England nurtured Beatrix's growing sense of freedom and creativity. Even in her youth, Beatrix Potter was inspired by the countryside with its animals, plants, and ordinary folks. The success of her "little books" financed her lifetime dream of buying property in the Lake District. In becoming the proud owner of Hill Top Farm, Beatrix Potter had come a long way in forging a new life for herself. The farmhouse provided a retreat where she could enjoy holidays away from the restrictions of her parents' house in London and a sanctuary where she could work on her books. Tourists who visit Beatrix Potter's house at Hill Top recognize the similarity between that charming setting and familiar scenes from her picture books.[11]

Eventually, Beatrix Potter became so involved in rural life that she assumed a leadership role in the conservation movement. She continued to purchase property in hopes of preserving the beautiful English countryside. In order to facilitate the business of buying property, Beatrix Potter procured the services of a country lawyer named William Heelis. In time, Beatrix's relation with Willy Heelis developed from a professional endeavor into a personal friendship. Eventually, they became engaged. Even though Beatrix was nearly forty-seven years old when Willy proposed to her, her parents were vehemently opposed to the prospective marriage. Beatrix asserted her independence by permanently leaving her parents' house and setting up household with her new husband. Beatrix Potter, the middle-aged spinster, became Mrs. William Heelis and committed herself to being a wife and farmer. Country living that she had romanticized in her stories now became her way of life.

It is interesting to note that the more immersed Beatrix actually became in rural life, the less inclined she was to write about it. Admittedly, her diminishing eyesight made it increasingly difficult for her to do the art and composition for her "little books." Also, her responsibilities on the farm did not provide much time to continue her career as an author of children's books. Nevertheless, one cannot dismiss the suspicion that Beatrix did not need to live vicariously through her writing after she felt fulfilled in real life. Ultimately, Beatrix Potter succeeded both in the world of children's literature and in her personal ambition to become part of the country life that she depicted in her books.

Immortality and Beatrix Potter

In the process of overcoming obstacles, the child archetype develops from a former existence into a future state of being. "The child motif represents not only something that existed in the distant past but also something that exists *now*."[12] Furthermore, there is an integral connection between past, present, and future: "One of the essential features of the child-motif is its *futurity*."[13] Stages of time seem to coalesce in the archetypal child. According to Jung's psychology, the " 'child' symbolizes the pre-conscious and the post-conscious nature of man. His pre-conscious nature is the unconscious state of earliest childhood; his post-conscious nature is an anticipation by analogy of life after death."[14] Jung believed that the child archetype evolves from a "dubious beginning" to a "triumphal end."[15] In referring to the "eternal child,"[16] Jung bestowed an aura of immortality on the archetype.

Because *The Tale of Peter Rabbit* has endured as such a popular classic for the past century, that little bunny seems to defy the limitations of time. Peter Rabbit never ages, while his readers continue to grow older and pass on. Although Beatrix Potter never gave birth to any biological children, her spirit remains forever alive in the generations of children who are the beneficiaries of her "little books."

THE CHILD ARCHETYPE AND PETER RABBIT

After considering how the child archetype seems to have been operative within Beatrix Potter herself, we might consider the possibility of how that archetype is reflected in her creation of *Peter Rabbit*. Of the many books that Beatrix Potter produced, *Peter Rabbit* was the first and most famous. With that in mind, it might be helpful to consider Beatrix Potter's relation to *Peter Rabbit* and her first pet rabbit, Peter Piper.

Because Potter was, for the most part, deprived of peer companionship during the early years of her life, her pets literally became her best friends and symbolically became extensions of herself. In her biography, *Beatrix Potter: Artist, Storyteller and Countrywoman,* Judy Taylor described Beatrix Potter's attachment to her pet rabbit saying that she "was utterly devoted to him."[17] When the rabbit died, Beatrix recorded in her journal that "his disposition was uniformly amiable and his temper unfailingly sweet. An affectionate companion and quiet friend."[18]

Based on the strong, personal affinity that Beatrix Potter felt for her pet rabbit, it is not surprising that he was reincarnated as a character in a picture letter that she wrote to Noel Moore, the first-born child of her favorite governess and faithful friend. It seems fitting that Beatrix would compose a story about Peter Rabbit recuperating in his mother's care in a letter to Noel while he was sick in bed with scarlet fever. Although that picture letter was only one of many letters that Beatrix wrote to children, it was the one that stood out in her mind seven years later when "Annie Moore suggested to Beatrix that some of her letters to the children might be turned into books."[19] How fortunate that young Noel had so treasured the picture letter that he still had it when Beatrix asked him to lend it to her! That letter became the basis for Beatrix Potter's first publication, *The Tale of Peter Rabbit*.

The life of Beatrix Potter and the spirit of the child archetype seem to infuse the creation of Peter Rabbit. It might seem appropriate, at this point, to explore how characteristics of Jung's archetypal child are also reflected in *The Tale of Peter Rabbit*.

Abandonment and Peter Rabbit

Many children in archetypal literature suffer an experience of abandonment because of the death of a parent. Peter's father had come to a tragic end when Mrs. McGregor made a pie out of him. Like the orphaned child in fairy tales, Peter has to confront the world on his own. This literary motif addresses a primeval fear of losing one's parents. What is significant is that the lone child survives and ultimately achieves a sense of independence and victory. This success bolsters confidence in the reader that he or she can also be self-sufficient enough to survive the vicissitudes of life.

Wholeness and Peter Rabbit

Self-reliance demands a sense of archetypal wholeness. A child archetype manifests complementary characteristics of child and adult, as well as male and female. Because Peter Rabbit is immature, he needs an adult to protect and nurture him. Although Peter is quite resourceful in his efforts to escape from Mr. McGregor, he reverts to the position of a dependent child who needs his mother to take care of him when he comes home sick. Children of all ages can relate to these contradictory urges of wanting to be free and yet wishing to be cared for in times of need. The scene of Mrs. Rabbit tending her child circumscribes *The Tale of Peter Rabbit* from the frontispiece to the concluding description of how, "His mother put him to bed, and made some camomile tea."[20] The familiar picture of Mrs. Rabbit and Peter is somewhat reminiscent of a classic portrait of Madonna and child. In fact, a portrait of Madonna and child might be regarded as an expression of Jungian wholeness representing the union of child and adult, as well as male and female.

The most charming aspect of Peter's duality is in terms of his human and animal attributes. As his name implies, Peter Rabbit is a hybrid of boy and animal. Potter's watercolors accurately depict the physical characteristics of a real rabbit. Peter performs activities that are possible for a rabbit, but impossible for a human. He squeezes under the gate leading to Mr. McGregor's garden. In trying to escape from the garden, Peter gains speed by running on four legs. Then, Peter Rabbit hides inside a watering can, jumps out a window, and props himself in a wheelbarrow.

It is delightfully ironic that the little rabbit dresses like a child wearing a blue jacket with brass buttons and a pair of black shoes. In that regard and in many others, Peter seems more like a little boy than a bunny. He cries when he feels frightened. He sneezes, sits down to rest, and asks for directions. The narrator mentions his cognitive activities of forgetting the way, plotting an escape, and deciding not to talk to the cat. When Peter returns home, he goes to bed and is given a tablespoonful of camomile tea.

Because Peter Rabbit is presented as a composite of animal instincts and human behavior, we tend to apply a dual set of standards to his harebrained activity. On one hand, the reader is impressed with Peter's impulsiveness, but, on the other hand, one recognizes that he has been disobedient. Like Adam, the father of the human race, Peter commits the forbidden crime in the garden. Normally, the reader would just take it for granted that a bunny would romp freely in a garden without paying attention to anyone who cautioned him not to do so. Who would expect a rabbit to function within the restraints of a jacket and shoes? If Peter Rabbit were judged as an animal, one would simply think that he was acting like a typical bunny. Because Peter is judged by human standards, he is dubbed as a naughty rabbit.

The reader can identify with the plight of Peter Rabbit, who is criticized for succumbing to his natural instincts. M. L. von Franz, an associate of Jung, said that, "The Self is often symbolized as an animal, representing our instinctive nature and its connectedness with one's surroundings."[21] Jungian psychology addresses the tension of trying to reconcile our noble desires with the shadow of our lower drives. According to Jung, the pinnacle of human development is achieved in a fully integrated personality that accepts the darker shadow of one's personality while striving to a higher level of development. Jung discussed the human struggle of dealing with one's lower or animal instincts that he refers to as the "shadow":[22] "Taking it in its deepest sense, the shadow is the invisible saurian tail that man still drags behind him."[23] Jung recognized that the repressed instincts of the human shadow are not essentially bad, but unacceptable according to social conventions. He believed that "the shadow is merely somewhat inferior, primitive, unadapted, and awkward; not wholly bad. It even contains childish or primitive qualities which would in a way vitalize and embellish human existence, but—convention forbids."[24] When we reflect on Peter Rabbit's behavior, we recognize that although he might be regarded as a naughty rabbit, there is something endearing in the fact that he gives vent to his basic instincts. The little rabbit simply does what comes naturally to him.

The child-like reader champions Peter Rabbit's freedom to be himself, while many adults harbor a hidden desire to cast off human conventions and to follow their own impulses. Inwardly, we delight in Peter's impetuous nature and his ability to survive. In discussing *The Tale of Peter Rabbit,* Alison Lurie recalls that when she "asked a class of students which character in the book they would have preferred to be, they voted unanimously for Peter, recognizing the concealed moral of the story: that disobedience and exploration are more fun than good behavior, and not really all that dangerous, whatever Mother may say. Consciously or not, children know that the author's sympathy and interest are with Peter."[25]

Invincibility and Peter Rabbit

Whether the child archetype is represented as a child or an animal, invincibility is a distinguishing characteristic of the archetype. Characteristically, the archetypal child is "delivered helpless into the power of terrible enemies and in continual danger of extinction."[26] Nevertheless, the classic myth of the archetype emphasizes "that the 'child' is endowed with superior powers and, despite all dangers, will unexpectedly pull through."[27] The archetype survives; the child triumphs. Invariably, the archetypal child embarks on a journey that symbolizes the transformation that takes place as one progresses from the area of the conscious to the realm of the unconscious.

We recognize changes in Peter Rabbit as he journeys into Mr. McGregor's garden. Peter follows the pattern of the archetypal hero who sets out in quest of his lost father. He ventures toward Mr. McGregor's garden to the place where Mr. Rabbit had come to his demise. During his dangerous adventure in the garden, Peter undergoes the rites of passage that test his endurance. Peter confronts obstacles and dangers along the way. He feels frightened and lost as Mr. McGregor pursues him. Peter's experience resembles the perennial theme of the fairy tales in which the youngster wanders into the primeval forest. Invariably, the estranged youngster overcomes obstacles with the assistance of a mentor figure such as a fairy godmother. The mentor seems to bestow power that enables the archetypal child to move beyond the limitations of childish fears. In the case of Peter Rabbit, the troubled bunny rallies the incentive to overcome his plight in Mr. McGregor's garden through the inspiration of the friendly sparrows who "implored him to exert himself."[28]

Peter Rabbit survives. Ultimately, Peter outwits Mr. McGregor. The reader rejoices in the triumph of the underdog. Peter escapes from Mr. McGregor, and the "prodigal son" returns home.

Immortality and Peter Rabbit

In addition to attributes of abandonment, wholeness, and invincibility, the archetypal child characteristically emanates an eternal quality. The story opens with an aura of timelessness. The familiar phrase, "Once upon a time," magically transports the reader into a realm beyond the physical limitations of time and space.

As an archetype of the child, Peter Rabbit begets an ongoing cycle of generativity. Because the rabbit is such a prolific animal, it has long been regarded as a symbol of immortality. Peter himself belongs to a long line of Rabbits who will live after him. In the subsequent series of Beatrix Potter's stories, Peter's cousin, Benjamin Bunny, marries Peter's sister, Flopsy, who gives birth to many "Flopsy Bunnies."

More importantly, *The Tale of Peter Rabbit* lives on. It is a good story that has withstood the test of time. An editorial that appeared in the *New York Herald Tribune* on January 6, 1944, commemorating Beatrix Potter's death proclaimed that, "Her greatness lies in the fact that she was able again and again to create that rare thing—a book that brings grown-ups and children together in shared delight."[29] Because a good story has universal appeal, *The Tale of Peter Rabbit* has remained popular for a century and certainly gives promise of continuing appeal for subsequent generations.

UNIVERSAL APPEAL OF BEATRIX POTTER'S ARCHETYPAL RABBIT

An examination of the text of *Peter Rabbit* and the life of Beatrix Potter reveals similarities in their archetypal journeys. We might say that writing *The Tale of Peter Rabbit* assisted Beatrix Potter in her process of self-realization. Through the dynamic interplay of her unconscious and conscious, Beatrix Potter's imagination gave birth to Peter Rabbit. The organic unity and unrivalled craft of her story and illustrations continue to speak to the hearts and minds of readers of all ages. Children identify with Peter, while adult readers recapture the spirit of childhood.

Because *Peter Rabbit* emanates from the core of Beatrix Potter's being, her creation resonates with all humanity. The depth of the author's inspiration and the reader's response suggests the archetypal quality of the story and accounts for the undying appeal of *The Tale of Peter Rabbit*.

NOTES

1. Ira Progoff, *Jung, Synchronicity, and Human Destiny* (New York: Julian Press, 1973), 78.
2. Carl Jung, "The Relations between the Ego and the Unconscious," in *The Basic Writings of C. G. Jung*, ed. Violet Staub DeLaszlo (New York: Modern Library, 1959), 127.
3. Carl Jung, "The Psychology of the Child Archetype," in *The Archetypes and the Collective Unconscious*, Vol. 9, Part I, ed. Herbert Read, Michael Fordham, Gerhard Adler, and William McGuire, translated by R. F. C. Hull (Princeton: Princeton University Press, 1969), 156.
4. Jung, "The Psychology of the Child Archetype," 151–81.
5. Margaret Lane, *The Tale of Beatrix Potter* (London: Frederick Warne, 1946), 16.
6. Lane, *The Tale of Beatrix Potter*, 54.
7. Lane, *The Tale of Beatrix Potter*, 54.
8. Lane, *The Tale of Beatrix Potter*, 54.
9. Timothy Foote, "A Tale of Some Tails, and the Story of Their Shy Creator," *Smithsonian* (January 1989): 90.
10. Lane, *The Tale of Beatrix Potter*, 53.
11. Judy Taylor, *Beatrix Potter and Hill Top* (London: The National Trust, 1989).
12. Jung, "The Psychology of the Child Archetype," 162.
13. Jung, "The Psychology of the Child Archetype," 164.
14. Jung, "The Psychology of the Child Archetype," 178.

15. Jung, "The Psychology of the Child Archetype," 179.

16. Jung, "The Psychology of the Child Archetype," 179.

17. Judy Taylor, *Beatrix Potter: Artist, Storyteller and Countrywoman* (London: Frederick Warne, 1986), 61.

18. Taylor, *Beatrix Potter: Artist, Storyteller, and Countrywoman*, 61.

19. Judy Taylor, *Letters to Children from Beatrix Potter* (London: Frederick Warne, 1992), 81.

20. Beatrix Potter, *The Tale of Peter Rabbit* (London: Frederick Warne, 1902).

21. M. L. von Franz, "The Process of Individuation," in *Man and His Symbols*, ed. Carl G. Jung (New York: Laurel, 1968), 220.

22. Jolande Jacobi, *The Psychology of C. G. Jung* (New Haven, Conn.: Yale University Press, 1973), 109–14.

23. Carl Jung, *Psychological Reflections*, ed. Jolande Jacobi and R. F. C. Hull (Princeton: Princeton University Press, 1970), 243.

24. Jung, *Psychological Reflections*, 242.

25. Alison Lurie, *Don't Tell the Grown-Ups Why Kids Love the Books They Do* (New York: Avon, 1990), 95.

26. Jung, "The Psychology of the Child Archetype," 170.

27. Jung, "The Psychology of the Child Archetype," 170.

28. Potter, *The Tale of Peter Rabbit*.

29. *New York Herald Tribune,* 6 January 1944, Editorial, 18.

BIBLIOGRAPHY

Foote, Timothy. "A Tale of Some Tails, and the Story of Their Shy Creator." *Smithsonian* (January 1989): 80–90.

Jacobi, Jolande. *The Psychology of C. G. Jung*. New Haven, Conn.: Yale University Press, 1973.

Jung, C. G. "The Psychology of the Child Archetype," Pp. 151–81 in *The Archetypes and the Collective Unconscious*. 1934. Vol. 9, Part I. 2nd ed., edited by Herbert Read, Michael Fordham, Gerhard Adler, and William McGuire, translated by R. F. C. Hull. Princeton: Princeton University Press, 1969.

———. *The Basic Writings of C. G. Jung,* edited and introduced by Violet Staub DeLaszlo. New York: Modern Library, 1959.

———. *Psychological Reflections*, edited by Joland Jacobi and R. F. C. Hull. Princeton: Princeton University Press, 1970.

Lane, Margaret. *The Tale of Beatrix Potter.* London: Frederick Warne, 1946.

Lurie, Alison. *Don't Tell the Grown-Ups Why Kids Love the Books They Do.* New York: Avon, 1990.

New York Herald Tribune, 6 January 1944, Editorial: 18.

Potter, Beatrix. *The Tale of Peter Rabbit*. 1902. London: Frederick Warne, 1997.

Progoff, Ira. *Jung, Synchronicity, and Human Destiny*. New York: Julian Press, 1973.

Taylor, Judy. *Beatrix Potter and Hill Top*. London: The National Trust, 1989.

———. *Beatrix Potter: Artist, Storyteller, and Countrywoman*. London: Frederick Warne, 1986.

———. *Letters to Children from Beatrix Potter*. London: Frederick Warne, 1992.

Von Franz, M. L. "The Process of Individuation." Pp. 157–254 in *Man and His Symbols*, edited by Carl G. Jung. New York: Laurel, 1968.

Beatrix Potter, *The Tale of Peter Rabbit,* p. 20 (1902 edition).

10

Why Children Come Back: *The Tale of Peter Rabbit* and *Where the Wild Things Are*

Melissa Gross

There are many reasons why a particular book may retain its popularity over time. Certainly excellence of story, writing, and illustration are expected and, when evaluating picture books, the integration of the writing and pictures in telling the story is essential. However, beyond any technical measures of quality, *appeal,* that connection readers feel to a book, is essential to its longevity.

Some characters from children's literature become so strongly associated with childhood itself that exposure to a particular book at the appropriate age is seen by many as a highly desired experience, one not to be missed. Such books have something to say to children that adults and the culture at large feel they need to hear. The ability of a book to serve children in this way is worth exploring. Over the past hundred years, the views of childhood, children's literature, and the experience of being a child, have changed and yet certain messages continue to be pertinent. For instance, *The Tale of Peter Rabbit,*[1] written in Victorian times by Beatrix Potter, continues in multiple editions and through a wide variety of spin-off products to appeal to children the world over.[2] Likewise, *Where the Wild Things Are,* written in 1963 by Maurice Sendak, for what might seem a very different child from Potter's intended reader, meets the new millennium commodified in much the same way that Peter Rabbit has been and as avidly enjoyed by a new generation of children.[3]

What is of interest here is the strong similarity of message that these two books share and the ways in which this message is deeply reflective of issues and developmental tasks with which the child struggles. That these books are works of great literary and artistic merit is taken as a given in this essay. This exploration will look at their deep connection to the life of young children and at the adult messages they convey.

BOOKS AS INSTRUMENTS OF SOCIALIZATION

From age to age the trappings of childhood can change, and yet growing up involves developmental phases and experiences that can supersede an individual historical era or society. One such experience that children go through is that of being socialized to understand how to behave in the society in which they are born. Early in babyhood tutelage in correct behavior, how to be one of the group, begins. While the study of children has only recently begun to interest sociologists, new interest in this group has already resulted in a fair amount of work, and several models are available to describe socialization, "the process by which children adapt to and internalize society."[4] These models range in type from deterministic, those models that see the child as a force to be tamed and contained by society (primarily through the parents), to constructivist, models that see the child as an active participant in the socialization process.[5]

The idea that children's books are instruments of socialization has been recognized by many.[6] As Nodelman puts it, "whatever else literary texts are, and whatever pleasure they might afford us, they are also expressions of the values and assumptions of a culture and a significant way of embedding readers in those values and assumptions."[7] Both of the books considered here have been discussed elsewhere as being about socializing the child out of naughty behaviors and dealing with the child's need to rebel.[8]

However, other writers point out that the story can also reveal the individual's response to the process of being socialized. For instance, perhaps what we see in Potter's stories is an expression of her own need to rebel against the constraints of Victorian society.[9] Likewise, Shaddock suggests that "the motive for the adventure at the core of *Where the Wild Things Are*—the desire for the freedoms of the uncivilized—is founded upon the restraints of the domesticated world."[10] She sees Max as reacting to "his confrontations with the civil boundaries of a 'mature' society" and "the taming force of women, particularly mothers."[11]

In both of these works, the implied child reader is a wild thing, constrained by socialization and the civilizing interests of adults, who is working to integrate these conflicting demands into a growing sense of self. Socialization, of necessity, is embedded in the child's developmental sequence. The child can make sense of rules and manage impulses and feelings only in relation to his or her developmental place within the context of the behaviors and lessons of socializing others (including parents, siblings, friends, and the society at large).

For both Peter and Max, "naughtiness" has something to do with movement toward individuation and autonomous function, developmental issues that are prime between the ages of 18 to 36 months and that arise again in adolescence. Individuation is about the development of a sense of "self" as the child begins to internalize mother as object and acclimates to the realization that mother and child are separate entities.[12] Autonomous functions are the skills children develop, such as sitting, crawling, standing, and particularly walking, that give them increased mobility and independence. It is through the development of such skills that children begin to be aware of the world. Children in this phase of development spend time "practising" their new skills, and as they become more proficient, experience a sense of self, independent from mother. Of course, the child still needs the mother, and so individuating is not always a comfortable experience. The awareness, for instance, of selfhood makes the child fearful because the child is not yet able to hold a sense of mother internally. In what is called the rapprochement subphase, the child returns to the mother and shows dependence on her again. Both steps, separating and returning, are part of the normal developmental sequence.

Peter and Max can be described as toddlers moving through the practising and rapprochement subphases of the separation-individuation phase of development, depicting experiences that are highly pertinent to the young children to whom these books are addressed. *The Tale of Peter Rabbit* and *Where the Wild Things Are* speak especially well to this audience by mirroring the developmental wishes and experiences that young children are engaged in resolving.

THE CHILD AND THE NATURAL WORLD: WHO'S A WILD THING?

It has been suggested that Sendak developed the term *wild thing* from "the common Yiddish expression 'wilde chaye.' "[13] Regardless of its origin, wild thing can be taken as indicating both a creature that is not integrated into society, in the sense of being civilized or socialized, and also as a creature that inhabits the natural world. Webster's, for example, defines *wild* in three ways: "living or growing in its original or natural state and not normally domesticated or cultivated [*wild* flowers, *wild* animals]," "not easily restrained or regulated [*wild* children]," and "characterized by a lack of social or moral restraint."[14]

The relationship between each of these protagonists and the natural world presents interesting contrasts. As a rabbit, Peter is clearly a creature of nature. His home is in the sandbank under a fir tree. Although the tale is foreshadowed on the cover, endpapers, and front matter, Peter and his family are depicted as wild rabbits in their natural setting as the story begins. The reader does not know yet that "Peter . . . is as much boy as rabbit."[15]

Max, on the other hand, is presented in a highly domestic environment, the modern home, and must approximate nature through imagination and imitation. He wears his connection to the natural world, his wolf suit, indicating that he is as much wolf as boy. The wolf is well known in children's literature. Children know not to talk to one or open the door, for the wolf is tricky and hungry, and a threat to their safety. Max wears the wolf suit to indicate that there is something about him to be overcome, his wildness, in service to preserving domestic tranquility.

Clothing As Socialization: How It Begins

Both Peter and Max are presented as part wild thing and part little boy. In each case, clothing is used to symbolize the character's level of socialization, which for each boy is incomplete. One is a wild animal dressed as a human child; the other is a human child dressed as a wild animal. The wildness of each is fairly tempered, however, because neither bunnies, nor wolf suits, nor even little boys are very intimidating.

For Peter the attempted socialization begins when he and his sisters are dressed to go out into the world. This adornment of clothing is important, for it signals that a certain code of behavior is required in "public." As Scott notes, "For Potter clothes are what people must learn to wear as they grow up and go out into the world . . . for her animals merge their own natures so aptly with the behavior and personalities of children that we wonder whether her animals have become children or vice versa."[16]

Max, on the other hand, is a boy dressed like a wolf. At first it seems that his face is his only human aspect, but on closer inspection, the buttons on his wolf suit further betray his hidden identity: "Max's costume looks suspiciously like a baby suit, a sleeper or pajama."[17] In that sense, it is hardly more frightening than a wild bunny. Like Peter, his nature is merged so that we recognize him as part animal, part boy. Recognition of their natures also involves understanding how very young they are. Potter's dressed-up rabbits are toddler-like, with their big heads and round bodies.[18] Max, for all his wildness, is dressed in baby pajamas. These clues to the age and identity of the protagonists help to set the context for these stories and for the social and psychic rationale of the adventures that follow.

ADVENTURE AS AUTONOMOUS FUNCTION

The adventures that Peter and Max have can be described as representing the practising subphase of the separation-individuation schema. At this point in development, the world opens up for the toddler. The bond the child feels with the mother continues to be very strong, but the ability to move about and away from mother allows the child to develop the sense of being separate from her and also of him or herself as a separate person. This sense is a very exciting development for the child. Learning to stand and walk changes the child's experience of the world. As mobility increases, the child becomes even more interested in developing his or her abilities. Discovery and mastery are the toddler's aims. As skills increase, the sense of individuality grows. Both Peter and Max have adventures that express movement toward individuating from the mother and the desire to practise and develop skills they need ultimately to internalize the mother and become separate (socialized) individuals. Therefore, what appear to be acts of will that are contrary to the socialization process, in the end serve only to feed it because this developmental process, like the socialization process, is necessary if the child is ultimately to join the society as a fully-functioning member.

For Peter and Max, this process means going immediately toward the exact thing mother has told them not to do. Peter goes directly to the garden and the threat of becoming pie filling. Max "leaves" his room and ventures into the forbidden natural state that he desires. Both pursue their goals independently.

Peter's adventure is an exploration of the socialized world, symbolized by Mr. McGregor's garden. Here he practises his ability to move away from mother and to act autonomously in the world. He begins with a feast of lettuces, French beans, and radishes. Things shortly take a downward turn, however, with an ensuing stomachache and an encounter with Mr. McGregor himself. Almost immediately the sign of Peter's socialization, his clothing, begins to work against him, as though wearing jacket and shoes supports a code of behavior that he eschewed when he entered the forbidden garden.

It becomes clear that, in order to deal with Mr. McGregor and his predicament, Peter must revert to his natural self and depend on his wildness to survive. The clothes (socialization) prove to be impediments. First the shoes go. One is lost among the cabbages, another in the potatoes: "After losing them, he ran on four legs and went faster."[19] He travels now more like a bunny, or perhaps he crawls like a baby in the way a toddler will revert to crawling to move faster. This mode of moving is a big help, but then his jacket gets him caught in the gooseberry net. The coat also has to go. As he loses each article of clothing, his wildness becomes more apparent until, as Scott expresses it, "Peter looks once more like generic Rabbit, for both he and the reader are for the moment lost in the purely animal emotion of escape."[20] Peter is now stripped down to his wildness and must find his way out of the civilized garden rows and return to mother.

Max also moves away from mother in hopes of showing some mastery of the world. However, as an urban child with limited access to the natural world, to go there he must take it on (wear it) and conjure it up in imagination or in a virtual sense. Max does not go out into the natural world; rather, he goes into the world of imagination to construct a forest, an ocean, and a land where his wolf suit, baby buttons and all, fits in.

Max's adventure is a return to nature that helps him to realize a return to a more "natural," unsocialized world and to demonstrate a wide range of autonomous activities including sailing a boat and taming wild things himself. This autonomy is symbolized, first, by the appearance of Max's private boat, which represents his journey toward becoming an individual. He looks quite happy and confident. He is separating from his mother and is unconcerned about it.

The first thing Max does, when he arrives where the wild things are, is to tame them using language that is reminiscent of things his mother may have said to him ("BE STILL!") and a child's game of who will blink first to frighten them into submission. He treats the wild things like children; that is, as he is treated when he behaves in a wild way. It is as a child who uses the socializing words of grown-ups that he becomes their king. And having established his dominance, he begins his true descent into wildness. Now the wild rumpus starts! Pictures fill up the space, and we lose the text because animals (wild things) do not have words the way we do. Max's return to nature is a deep regression that reaches its apex as he and the wild things dance, hang from trees, and parade *wordlessly,* for this is a regression that goes back to a place before language to the expressions of babies and of beasts.

The behaviors that Max has engaged in are highly representative of the dramatic behaviors young children demonstrate as they reach a rapprochement crisis in the separation-individuation phase. These behaviors often include temper tantrums and general moodiness. When Max speaks again, it is a signal that he is on his way back to socialized behavior and to mother. His wordlessness is analogous to Peter's being stripped down to a "wild thing" in Mr. McGregor's garden. Max's return to language likewise is similar to Peter's use of his socialized knowledge to get back home.

Peter descends into wildness in his panic to escape. However, it is not being wild that gets him out of the garden; rather, it is his ability to understand the order of the garden world he has invaded and to recognize that safety is to be found in the domestic life at home. As a dressed-up boy-rabbit, he explores civilization, regresses to his rabbitness, and then finds his way home. Max, the wolf-boy, explores his wildness, regresses to babyhood, and then returns home. Both have had a cathartic experience.

When Max reaches the deepest, wordless part of himself and conquers it, he too begins to look out from it, and to desire the context he had wished to leave behind. He takes this opportunity again to socialize the wild things in the manner he is accustomed to. "Now Stop!" he says and sends them "off to bed without their supper."

But something else has happened here. During the rumpus, the moon, which has hesitated since before "night and day and in and out of weeks and almost over a year," has grown full and is still full when Max gets back to his room. The image of the werewolf's transformation with the full moon is called up here, and it makes sense that Max's full transformation to wild thing is aligned with the moon. But another change has happened for him at that apex. Max has grown. He has internalized the socializing behavior exhibited by his mother and shown his mastery of it by using it to subdue the wild things of his imagination. Like the wolfman he will now begin to return to his prior form, and he is ready to come back. Peter, too, has given himself an experience that may well help him to control his behavior. Both boys are triumphant in a sense. Max has tamed the wild things. Peter not only has his life, but also has succeeded where his father could not.

THE ROLE OF FOOD: "I'LL EAT YOU UP!"

Food plays many roles in *The Tale of Peter Rabbit* and in *Where the Wild Things Are*. Because these books are meant for young readers and portray young protagonists, it is important to note that, in a psychological sense, food and the mother are deeply connected. For babies, food and mother are much the same thing. As children grow, they remain dependent on adults to feed them, even when weaned from the breast. The child's relationship to food is entwined with a basic drive to survive, with mother's love, and with comfort, punishment, motivation, and reward.

It was food that lured Peter (and his father) to Mr. McGregor's garden. It is food that lures Max back from where the wild things are. Peter goes to the garden even though his father perished there. He goes to the garden even though there is plenty of food at home. His mother has gone to the baker for "a loaf of brown bread and five currant buns." His sisters are gathering blackberries while he is losing his coat and shoes and "exerting" himself (or practising, if you please). Peter is in many ways the thief that Mr. McGregor accuses him of being. He is also something of a glutton, eating himself sick in short order. Food, for Peter, provides motivation, reward, punishment, and comfort for his "naughty" behavior. The prize of the garden lettuce provides motivation and reward. The resulting stomachache and absence of dinner is punishment. Being cared for with a dose of curing camomile tea (an instant cure for stomachaches, highly recommended) is comfort to those who know its healing powers.

However, Peter hides in his bed in the frontispiece as mother dips the spoon in for his "dose," and more than one interpretation of this illustration has been made. For example, Carpenter interprets the dose of tea as "the disobedient boy meets his deserts" indicating that the tea is a punishment.[21] Frey sees Peter as snug in his bed resisting his medicine.[22] Kutzer, however, questions whether Peter has been punished at all, since he has enjoyed the garden and now has "his mother's undivided attention."[23] Yet another interpretation of this illustration is that he is not hiding from the tea, but rather, is reluctant to look at mother in the aftermath of his misbehavior. For the child reader, any of these interpretations is possible, but the comfort of being cared for, even when this entails taking medicine that might taste bad, still comes through.

Max's major infraction is also related to food. Although Max has made "mischief of one kind and another" (including chasing the family dog with a fork) and "his mother called him 'WILD THING!'," it is not until he makes a threat of oral aggression, "I'LL EAT YOU UP!" that he is sent to bed (like Peter) without supper.

But considering that Max is in his wolf suit, is his oral aggression surprising? He is a wolf after all, and wolves are always eating things up, things like grandmas, goat children, and little pigs.[24] What happens, though, is that "he loses her. He loses food, and food equals mother."[25] And so, the loss of a meal and the loss of mother are the punishments used in the socialization process. In his turn, Max, too, in his role as parent (king and patriarch) to them, sends the wild things to bed without their supper.

However, in each case, the loss of supper does not disrupt the bond. Peter still finds comfort; Max still wants to be "where someone loved him best of all." For both of them, nurturance continues to lie with mother despite events. Even the wild things, sent to bed without their supper, threaten lovingly, as adults often do to children, "we'll eat you up—we love you so!"

When Max gets back, the food is there for him, but his mother is not.

LIFE WITH MOM: RAPPROCHEMENT AND SOCIALIZATION

At some point in the practising phase, the child remembers mother and wishes to return to her, as Max, smelling good things to eat, thinks about home. What happens here is that Max suddenly becomes aware that his mother is not with him, begins to experience separation anxiety, and wants "to be where someone love[s] him best of all."

On the way back, the boat does not say "Max" on the side anymore, for he is coming back in hopes of merging with mother again. Peter, concluding his practising phase, runs directly home: "[He] never stopped running or looked behind him till he got home to the big fir tree."

The child now begins to understand that mother, too, is a separate person and does not always want what her child wants. In response to this awareness of separateness, young children may become more needy and negative, and feel separation anxiety. While the child wants to share his or her achievements with mother, the feeling of mastery is fading and is replaced with the sense of being small and helpless.

As Peter and Max return home, it is striking to perceive how these two households, born more than sixty years apart, are so similar. First, both boys appear to come from single parent, mother-run homes. The absence of fathers in these stories can be interpreted as representative of the young child's fixation on the mother and also the mother's role as traditionally responsible for the children, although an increased awareness of the father often occurs in the practising subphase as part of the child's expanding sense of the world. This awareness may in part explain Peter's desire to go to Mr. McGregor's garden.

Max's father is totally outside the reader's awareness. His mother is perpetually offstage. Reflecting historical changes in generativity rates in the western world, Peter has several sisters; Max appears to be an only child, left to amuse himself as he can.

Both mothers, while present, do not seem particularly interested in where their children have been or what has transpired with them. They are attentive in the sense of providing for their children's basic welfare. Both mothers have been busy cooking during their boys' absence. Peter's mother is cooking when he gets home. She wonders about the lost clothes but is unconcerned about his exhaustion.

Max's mother is offstage, but we know that she has been preparing food because it is the smell of it that brings Max home. Apparently, she put the food in his room and left. Apparently she did not notice his absence. Apparently she did not try to engage with him, or he, in understandable toddler behavior, ignored her. Although on one level the reader thinks that he was there all the time, engrossed in fantasy or having a tantrum, the reader also knows that Max was very far away in time "through night and day and in and out of weeks and almost over a year"! How is Max's mother able to ignore this?

Both Peter and Max's mothers are attentive to some things, but are not perceived as fully attentive to what is going on with the child. There is no sharing of the achievements of each adventure here, which seems to stress the separateness and individuation of the child. The adventure belongs to the child although, given the nature of these adventures, the words of Dr. Seuss from *The Cat in the Hat* seem most pertinent, "Well . . . [*sic*] what would you do if your mother asked you?"[26]

CLOTHING AS SOCIALIZATION: AT DAY'S END

The use of clothing in the illustrations in these two books continues to reflect the status of each child in terms of his level of socialization. As Peter loses and is forced to give up articles of clothing, he becomes more and more rabbit-like. He achieves what his father could not and comes back to the family a wild natural thing. He no longer has any clothes; his mother will have to replace them (socialize him some more). On the other hand, he ends up swaddled in bed. The practice of swaddling was used both to restrain and to mold children:[27] "Short of killing the child, swaddling represented the most effective method of control . . . If swaddling offered as one of its chief aims physical restraint, along with this went the desire to restrain the child morally and emotionally."[28] As Kutzer describes it, "Peter is swaddled into immobility in that bed, bound in by coverlet and mother both, finally caught much more firmly than if he had uncomplainingly accepted his jacket in the first place."[29]

Max comes back "King of all Wild Things"; however, he is less wild now. The wolf suit is still on, but the hood is pushed back. He looks calmer. Neither boy is yet completely socialized. The promise of future freedoms is still there.

IN THE END: LIVE TO FIGHT ANOTHER DAY

The final subphase of the separation-individuation process occurs sometime in the third year of life or later. The developmental sequence is described in a linear fashion, but there is much movement back and forth before its aims are achieved, though in some sense they are never totally attained: "Like any intrapsychic process, this one reverberates throughout the life cycle."[30] Such reverberation is true of the socialization process as well, which often takes many lessons, and is not always fully successful anyway.

Clues to the iterative nature of the developmental process and the multiple applications that socialization may require are also provided to the reader of *Peter Rabbit* and *Where the Wild Things Are*. There are two clues in *Peter Rabbit*. One is that his father got caught exhibiting the behavior Peter is emulating. The other becomes apparent when Mrs. Rabbit notes, "It was the second little jacket and pair of shoes that Peter had lost on a fortnight!" The reader knows how Peter loses his clothes and sees that this adventure was probably not his first one.

In *Where the Wild Things Are,* the foreshadowing portrait of the wild thing on the wall provides the indication that Max has made this voyage before. He has already met the wild things. In fact, his expertise at taming wild things may be attributable in part to "practice." Children learn through repetition, which is also something that the reading experience provides. Children can and do go back to these books again, and yet again, for the beauty of the texts and illustrations, but also for the truth they find there that mirrors their own experience and concerns.

Sendak has said that *Where the Wild Things Are* is modeled to some extent after *Peter Rabbit*.[31] He notes Potter's honesty and her ability to share a story from which we can all get something. The same, of course, must be said of Sendak's work. It is this honest depiction of the struggle and risks we face in becoming self-determining, competent individuals that moves these books along the tide of generations.

NOTES

1. All citations of *Peter Rabbit* refer to Beatrix Potter, *The Tale of Peter Rabbit,* (1901, reissue London: Frederick Warne, 1987).
2. An extensive discussion of the marketing of *Peter Rabbit* can be found in Margaret Mackey, *The Case of Peter Rabbit: Changing Conditions of Literature for Children* (New York: Garland Publishing, 1998).
3. All citations of *Where the Wild Things Are* refer to Maurice Sendak, *Where the Wild Things Are,* 25th Anniversary ed. (New York: HarperCollins Publishers, 1991).
4. William A. Corsaro, *The Sociology of Childhood* (Thousand Oaks, Calif.: Pine Forge Press, 1997), 8.
5. Corsaro, *The Sociology of Childhood,* 8–27.
6. Some examples of authors who espouse this view are: Anne Scott MacLeod, "An End to Innocence: The Transformation of Childhood in Twentieth-Century Children's Literature," in *Opening Texts: Psychoanalysis and the Culture of the Child,* ed. Joseph H. Smith and William Kerrigan (Baltimore, Md.: Johns Hopkins University Press, 1985); Gail Schmunk Murray, *American Children's Literature and the Construction of Childhood* (New York: Twayne Publishers, 1998); and Virginia A. Walter, *War and Peace Literature for Children and Young Adults: A Resource Guide to Significant Issues* (Phoenix: Oryx, 1993).
7. Perry Nodelman. *The Pleasures of Children's Literature,* 2nd ed. (White Plains, N.Y.: Longman Publishers USA, 1996), 68–69.
8. For examples of this treatment see Humphrey Carpenter, "Excessively Impertinent Bunnies: The Subversive Element in Beatrix Potter," in *Children and Their Books: A Celebration of the Work of Iona and Peter Opie,* ed. Gillian Avery and Julia Briggs (Oxford: Clarendon Press, 1989); Charles Frey, "Victors and Victims in the Tales of *Peter Rabbit* and *Squirrel Nutkin,*" *Children's Literature in Education* 18 (1987): 105–11; and Jennifer Shaddock, "*Where the Wild Things Are:* Sendak's Journey into the Heart of Darkness," *Children's Literature Association Quarterly* 22 (1997–1998): 155–59.
9. Two authors who deal with the constraints of Victorian life for Potter and

women in general are M. Daphne Kutzer, "A Wildness Inside: Domestic Space in the Work of Beatrix Potter," *The Lion and the Unicorn* 21 (1997): 205; and W. Nikola-Lisa, "The Cult of Peter Rabbit: A Barthesian Analysis," *The Lion and the Unicorn* 15 (1991): 63, 65.

10. Shaddock, "*Where the Wild Things Are,*" 156.

11. Shaddock, "*Where the Wild Things Are,*" 156.

12. Object relations is still best explained in the classic text, Margaret S. Mahler, Fred Pine, and Anni Bergman, *The Psychological Birth of the Human Infant: Symbiosis and Individuation* (New York: Basic Books, 1975).

13. Ellen Handler Spitz, *Inside Picture Books* (New Haven, Conn.: Yale University Press, 1999), 128.

14. *Webster's New World Dictionary of American English,* 3rd college ed. (New York: Webster's New World, 1988).

15. Frey, "Victors and Victims," 106.

16. Carole Scott, "Clothed in Nature or Nature Clothed: Dress As Metaphor in the Illustrations of Beatrix Potter and C. M. Barker," *Children's Literature* 22 (1994): 81, 83.

17. Spitz, *Inside Picture Books,* 126.

18. Frey, "Victors and Victims," 106.

19. Potter, *The Tale of Peter Rabbit,* 30.

20. Scott, "Clothed in Nature," 84.

21. Carpenter, "Excessively Impertinent Bunnies," 287.

22. Frey, "Victors and Victims," 106.

23. Kutzer, "A Wildness Inside: Domestic Space in the Work of Beatrix Potter," 212.

24. Spitz, *Inside Picture Books,* 126.

25. Spitz, *Inside Picture Books,* 128.

26. Dr. Seuss, *The Cat in the Hat* (Boston: Houghton Mifflin, 1957).

27. Joseph Zornado, "Swaddling the Child in Children's Literature," *Children's Literature Association Quarterly* 22, no. 3 (Fall 1997): 106.

28. Zornado, "Swaddling the Child," 106.

29. Kutzer, "A Wildness Inside: Domestic Space in the Work of Beatrix Potter," 212.

30. Mahler, Pine, and Bergman, *The Psychological Birth of the Human Infant,* 3.

31. "Sendak's Western Canon, Jr.," *HomeArts.* http://homearts.com/depts/relat/sendakb7.htm (25 March 2000).

BIBLIOGRAPHY

Carpenter, Humphrey. "Excessively Impertinent Bunnies: The Subversive Element in Beatrix Potter." Pp. 271–98 in *Children and Their Books: A*

Celebration of the Work of Iona and Peter Opie, edited by Gillian Avery and Julia Briggs. Oxford: Clarendon Press, 1989.

Corsaro, William A. *The Sociology of Childhood.* Thousand Oaks, Calif.: Pine Forge Press, 1997.

Frey, Charles. "Victors and Victims in the Tales of *Peter Rabbit* and *Squirrel Nutkin.*" *Children's Literature in Education* 18 (1987): 105–11.

Kutzer, M. Daphne. "A Wildness Inside: Domestic Space in the Work of Beatrix Potter," *The Lion and the Unicorn* 21 (1997): 204–14.

Mackey, Margaret. *The Case of Peter Rabbit: Changing Conditions of Literature for Children.* New York: Garland Publishing, 1998.

MacLeod, Anne Scott. "An End to Innocence: The Transformation of Childhood in Twentieth-Century Children's Literature." Pp. 100–17 in *Opening Texts: Psychoanalysis and the Culture of the Child,* edited by Joseph H. Smith and William Kerrigan. Baltimore, Md.: Johns Hopkins University Press, 1985.

Mahler, Margaret S., Fred Pine, and Anni Bergman. *The Psychological Birth of the Human Infant: Symbiosis and Individuation.* New York: Basic Books, 1975.

Murray, Gail Schmunk. *American Children's Literature and the Construction of Childhood.* New York: Twayne Publishers, 1998.

Nikola-Lisa, W. "The Cult of Peter Rabbit: A Barthesian Analysis." *The Lion and the Unicorn* 15 (1991): 63-65.

Nodelman, Perry. *The Pleasures of Children's Literature,* 2nd ed. White Plains, N.Y.: Longman, 1996.

Potter, Beatrix. *The Tale of Peter Rabbit.* 1901. London: Frederick Warne, 1987.

Scott, Carole. "Clothed in Nature or Nature Clothed: Dress As Metaphor in the Illustrations of Beatrix Potter and C. M. Barker." *Children's Literature* 22 (1994): 70–89.

Sendak, Maurice. *Where the Wild Things Are,* 25th anniversary ed. New York: HarperCollins Publishers, 1963, 1991.

"Sendak's Western Canon, Jr." *HomeArts.* http://homearts.com/depts/relat/sendakb7.htm (25 March 2000).

Seuss, Dr. [Theodor S. Geisel]. *The Cat in the Hat.* Boston: Houghton Mifflin, 1957.

Shaddock, Jennifer. "*Where the Wild Things Are:* Sendak's Journey into the Heart of Darkness." *Children's Literature Association Quarterly* 22 (1997–1998): 155–59.

Spitz, Ellen Handler. *Inside Picture Books.* New Haven, Conn.: Yale University Press, 1999.

Walter, Virginia A. *War and Peace Literature for Children and Young Adults: A Resource Guide to Significant Issues.* Phoenix: Oryx, 1993.

Zornado, Joseph. "Swaddling the Child in Children's Literature." *Children's Literature Association Quarterly* 22, no. 3 (Fall 1997): 105–12.

4

POST-TEXT

In this section, three authors explore different ways in which the story of Peter Rabbit has been readdressed and adapted. Peter Hollindale, in a persuasive account of Potter's naturalist accuracy, looks at the little books that act as sequels to *The Tale of Peter Rabbit*: *The Tale of Benjamin Bunny*, *The Tale of Mr. Tod*, and *The Tale of the Flopsy Bunnies*. Margaret Mackey looks at the commodification and marketing of the Beatrix Potter characters, and discusses questions of cultural and commercial values. Finally, Shin-ichi Yoshida gives an account of how Potter's works traveled abroad and were translated into Japanese, and follows this with the story of his own deepening acquaintance with Potter's world as he himself traveled back to England to explore the terrain that the whole world recognizes as the home of Potter's little stories.

11

Humans Are So Rabbit

Peter Hollindale

"Master Rabbit I saw." Walter de la Mare's line is the epigraph for the most substantial rabbit story ever written, Richard Adams's *Watership Down*.[1] But which "Master Rabbit" does one see, whether in Adams, or Uncle Remus, or Alison Uttley, or Beatrix Potter? Is it at root the wild creature, even if temporarily adorned with human dress, habits, and speech? Or is it essentially the human being, derived from folktale and fable, perhaps naturalized in biological separateness to accord with modern natural history, but still pre-eminently *homo sapiens,* transferred elsewhere in the animal kingdom to give us a new angle on ourselves? Both claims are regularly made about Beatrix Potter, reinforced by our knowledge that her background qualifies her for any permutation on the roles available. She was at once a natural scientist, a fine field naturalist, a reader of fable and folktale schooled in Aesop and Uncle Remus, and (as her *Journal* amply testifies) a merciless satirical observer of the human scene. She was also a keeper of pets, and demonstrably interested more than any others in animal species that lie on the border between wild and tame, independent and domestic—cats, rats, mice, hedgehogs, and especially rabbits.

We should heed the injunction of John Goldthwaite to remember that Potter was not always doing the same thing: "You see her twenty-three little titles standing shoulder to shoulder on the bookstall shelf in their regimental jackets and they look to be not the twenty-three separate and often fitful starts that they were but twenty-three chapters mustered from one serene act of imagining."[2] And again, "The uniform set of Potter's books soothes us with the illusion that they are all of a kind. They are not. No more was Potter all of a kind."[3] The abundant evidence that Goldthwaite is right lies not only in the manifest diversity of the little books but even in apparently contradictory attitudes expressed side by side in the same letter, as in this to Freda Wright on October 6th, 1902, just before the first colored edition of *Peter Rabbit* was published: "My brother has been shooting pheasants & rabbits; the gardener puts a ferret into the hole & then the rabbit rushes out; he got 11 today. I have a little rabbit which I tamed; it jumps over my hands for a bit of biscuit, but it is so frightened of everyone else I cannot show off its tricks to people."[4]

Further evidence that diversity in the books was produced by diversity in the life is provided by Potter's *Journal* entry for October 30th 1892, which is full of conflicting attitudes and mixed signals. On holiday in Scotland, Potter found herself "in time to rescue a poor little rabbit, fast in a snare":

> I had great difficulty in slackening the noose round its neck. I warmed it at the fire, relieved it from a number of fleas, and it came round. It was such a little poor creature compared to mine. They are regular vermin, but one cannot stand by to see a thing mauled about from ones [*sic*] friendship for the race. Papa in his indignation pulled up the snare. I fancy our actions were much more illegal than Miss Hutton's.[5]

In such brief extracts as these one can see, side by side in the same statement, Potter the unsentimental countrywoman and future farmer, and Potter the amused and compassionate animal-lover. Behind such activities and attitudes lie Potter the detached, observant, scientific naturalist and Potter the anthropomorphic comedian. Those who see Potter's books as covertly (or openly) subversive, allied with Peter's or Benjamin's disobedient roguery, will find confirmation in her rescue of the rabbit and support for Papa's destruction of the snare; those who see her as conservative will notice the word "vermin" and the momentary qualm about illegality. The rescue and its *Journal* record are analogous to the ambivalence that Suzanne Rahn discovers in *The Tale of Two Bad Mice:*

> we might assume Beatrix Potter to be in sympathy with the revolutionary uprising she has depicted; certainly she is in sympathy with the mice rather than the passive and uninteresting dolls. The ending, however, reveals a political stance unmistakably Conservative.[6]

I know of one British university where the Faculty of Law, in a course on "Law and Literature" has used *The Tale of Peter Rabbit* as a set text to illustrate the socialising role of children's literature, representing Peter's crimes of trespass and theft, and his punishment by fear, illness, and camomile tea, as indoctrination to promote law-abiding values. The books enable such an interpretation to coexist with the opposite view of Humphrey Carpenter (and many others) that "the narrator of *Peter Rabbit* and its successors is striking a blow for independence and a freer moral attitude towards children."[7]

My own view is that the spectrum from exact behavioral realism to anthropomorphic comedy in the "Peter Rabbit" stories is closely interwoven with the war in Potter between subversion and conformity, and that the noticeable differences between these books (masked as Goldthwaite says by their deceptive uniformity) are concentrated in Potter's successive re-readings of Peter, in the course of which he gradually ceased to be a rabbit. Although Goldthwaite's remarks, quoted above, refer to the whole range of Potter's work, I hope to show that they apply with equal force to the much smaller group of rabbit stories in particular, which may seem at first sight to represent a more self-contained and homogeneous unit.

Before turning to the stories themselves, it is helpful to set Potter in the context of general human attitudes towards rabbits, especially when the overall approach is scientific. In a short popular monograph on the species, Michael Leach finds more general evidence of the ambivalence I have pointed to in Potter:

> Man has an ambivalent attitude towards the rabbit. It is condemned as an agricultural and horticultural pest, being hunted for its fur and commercially farmed for its meat. On the other hand it is the hero of many children's stories such as those of Brer Rabbit, Peter Rabbit and *Watership Down*. Rabbits are also adored, and abused, in garden hutches everywhere, often being the first introduction that many people have to keeping and looking after animals. The life of the wild rabbit extends much beyond either of these images.[8]

One of the largest studies of wild rabbits ever undertaken is that documented by R. M. Lockley in his book *The Private Life of the Rabbit*.[9] This was a scientific study of several discrete and controlled rabbit communities on Lockley's estate at Orielton in Wales. The nature of the species seems such that even a scientist like Lockley sometimes finds ambivalent responses irresistible. They can be seen in this part-anthropomorphic, part-scientific account of a buck rabbit's behavior after the threat of attack by a buzzard has been removed:

> The buck rabbit relaxed as if a load had been lifted from his mind. He suddenly frisked, gave a little jump into the air, twisting sideways so as to come down facing half backwards. He then ran easily in a wide circle round the warren, pausing to press his chin at intervals to the ground in a forward-thrusting, almost affectionate, action. He was feeling good and playful . . .
>
> The old buck seemed happy. He gave another little jump into the air. . . . Then he pressed his chin against a plant stem.
>
> The secretion of a colourless fluid from the glands beneath the jaw, which are much larger in the male, occurs when a rabbit "chins" the ground or some plant or other object in its territory. This laying of a scent has a territorial function.[10]

In Lockley's account of the evolving observation of individual rabbits, it is clear that a Potter-like spectrum from impersonal mass observation to unique identities was present in the work, and also—as is clear in this passage—that Lockley himself was quite conscious of the link:

> In our study of individual rabbits at Orielton it was some months before certain leading rabbits became familiar to us by their frequently observed behaviour and characteristic habits. But as soon as they exhibited these idiosyncrasies regularly we began to apply names—at first without a plan, and most of them uncomplimentary. Thus Buck Seven became known as "Rough Stuff", Buck Three was nicknamed "Weary Willie", Buck Twenty became "Timid Timothy" . . . while the powerful Doe Four was dubbed "Mrs. Potter" (afterwards changed to "Beatrix").[11]

In the course of his observations Lockley became conscious of parallels and resemblances between the behavior of rabbits and of human beings. Although he enjoyed moments of tongue-in-cheek humanizing, the connections he made were not sentimental, whimsical, or fanciful. They were based on his scientific awareness of the shared mammalian condition and biological processes that underlie the observable behavior of humans and rabbits alike:

> The same organs and nerves in man, rabbit and bird achieve . . . self-preservation by their co-ordinated response to changes in the external scene, by interpreting and acting correctly on these external stimuli. The organs of hearing, touch, smell and taste are each connected with the seat of intelligence in the same ways as are the eyes, the organs of sight, by

> nerves communicating between the external sensory cells and the internal brain. External movement or stimulus causes a reaction which is automatic, and of which we and the animal are consciously aware in a greater or lesser degree.[12]

An instance of this similar behavioral pattern in practice can be drawn from the observations of the vet and animal behaviorist Caroline Bower, in an article first written for the award-winning exhibit "Mr. McGregor's Garden" at the Chelsea Flower Show in 1999, and later reprinted in the Newsletter of the Beatrix Potter Society. Bower compliments Potter on her precision as an observer and the accuracy of her illustrations in depicting rabbit behavior:

> For example, look at Peter Rabbit with "eyes as big as lolly-pops" when startled in *The Tale of Benjamin Bunny,* and his terrified expression when fleeing from the distant figure of Mr. McGregor and his rake in *The Tale of Peter Rabbit*! Contrast this expression with the half-closed contented eyes and relaxed ears while he guzzles lettuces, French beans and radishes in the garden.[13]

This is certainly an accurate depiction of rabbit behavior, but also closely akin to the typical eye-and-brain reactions of human beings in response to equivalent contrasting stimuli! It is hardly surprising that the closing statement of Lockley's meticulous study is "Rabbits are so human. Or is it the other way round—humans are so rabbit?"[14]

It is evident from these observations that Beatrix Potter's work is interesting, and convincing—a relevant memory, so to speak—for scientists who are interested in the behavior of wild rabbits and find themselves reaching almost automatically for the language of human behavior to express what they see. Lockley first wrote up his experiments in the 1960s, before Leslie Linder had transcribed and published Potter's *Journal,* and long before her work as a naturalist had undergone the detailed study of recent years—at a time, in fact, when her image and reputation rested solely on the little books themselves—yet when he came to ask how close the sensory perceptions of rabbits are to those of humans, he found her in need of only slight indulgence on the grounds of humanizing excess: "And how near are [the rabbit's] perceptions to those of the human observer? Not as near as Beatrix Potter's caricatures of rabbits would suggest, but perhaps nearer than the sceptics suppose."[15]

These "caricatures" of rabbits, on the scale from species realism to humanized status, differ from one of Potter's little books to another and sometimes within the same book, and they are closely bound to the evolving character of Peter. Leaving aside his walk-on appearances (to patronize the shop in *The Tale of Ginger and Pickles,* and to collect his washing in *The Tale of Mrs. Tiggy-Winkle*) there are four "Peter Rabbit" books, falling into two neat pairs—first *Peter Rabbit* and *Benjamin Bunny,* where Peter is a child, and then *The Tale of the Flopsy Bunnies* and *The Tale of Mr. Tod,* where he is adult. This is the order of publication also, but the date of composition of *Mr. Tod* is problematic; when Potter submitted it to Warne's in 1911, she said "I wrote it some time ago,"[16] and John Goldthwaite is in no doubt that *The Flopsy Bunnies* intervened at some point during its slow progress from writing to publication. He demonstrates conclusively that both stories, with their close similarities of plot, are indebted to the *Uncle Remus* story "The Bag in the Corner," and declares: "Potter had digressed into this lighter-hearted version of 'The Bag in the Corner' [i.e., *The Flopsy Bunnies*] at some point during her long hesitation over whether or not to publish *Mr. Tod.*"[17] It seems sensible to treat these two stories as contemporary, but with the likelihood that *The Flopsy Bunnies,* rather than *Mr. Tod,* represents her last word on Peter himself.

I will take the two "child" stories first, ignoring the well-known "letter-story" origins of *Peter Rabbit* and starting with the published book. Much of the commentary that has gathered around *Peter Rabbit* rests on the question whether the story is moralising and tutelary or subversive. Does Potter condone Peter's naughtiness, or does she show him getting a deserved comeuppance for his crimes of trespass and theft? The question is best answered by taking *Peter Rabbit* and *Benjamin Bunny* together, and treating them respectively as the Songs of Innocence and Experience of Peter's childhood.

Peter's family life with his mother and his good little sisters is one of Potter's acts of inventive unrealism. As Caroline Bower points out: "There are many references to parental care, with Mrs. Rabbit fussing over her young. One of the characteristics of rabbit biology is that they have as little to do with their offspring as possible, usually feeding them once a day and leaving them to get on with it the rest of the time."[18] The domestic scene is humanized fabrication, and what we are shown in *Peter Rabbit* is an indulgent and caring one-parent household. Peter is not in this story punished for disobedience; he suffers for it by being dosed with camomile tea while his sisters guzzle milk and blackberries, but this diet is curative, not punitive. A universal hazard of childhood is to be deprived by illness of the gastronomic treats that your siblings are enjoying, and the fact that Peter has brought his illness on himself is not a finger-wagging admonition by Potter to her readers. At home Peter is a typical human child.

In Mr. McGregor's garden, however, he is a rabbit. Like all young animals (including boys), he explores, forages, trespasses, nicks things, and loses things, but he does all this in a "rabbit" way, squeezing under gates, dining illicitly, reconnoitering alertly, dodging, weaving and fleeing for cover, as rabbits do. He is also terrified by physical entrapment (the gooseberry net, the sieve), as all wild creatures are, and takes perilous refuge in the watering-can, thus inaugurating a series of dangerous hiding-places and confinements that run through all the books (the onion basket in *Benjamin Bunny,* the new burrow in *Mr. Tod,* the sacks in *The Flopsy Bunnies* and *Mr. Tod,* the oven at Bull Banks). Peter makes a risky expedition such as parents fear but children need. Without such adventures, there is no independence for a young animal, and parents (certainly the human, but not humans only) act to forbid, prevent, and sometimes punish what they must nervously desire. All this Potter knew, and had good cause to know. Wordsworth in *The Prelude* said that he grew up "fostered alike by beauty and by fear." In *Peter Rabbit* Peter is punished not by camomile tea but by fear, yet he is also fostered by it. Thus, balancing humanized domesticity against wild rabbit foraging, Potter subverted parental authority and its built-in hypocrisy while also, in a minor key, endorsing prudence and property rights.

Benjamin Bunny is Peter's Song of Experience, and painfully furthers his education. Goldthwaite downgrades this story because of the connotations he perceives in "bunny": "Putting pants on a bunny is not the same as putting them on a rabbit. A trousered rabbit is free to have his story told; the bunny, merely by being called a bunny, is now promised in advance to the audience as an emotional treat."[19] This is anachronistic, and blurs the point of the story. Margery Fisher puts the matter correctly: "So long as a rabbit behaves like a rabbit, I see no reason why she should not have human attributes as well as a human name, but the very word 'bunny' has picked up a sentimental connotation since the days of Benjamin Bunny and his uncompromising papa."[20]

If we unpick the subsequent "bunny" connotations, we see that Benjamin (once removed from the humanized domestic circle) is now occupying Peter's role but is less "rabbit" than Peter was. Peter concentrated on food, not tam o' shanters. Benjamin is not a cute bunny, but he is nearer the human end of Potter's spectrum than Peter was. He is a mischievous boy, leading his chastened cousin into further trouble. Moreover, he gets Peter (still dazed and shell-shocked from his earlier trauma) to do all the heavy work. Benjamin loots the onions, but gets Peter to carry them. Peter, now nervous of theft and afraid of the garden, first drops half the onions and then the rest, but in one of Potter's subtle masterstrokes of pictorial narrative, we turn over the page and find that he is carrying them yet again.[21] Benjamin, meanwhile, brings up the rear with the air of one in control of the game; the difference in the two rabbits' facial expressions on this page is beautifully done.

It does not matter that Benjamin is relatively un-rabbit like. This is not because he is "bunny," but because he is a foil to Peter. The subject of *Benjamin Bunny* is Peter's fear, which he learned in the first story, and pictorially it is best caught on page 27, as Benjamin takes ingenuous interest in their footmarks while Peter looks around in the (realistically caught) alert paralysis of terror. At the anthropomorphic level, he is learning through fear to behave himself and respect other people's property. As a wild rabbit, he is learning the need for constant monitoring of dangerous terrain. In this story he is the wilder of the two, and the second role is dominant, but as Potter re-read him for the later stories, the positions were reversed, leaving Peter—in fictional terms—as a socialized ex-rabbit.

If Potter did see *The Tale of Peter Rabbit,* at some secondary level, as a moralistic story of Peter's crime and punishment, she certainly discarded such legalism when she re-read Peter for *The Tale of Benjamin Bunny*. In this story Peter is comprehensively punished as he never was in *Peter Rabbit,* and quite undeservedly. Throughout this second visit to the garden, he is in a trance of fear; again a refuge becomes an uncomfortable temporary prison; and after all his tribulations he suffers not mere camomile tea but Uncle Benjamin's switch. This second expedition is at Benjamin's instigation. Peter is merely a reluctant and bemused accessory. Benjamin does not just forage on the spot, as Peter did; he loots the onions. For this behavior he has the authority of parental example: "He said that he was in the habit of coming to the garden with his father to get lettuces for their Sunday dinner."[22]

The little rabbits certainly owe their rescue to Benjamin's father. In his brave and ferocious attack on the cat he is authentically a wild rabbit, which can be a formidable fighter: "When an adult is attacked it can fight back with a series of powerful kicks from its hind legs. It can also inflict deep bites with its long incisors."[23] Once the children are retrieved, however, he becomes the unmistakably hypocritical, punitive parent (and uncle). He whips Peter (the vivid picture on page 52 gaining force from the text's significant reticence) for something that is not Peter's fault. He whips Benjamin for emulating his own example. He takes possession of the stolen onions, having opportunistically seized some lettuce to go with them. Home with his sisters once more, Peter is received indulgently: "his mother forgave him," though her tolerance is noticeably sweetened by Peter's recovered clothing and a bonus of onions. Despite his mother's kindness, where Peter is concerned both adventure and domestic reception are far worse than those in *Peter Rabbit,* and both are incurred because he is led on by Benjamin. This time he is an undeserving victim. A conventional moral tale is not to be found.

A conventional moral Peter, on the other hand, is well forward in the making. Peter and Benjamin, indeed Peter and Benjamin's family, are on divergent paths. Peter may be the "wilder" rabbit in physical reactions, but Benjamin *père et fils* are the wilder rabbits in social behavior, as opportunistic thieves. The clues are here for a socialized Peter, taught by bitter experience. This is the adult Peter whom we find in *The Tale of Mr. Tod.*

Although the rabbit family of Benjamin and Flopsy is humanized as before, their prolific breeding is all rabbit. Potter was never again to occupy "rabbit consciousness" so convincingly and sustainedly as she had in *Peter Rabbit,* but throughout the quartet it makes sporadic appearances in a more anthropomorphic context. Most of the realistic rabbitness of *Mr. Tod* is Benjamin's, notably his beautifully observed reaction to Mr. Tod's stick house: "Benjamin Bunny sat up, staring; his whiskers twitched. Inside the stick house somebody dropped a plate, and said something. Benjamin stamped his foot, and bolted." This is a rabbit's instinctive reaction to danger. Later, when Peter has joined Benjamin on their search-and-rescue expedition in pursuit of Benjamin's kidnapped offspring, the two show another instinctive reaction, which Potter humanizes as "foolish." Peter and Benjamin hear the yelp of the approaching Mr. Tod: "Then those two rabbits lost their heads completely. They did the most foolish thing that they could have done. They rushed into their short new tunnel, and hid themselves at the top end of it, under Mr. Tod's kitchen-floor." Foolish it may have been, rationally considered, but it is automatic rabbit behavior, and not far removed from instinctive human behavior in equivalent situations!

Such occasional moments apart, however, Peter is now a strongly humanized figure. He is solitary and independent, where rabbits are gregarious, and his altered status is registered by his speech—by its style, which is formal, rotund and pompous, and by its content, which consists almost totally of disapproval. "Let me use my mind," he says; and does, almost wholly avoiding the impulsiveness of rabbit-panic. The crisis is all due to the negligence of Benjamin's father, he who so painfully and unjustly chastised Peter in the earlier story. What pleasure Potter must have taken in giving Peter the excuse for verbal revenge: "My Uncle Bouncer has displayed a lamentable want of discretion for his years." (The original Benjamin Bunny, Potter's pet rabbit, was commonly called Bounce, and the names are interchangeable.) Peter reproves the afflicted parent's desperation: "Cousin Benjamin, compose yourself." Furtively observing Tommy Brock's coarse proletarian behavior, he is shocked. " 'He has gone to bed in his boots,' whispered Peter." While Benjamin is "all of a twitter" about the fight between fox and badger, Peter finds time for moral censoriousness: "What dreadful bad language!"[24] The Peter of *The Tale of Mr. Tod* is a highly respectable citizen.

In what I regard as Peter's finale, in *The Tale of the Flopsy Bunnies,* his transformation is complete. Benjamin and his family, "improvident and cheerful," are a rabbit-like company, scrounging provisions where they can. "Benjamin used to borrow cabbages from Flopsy's brother, Peter Rabbit, who kept a nursery garden;"[25] here, "borrow" has much the same sense in which lettuces and onions were "borrowed" from Mr. McGregor. The rabbit-like image of Benjamin's family is one of haphazard fecundity, provided for by any means to hand.

Peter, on the other hand, is now a person of means, and must husband his resources against the amiable depredations of his relatives. "Sometimes," says the lovely brief text on page 14, "Peter Rabbit had no cabbages to spare," and the facing illustration is full of significance. While the unnamed Mrs. Peter Rabbit holds out her skirts to conceal the flourishing cabbage patch at the rear, Peter indicates a discouraging foreground view of bare earth and cabbage stalks. He is holding a spade, and his partner, still more expressively, is holding a rake. The rake, utilitarian and menacing, calls up images of Mr. McGregor, in angry pursuit of the youthful Peter. Now the wheel is come full circle. Peter has his own spade and rake, his own fence, his own vegetable produce, and the improvident Bunnies peep into his demesne just as he once did at Mr. McGregor's. He is a person of consequence, and his name a guarantor of respectability. When Mrs. Tittlemouse disturbs the Bunny family's siesta, she "apologized profusely, and said that she knew Peter Rabbit."[26] If Benjamin and Flopsy's subsequent confounding of Mr. McGregor subverts the established order with gleeful disruption, Peter himself stands apart as a conservative figure, on his own inviolate patch.

Beatrix Potter knew rabbits and humankind. Like the natural scientists who followed her, she knew that both are territorial. She observed the spectrum of behavior that both linked and distinguished them, and through Peter's adventures she picked up her own cues for his progress from youthful raider to rabbit of property. As we see Benjamin's family looking into Peter's territory, we may be reminded of another famous group of animals. In George Orwell's *Animal Farm,*[27] the beasts expel their human oppressor, only to find his place usurped from their own number, by their comrades the pigs. At the end they see the pigs consorting with the neighboring human farmers, and find so little difference that they wonder which is which. Long before *Animal Farm,* Potter had anticipated the joke. Her ultimate stroke of comic anthropomorphism was to reconstitute Peter Rabbit as Mr. McGregor.

NOTES

1. Richard Adams, *Watership Down* (Harmondsworth: Penguin, 1973), 5.
2. John Goldthwaite, *The Natural History of Make-Believe* (New York and Oxford: Oxford University Press, 1996), 288.
3. Goldthwaite, review of *Beatrix Potter as Writer and Illustrator,* in *Children's Books History Society Newsletter* 66, April 2000, 37.
4. Judy Taylor, ed., *Beatrix Potter's Letters* (London: Frederick Warne, 1989), 68.
5. Beatrix Potter, transcribed by Leslie Linder. *The Journal of Beatrix Potter, from 1881 to 1897* (London: Frederick Warne, 1966), 300.
6. Suzanne Rahn, "Tailpiece: *The Tale of Two Bad Mice.*" *Children's Literature* 12, (1984): 81.
7. Humphrey Carpenter, "Excessively Impertinent Bunnies: The Subversive Element in Beatrix Potter," in *Children and Their Books,* ed. Gillian Avery and Julia Briggs (Oxford: Clarendon Press, 1989), 289.
8. Michael Leach, *The Rabbit* (Princes Risborough: Shire Publications, 1989), 2.
9. R. M. Lockley, *The Private Life of the Rabbit* (London: Deutsch, 1964; reissued Woodbridge: The Boydell Press, 1985).
10. Lockley, *The Private Life of the Rabbit,* 23–24.
11. Lockley, *The Private Life of the Rabbit,* 37.
12. Lockley, *The Private Life of the Rabbit,* 22.
13. Caroline Bower, "Closely Observed Rabbits," *The Beatrix Potter Society Newsletter* 74 (October 1999): 9.
14. Lockley, *The Private Life of the Rabbit,* 144.
15. Lockley, *The Private Life of the Rabbit,* 20.
16. Taylor (ed.), *Beatrix Potter's Letters,* 189.
17. Goldthwaite, *The Natural History of Make-Believe,* 308.
18. Bower, "Closely Observed Rabbits," 10.
19. Goldthwaite, *The Natural History of Make-Believe,* 295.

20. Margery Fisher, *Intent upon Reading: A Critical Appraisal of Modern Fiction for Children* (Leicester: Brockhampton Press, 1961), 51.

21. Beatrix Potter, *The Tale of Benjamin Bunny* (London and New York: Frederick Warne, 1904), 35, 39, 40.

22. Potter, *The Tale of Benjamin Bunny,* 33.

23. Leach, *The Rabbit,* 9.

24. Beatrix Potter, *The Tale of Mr. Tod* (London and New York: Frederick Warne, 1912), 23, 44, 27, 28, 36, 78.

25. Beatrix Potter, *The Tale of the Flopsy Bunnies* (London and New York: Frederick Warne, 1909), 13.

26. Potter, *The Tale of the Flopsy Bunnies,* 25.

27. George Orwell, *Animal Farm* (London: Secker and Warburg, 1945).

BIBLIOGRAPHY

Adams, Richard. *Watership Down*. Harmondsworth: Penguin, 1973.

Bower, Caroline. "Closely Observed Rabbits," in *The Beatrix Potter Society Newsletter* 74 (October 1999): 9.

Carpenter, Humphrey. "Excessively Impertinent Bunnies: The Subversive Element in Beatrix Potter." Pp. 271–98 in *Children and Their Books,* edited by Gillian Avery and Julia Briggs. Oxford: Clarendon Press, 1989.

Fisher, Margery. *Intent upon Reading: A Critical Appraisal of Modern Fiction for Children.* Leicester: Brockhampton Press, 1961.

Goldthwaite, John. *The Natural History of Make-Believe*. New York and Oxford: Oxford University Press, 1996.

———. Review of Enid Bassom et al., eds., *Beatrix Potter as Writer and Illustrator*, in *Children's Books History Society Newsletter* 66, April 2000.

Leach, Michael. *The Rabbit.* Princes Risborough: Shire Publications, 1989.

Lockley, R. M. *The Private Life of the Rabbit*. Woodbridge: The Boydell Press, 1985.

Orwell, George. *Animal Farm.* London: Secker and Warburg, 1945.

Potter, Beatrix, transcribed by Leslie Linder. *The Journal of Beatrix Potter, from 1881 to 1897* London: Frederick Warne, 1966.

Potter, Beatrix. *The Tale of Benjamin Bunny.* London and New York: Frederick Warne, 1904.

———. *The Tale of Mr. Tod.* London and New York: Frederick Warne, 1912.

———. *The Tale of the Flopsy Bunnies.* London and New York: Frederick Warne, 1909.

Rahn, Suzanne. "Tailpiece: *The Tale of Two Bad Mice*." *Children's Literature* 12 (1984): 78–91.

Taylor, Judy, ed. *Beatrix Potter's Letters*. London: Frederick Warne, 1989.

12

The Mediation and Multiplication of *Peter Rabbit*

Margaret Mackey

When he was about five years old, my nephew Peter made a tape recording of *The Tale of Peter Rabbit* to send to his cousins, my daughters. Not long ago, they rediscovered this audiocassette in a bedroom, and, fifteen years after it was originally recorded, we listened once again to his childish voice warming to the excitement of the story. It has never been clear to us, then or now, whether Peter was reading or reciting, or some combination of both. What is abundantly clear is that this little boy relished every aspect of the book: liked the fact that the hero was called Peter, enjoyed the suspense and the drama, savored the opportunity to roll the language around his mouth. The tape recording gave him a vehicle to forward the pleasure of this experience to his cousins, and it enables us to continue to listen to him today.

In the same week that we found the tape, I made a very different acquisition: a Peter Rabbit Barbie doll (fig. 12.1). This Barbie is a "storyteller doll," which means that she has extra-long blonde curls and is dressed in a Bo-Peep kind of dress, the pale pink skirt of which is decorated with half a dozen panels of illustrations from *The Tale of Peter Rabbit*. Her presentation box, decorated with Potteresque woodland scenes, also contains a small paperback of the book, and the whole kit is produced through cooperation between Frederick Warne and Mattel. The box is sprinkled with commercial symbols: R for registered (8 appearances on the box), TM for trademark (23 appearances), and C for

Figure 12.1. Peter Rabbit™ Barbie® doll.

copyright (3 appearances), allocating ownership of the two powerful brands of Barbie and Peter between Mattel and Warne.

With help from a doll collector, I discovered the Peter Rabbit Barbie on the Internet.[1] The doll is one of the more extreme examples in my collection of well over a hundred Peter Rabbit adaptations and variant texts.[2] Some of my versions are pirated American reworkings of the stories; others are authorized by Frederick Warne and its numerous license-holders.

These two renditions of the story, the tape and the doll, which by coincidence appeared in my life at the same time, provide a useful starting-point for exploring the mediation and multiplication of Peter Rabbit at the end of his first century of life. They represent extremes of contrasting interactions with a much-loved story and offer an opening for a discussion of some contemporary realities of children's literature.

ENGAGING WITH AN AESTHETIC EXPERIENCE

It is very clear that *The Tale of Peter Rabbit* has engaged the hearts and minds of young readers since its original publication. The tape recording of my nephew's reading of the story, simple as it is, represents one way in which contemporary children may mark their ownership of a text, in the psychological as well as material sense of the term. This kind of recording provides the child and his family with an artifact that both celebrates and preserves the dynamics of his engagement with a loved story. Often, as in the case of Peter and his cousins, it allows a child the opportunity to make a gift of this engagement to someone else, someone outside the immediate domestic circle.

Furthermore, this simple tape recording demonstrates an important feature of contemporary children's encounters with stories: their engagement is often filtered through media other than print. In my nephew's case, the book came first and the recording later, but the order is often reversed, and in many cases children meet a variant version long before they meet the original. It is easy for purists to fear that this approach necessarily represents an inferior aesthetic experience for the child, but it is not necessarily so. Recently I had the pleasure of observing Olivia, fifteen months old, as she watched the Royal Ballet video *Tales of Beatrix Potter*[3] for the first time. Olivia was clearly both thunderstruck and enchanted: she pointed and exclaimed, laughed, and danced in her seat, remaining riveted to the screen for the best part of half an hour. Nobody could ask for a more joyful introduction to the world of the little books.

The Tale of Peter Rabbit, in its original incarnation, has enormous virtues as an early book for very small children. It may introduce them, long before they can read for themselves, to the pleasures of subtle comedy, elegant language, delicate perception, and eloquent ellipsis. The impetus to retell is often a positive one (and indeed what we consider the original story is itself a retelling of Noel Moore's letter), yet, when the first version is so supremely crafted, almost any kind of reworking is a diminishment.

Some "adaptations" can even be described as destructive of the qualities of the original. *The New Adventures of Peter Rabbit,*[4] for example, which exists in animated video, audio, and book forms, turns Peter Rabbit into a debased reincarnation of Bugs Bunny. In *The Parables of Peter Rabbit,*[5] two videos featuring a giant puppet of Peter, four children, and a window-box full of singing vegetables, proselytize for fundamentalist Christianity. Whatever their virtues as independent texts, their relationship to *The Tale of Peter Rabbit* is a negative one.

Nevertheless, it is too easy to produce a list of horrors and to dismiss all variant *Peter Rabbit*s as simply inferior and distracting. Given that children, whether we like it or not, are coming to *The Tale of Peter Rabbit* via many versions, this approach is neither useful nor interesting. Yet there is a genuine question of the value of literature to children; if we appreciate the qualities of the original *Peter Rabbit,* then it seems reasonable to wish to ensure children meet that version in preference to others.

Even though it is now a century old, *The Tale of Peter Rabbit* provides a good focus for discussing issues that profoundly affect contemporary children and their routes to literature. It is easy to feel beleaguered by the quantity and scale of commodification of children's texts today, but the actual issue is not a new one. There are positive and negative aspects to this fact of contemporary life, and there is also a larger question concerning the permeation of marketing values throughout our own and our children's lives.

QUESTIONS OF JUDGEMENT

In the vast world of *Peter Rabbit* versions and commodities, complex and fascinating questions arise when we explore the gap between the particularity and delight of individual responses to a story and the overwhelming and arguably cynical nature of the production of adaptations and commodities. Many issues entwine, including questions of personal taste, issues of literary value and fidelity to a classic original, acquisition of perceived cultural capital, development of market susceptibilities, and institutional frameworks. Questions of value are inseparable from these issues, and different value systems now inflect the literary system we have come to take for granted.

David Rudd's useful and neutral category of the "post-text"[6] describes such a collection of reworkings, commodities, and adaptations. The post-text collective of Peter Rabbit materials is particularly large and aimed at more than just the children's market, but the fact of its existence is not new—nor is such a collection unique to the world of Beatrix Potter.

One approach to this enormous post-text assembly of different materials is simply to ignore it and focus on the purity of the classic original. Another way of thinking about the issue is to accept and even welcome the plurality of the contemporary hall of mirrors in which successful images are marketed and re-marketed. Neither of these approaches is completely helpful to the adults who engage with small children, namely parents, librarians, and teachers. Such adults normally cannot afford to acquire everything; in any case they may not want simply to open a bottomless cornucopia and stand back while children grab for the goodies. And there is the ongoing and permanent question of what it is we, as adults engaged in introducing children to books, value in literature and why. Irrevocably, questions about selection criteria arise. Developing such criteria is a complex business.

CLASHING DISCOURSES

Many assumptions about the distinctions between classics and bestsellers, and about good taste versus the mass market, are shaken by the multiple incarnations of Peter Rabbit. We are used to the idea of the media blockbuster that is commercially exploited at every turn, for example, the *Star Wars* industry. John Seabrook succinctly describes this phenomenon: "The marketing is the culture and the culture the marketing."[7] It is hard to think of Peter Rabbit as merely a piece of cultural merchandise. On the other hand, that role is certainly now one part of his contemporary identity. Seabrook says of *Star Wars* that "Star Wars is both something to buy (marketing) and something to be (culture) through the buying: a *Star*

Wars fan."[8] The Peter Rabbit motif can be fitted comfortably into such a framework: "Peter Rabbit is both something to buy (marketing) and something to be (culture) through the buying." In many cases, what the purchaser is acquiring through Potter purchases is an identity as *a person of taste who doesn't succumb to the crass appeal of the mass market but relates to literary classics instead*. The paradox of such consumption is one that should be familiar to us by now. The highly educated mother of a newborn son recently told me that nearly all the presents given to the baby by her own and her parents' friends featured Beatrix Potter designs. The role of commodities in what Ellen Seiter calls "status relations"[9] is not limited to the easily denigrated "vulgarities" of the mass market. Nor is it a case of vile marketers hijacking the literary image of Peter Rabbit; Potter herself was an enthusiastic commodifier of her little animals.

Yet the new scale of literary post-text is beyond anything Potter might have imagined. The numbers of reworkings, toys, and other objects is now daunting. The official Peter Rabbit website[10] lists twelve specialty shops in the United Kingdom, all bearing the trademarked name of "Peter Rabbit and Friends."[11] These stores are dotted throughout the British Isles; similar sub-shops are located within large toy stores in the United States and elsewhere. All of them are appealing, tasteful, and expensive places to shop. Compared to Disney stores and Warner Brothers stores, which are perhaps their closest equivalents in terms of merchandising text-based commodities, they are peaceful and restrained, with much less distraction in the form of flashing lights and raucous music. Nevertheless, it is possible to be overwhelmed in these pretty shops by the sheer volume of commodification of a small set of texts.

Is there a point at which too much proliferation of dainty artifacts shifts us across the divide from the tasteful to the vulgar? Is there a point at which ever-increasing efforts of marketing and branding risk the destruction of the cultural "golden egg"? Or does even asking this question reveal a backward-looking elitism that rejects any routes to the pleasures of a classic story other than the culturally approved austerity of the nursery story-time?

A CRITICAL VOCABULARY

Much of the world is awash in adaptations, retellings, and commodities based on literature aimed at children. We need a critical vocabulary for discussing the ways in which children's literature, popular culture, and commercialization overlap and impinge on each other. It is not good enough simply to dismiss the *Madeleine* dolls, the *Arthur* animations, the *Secret Garden* lockets as so much flotsam and jetsam on the deep waters of true literary quality. The hybridization of certain literary texts in the commercial marketplace means that many new readers are wading through the shallows of the adaptations, where the artifacts lie thickest, not even aware of the deep waters of great literature. They may meet many different texts and commodities, and may have a strong sense of a fictional character or world, long before they read the original work—if, indeed, they ever do. It is not enough just to dismiss the phenomenon of commodification; it is clearly a lively cultural construct, with a very real impact on children and, in this case at least, on adults as well.

The implications of this development in the children's market need to be teased out in terms of readers and reading experiences. What is the effect of heavy-duty salesmanship on the texts involved and on the readers involved? How should we make judgements about the quality and success of the reworked texts? What questions should we be asking, both from a theoretical and also from a practical perspective?

ISSUES OF PROLIFERATION

The following questions may be productive:

- Why this story?
- How do we judge a particular reworking?
- What is the role of the medium?
- How do institutional frameworks affect the text?

Why This Story?

What is it about *The Tale of Peter Rabbit* that makes it such a ripe candidate for proliferation? Sybille A. Jagusch, chief of the Children's Literature Center at the Library of Congress, says some books are "stuffable," that is, the characters "lend themselves to product development, advertising, and the other money-making enterprises that can make a children's book known."[12] Jagusch says "stuffable" is not necessarily a negative word. As it happens, she also reserves some of her highest praise for *The Tale of Peter Rabbit* as a book that stirs adults as well as children. It may be that some form of adult appeal is a component of the successful marketing of more literary "stuffable" stories. Adults will often purchase such items out of nostalgia for their own childhood, or as a way of introducing children to texts they perceive as valuable, or both. The role of the adult mediator matters greatly in almost every aspect of children's exposure to literature, but in the case of relatively expensive toys and other commodities, the adult must be particularly convinced of the value of the purchase.

Stuffability is one requirement, but it strikes me that, while necessary, it is not sufficient to sustain the quantity of marketing that feeds off *The Tale of Peter Rabbit*. Other factors are clearly at work.

Obviously, the story's status as a classic is beyond argument. In terms of cultural capital, it is hard to beat Potter's luster in the world of books for very small children. At the same time, it is a book that can be read in different ways by adults who hold very divergent standards concerning priorities for their babies. As a complex text for very small children, it has very few peers, even now, but many people contentedly read it as an exhortation about obedience and appreciate it for its perceived moral simplicities rather than responding to it as a morally open-ended book. Because of the story's inherent ambiguities, neither market is closed off. Similarly, it is possible to admire the book for its austerity *or* its cuteness; its pastel and pastoral charm can be interpreted either way. It may even be that it creates a category of its own: the "austerely cute," where the asperity of Potter's sensibility inflects the pastel world in many complex and different ways.

There are class issues at work too. Potter's work, fairly or not, is by now almost a by-word for gentility. She herself makes good use of the human-animal ambiguity in her little stories to query this gentility in many ways, but this acerbic approach does not survive in the world of china ornaments and silver christening mugs. The bland middle-class appeal of the artifacts is neither good nor bad in itself, but it is fair to question the impact of all these "tasteful" items on how we read the story.

How Do We Judge a Particular Reworking?

In my extensive acquaintance with many versions of *The Tale of Peter Rabbit*, I have found little that strikes me as even faintly approaching the quality of the original book. Not everybody would agree with me about any particular version of the story. In any case, there is no *a priori* argument that the inferiority of any later version is automatic. So what criteria can we legitimately bring to bear on a reworking, bearing in mind that such a remaking will often be created expressly to refer to the original as part of its actual makeup?

The issue of fidelity to the original is troubling; if you are going to be completely faithful to the first version, why not simply reissue it? Yet, even if people disagree about specific examples, there does appear to be a certain consensus that there is such a thing as playing false by a text. For example, Kevin Sullivan produced a television sequel to *Anne of Green Gables*[13] that featured Anne struggling through war-torn Europe disguised as a nun and acting as a spy. All the public discussion I heard and read was disapproving; a line appeared to have been crossed (though there is a question about whether such a crass reworking matters only to people who already care about such issues). Similarly, many people are deeply perturbed by my two Christian videos of *Peter Rabbit*. The 1987 publication of the first Ladybird edition of *The Tale of Peter Rabbit,*[14] which replaced Potter's watercolors with stuffed dolls, also ran into serious public disapprobation and disappeared in fairly short order.

Beyond the issue of fidelity to the spirit, if not the letter, of the original story and characters, there is also the question of making use of the medium in which you perform your reworking. If you are making a video, how do you exploit the qualities of video to maximum potential in order to render your retelling powerful? This question is probably easier to answer than the more amorphous issue of fidelity. My own personal favourite, among all the reworkings of *The Tale of Peter Rabbit* that I have seen, is the ballet, *Tales of Beatrix Potter,*[15] performed by the Royal Ballet and filmed in the Lake District. All the elements of ballet—performance, choreography, costume, setting—are fully exploited, in the most positive sense of that loaded word. The ballet is not in any straightforward way "faithful" to the story of *The Tale of Peter Rabbit;* Peter's story is never told directly, and he appears only as a continuity figure. Yet I find it as good a ballet as the book is a book. Furthermore, it is as good as it is *because* of its connection to the little books and *because* of the many ways in which the stories both create and limit what is possible. Knowing the books adds richness to the ballet; it both works in its own terms and plays joyful games with the world of the stories.

It is possible to argue that the ballet exists within the same middle-class, high-art cultural construction as the original stories and that there is less conflict in such a reinterpretation than in many others. There is some weight to this argument, but I believe that the issue of whether a reworking fully exploits the potential of the new medium is more substantial. As evidence, I turn to another reworking of the story that, to my eye, is also successful: the bath book.[16] Drawings based on the video are reproduced on the plastic pages of this book, and the text is reduced to a two-word mantra per page, for example, "crunch, munch" or "helter skelter." It is a good bath book, and it tells the story surprisingly effectively, given the severe constraints of the format. It clearly is not "high art," but what it does, it does well and even wittily. It, too, is enhanced by an acquaintance with the original story, and since both texts are within the range of quite young children, it is arguable that its potential contribution to advancing a form of literary sophistication is actually considerable.

What Is the Role of the Medium?

The issue of the medium is an important one. Warne has produced an animated video and several CD-ROMs,[17] all of which raise interesting questions about how you may tell the same story in different ways. A comparison of these versions with the original book lends itself to an exploration of McLuhan's aphorism that the medium is the message. How is the story necessarily changed as a result of its reformatting?

The most immediate consequence can be described in a pun: there is a *change of address*. The video necessarily introduces a fixed pace to the story, and, for each character, a specific voice and accent as well as a way of moving. The invitation to engage with the story is differently conducted in this (or indeed any) video. Other issues are less the result of generic qualities of animation and more the consequence of particular decisions. There is no voice-over, so Potter's own words are lost, and sometimes replaced by others. For example, instead of the sparrows abstractly imploring Peter to exert himself, they are given specific lines: "Come on, Peter!" "Hurry up, Peter!" At another level, it would be possible to conceive of an animation that preserved some of the white space that is such a feature of the book. This video, however, bleeds the images to the edge of the screen and produces a much more saturated effect than the book.

Similarly, the CD-ROM *The Adventures of Peter Rabbit and Benjamin Bunny* extends its own kind of invitation to the reader/player. The complete text is mounted on the screen, the illustrations preserve some of the qualities of the white space, and there is rather more potential for the child to be in charge of the pacing of the story. Furthermore, you can move into the pictures and snoop around. This activity certainly has its own appeal, and the landscape is very attractively rendered. At the same time, it is an absolute change from the reticence and stillness of the book illustrations.

I could continue listing examples, but one or two probably make the point: how the reader or viewer or player is invited to take part in the story is part of the story itself. Even this modest set of specimens offers a perspective on how attractively and easily young children may become very sophisticated consumers of text. Moving from one of these formats to another is not difficult, but it fosters a development of multiple skills and strategies that will serve young readers well as they mature in a world of many media.

How Do Institutional Frameworks Affect the Text?

I believe that much of our unease about the proliferation of multiple versions lies in concerns about the distributional network. Rightly or wrongly, we feel that those institutions that once preserved a disinterested frame for our aesthetic explorations are now colored by the marketplace. A few examples will make my argument clearer. *The Tale of Peter Rabbit* offers many specific examples of these issues in action.

The Publishing Industry

When *The Tale of Peter Rabbit* was published, the company of Frederick Warne was the epitome of the gentleman's profession. Successive takeovers mean that it is now owned by Pearson, a multinational conglomerate that bills itself as the largest educational publisher in the world. Different incarnations of Peter Rabbit come and go, partly according to Pearson's changing commercial priorities; the Potter CD-ROMs, for example, were published as part of Pearson's short-lived bid to move into multimedia publishing through their short-term purchase of the software company Mindscape. While there is no reason why Pearson should not seek to maximize its investment in the Potter properties, it does raise questions of how many incarnations of Peter Rabbit were produced because somebody had an *artistic* urge to rework an old story. We assume, probably too romantically, that there was a time when questions of aesthetics drove questions of publishing and profit. In our contemporary world of international conglomerates, we know the bottom line is more important than it used to be. Such a perspective reduces our faith in publishing companies as arbiters of artistic quality; our perception of their gatekeeping role is changing.

Public Libraries and Museums

Our connection with the official custodians of our cultural goods is also becoming more complex. Changes in public funding mean that our relationship with the large public archives is no longer an entirely civic exchange. Ironically, one of the most telling examples is in the new British Library, where the magnificent display of original documents that were once displayed in the neutrally labelled British Museum Manuscript Room is now beautifully laid out in the Pearson Gallery, which is named after Peter Rabbit's current owners. Other public institutions rely on various forms of fund-raising that may subtly undermine their capacity to stand for the power of independent aesthetic judgement. For example, in the gift shop of the New York Public Library, I purchased a talking Peter Rabbit doll. Press his ear, and he will "read" a highly truncated account of his own story from the little board book stitched to his paws. He is as beautifully made as all the Peter Rabbit stuffed toys, but his American accent jars any ear expecting a English voice, and his play value is reduced by the stiff book that makes him impossible to cuddle. Really, he is just a gimmick, yet another collectible. Does he carry the *imprimatur* of the New York Public Library in the same way as the collection of texts available in that institution for free public use?

Similarly, in the gift shop of the Victoria and Albert Museum in London, I purchased an expensive paperback price guide to Royal Doulton and Beswick china of Potter characters.[18] The aesthetic qualities of these objects may be open to debate, but their value, by another set of terms, is clearly demarcated in the many pages of price tables.

In the summer of 2000, the V&A was also displaying a cabinet of Potter artifacts as part of its artistic heritage; the New York Public Library is famous for the careful and loving way it displays the original stuffed animals who feature in the stories of Winnie the Pooh. It is not that these great institutions have lost their focus on preserving what they perceive as important artifacts in our culture. It is rather that the relatively recent fund-raising approach to visitors also marks a *change of address* and inflects the gatekeeper's role with alternative values from the marketplace. The postmodernist's argument might simply run, "So, get used to it," but it is hard to dismiss all feelings of uneasiness. Commercial priorities are not necessarily what we would choose to substitute for the master narratives of our archival institutions.

The Marketplace

"Value" is a loaded word, and in the marketplace it is often rendered as part of a more complex term such as "rarity value" or "curiosity value." Old pirate versions of *The Tale of Peter Rabbit* now command astonishing prices, no matter what their original contribution to the fictional universe of Beatrix Potter.

Despite my references to contemporary phenomena such as *Star Wars,* the commodification of *The Tale of Peter Rabbit* is nothing new, and even pre-dates Walt Disney, who is often perceived as one of the originators in the area of merchandising fiction. Numerous Potter commodities anticipated the explosion of such materials in the 1980s and 1990s by many decades. By their very nature, most of these materials are ephemeral; nevertheless, some have survived and now constitute a particular market of their own.

I recently received the Summer 2000 catalogue of second-hand books from a specialist in Potter materials.[19] From this catalogue, I could purchase a copy of *Peter Rabbit's Painting Book* (Warne, 1911), or an edition of *The Songs of Peter Rabbit* (Warne, 1951). The listing of American pirated reworkings is much longer and features variations, such as books with puzzle pictures, poster stamps, or red pictorial borders of animals, all published by 1915 or earlier. The catalogue also includes an intriguing set of other titles, such as *Peter Rabbit Goes to Market* (1920), *Peter Rabbit's Birthday* (1921), *Peter Rabbit and the Tinybits* (1924), *Peter Rabbit & His Ma* (1928), *Peter Rabbit with Great Big Cut-Outs* (1936), and so forth.

Presumably, at least some of the interest in the collectibles of today is based on the hope that they will accumulate in "value" and feature some day on high-priced lists of antiques. Such ambitions drive the market; to what extent is their impact on the *literary* world and experience of *The Tale of Peter Rabbit* intrusive and/or distracting?

CONCLUSIONS

The effects on young readers of the complex, post-text world of Peter Rabbit versions, adaptations, reworkings, commodities, and collectibles is difficult to sum up briefly, since every child will have a different experience. In some cases, a Peter Rabbit toy may become a beloved companion whose emotional value is enhanced by the delicacy of the original story. In some cases, a child will express utter commitment to a fictional universe by way of clothing, toys, and other related objects. In other cases, a truncated or bastardized version of the story may short-circuit any approach to the original version, and who is the arbiter of how much of a loss to a child this may be?

If I were to attempt to describe the effects of the current proliferation succinctly, I would argue that what we see is a potential for richness and diversity, permeated and perhaps undermined by confusion and uneasiness about what value systems are at work. Literary values, archival values, cultural and historical values, in our present social arrangements, are all porous to commercial values that may support or sabotage them. Small wonder that the very phrase "value judgement" is open to dispute. For, if we simply dismiss the question of "value" as too old-fashioned and prescriptive to be useful, then commercial values will triumph whether we wish it or not.

My own criterion for passing judgement in this welter of alternatives is subjective but also reasonably stringent. Conveniently, it can be fitted into the rubric I have outlined above. I am looking for *added* value. I am not personally interested in pseudo-replacements for the original *Tale of Peter Rabbit,* nor am I convinced that they have much to offer to children—though any individual child may love any particular version, whatever its merits. I *am* intrigued by those reworkings that gain in interest when viewed against or alongside the original story. Mindless plurality does not interest me, but an intelligent, playful plurality is exciting—and it opens doors for today's children who need to learn to function in a world where multiple incarnations are the norm. Children, who take for granted that their fictional favorites come in a variety of versions, are well equipped to join a fascinating conversation.

And the paradox of reworking a literary classic is fascinating in itself. *Peter Rabbit* is rightly considered a masterpiece, for its timelessness and the ways that it speaks to children in many different contexts. Yet the ramifications of the many variant texts and commodities call to mind another kind of timelessness, that of the marketplace. Peter Lunenfeld says, "Final closure of narrative cannot occur in such an environment because there is an economic imperative to develop narrative brands: product that can be sold and resold."[20] Just as the aesthetic complexities and virtuosities of *The Tale of Peter Rabbit* are constantly refreshed under readers' eyes, so there is seemingly always a new way of selling the story—even to the extent of stretching to an unlikely contract with Barbie.

The Tale of Peter Rabbit provides a major case study of multiple reworkings. Among the many specimens of proliferation-for-profit are those texts and commodities that may illuminate and add interest to the original story. In a world where commercial reworking is now a given, to find ways of discovering, valuing, and putting such versions into the hands of children, seems to me to be a necessary step forward.

NOTES

1. You can see the Peter Rabbit™ Barbie® at http://www.barbie.com/collectors/ pshow. Accessed 14 January 1999.

2. This topic is discussed in much greater detail in Margaret Mackey, *The Case of Peter Rabbit: Changing Conditions of Literature for Children* (New York: Garland, 1998).

3. *Tales of Beatrix Potter*. Dancers of the Royal Ballet in association with the Royal Opera House, Covent Garden (EMI Film Productions, 1971).

4. Bonnie Trachtenberg, adapter, *The New Adventures of Peter Rabbit* (New York: Sony Wonder, 1995), in three formats: audiotape, picture book and video.

5. *The Parables of Peter Rabbit: Friends* (Brentwood, Tenn.: Brentwood Music, 1994) and *The Parables of Peter Rabbit: Faith over Fear* (Brentwood, Tenn.: Brentwood Music, 1995).

6. David Rudd. *Enid Blyton and the Mystery of Children's Literature* (Basingstoke: Macmillan, 2000), 66–67.

7. John Seabrook, *Nobrow: The Culture of Marketing—The Marketing of Culture* (New York: Alfred A. Knopf, 2000), 153.

8. Seabrook, *Nobrow*, 153.

9. Ellen Seiter, *Sold Separately: Parents and Children in Consumer Culture* (New Brunswick, N.J.: Rutgers University Press, 1995), 42.

10. The official site is located at http://www.peterrabbit.co.uk. Accessed 12 June 2000.

11. The list of gift shops may be located at http://www.charactergifts.com/peterrabbit/shops.cfm. Accessed 12 June 2000.

12. Von Hoffman, http://www.britannica.com.bcom/origina./article/print/0,57499,3162,00.html. Accessed 22 March 2000.

13. Broadcast by the Canadian Broadcasting Corporation on March 5, 2000.

14. David Hately, adapter, *The Tale of Peter Rabbit* (Loughborough: Ladybird Books in association with Frederick Warne, 1987).

15. *Tales of Beatrix Potter* (EMI Productions, 1971).

16. *Peter Rabbit: A Beatrix Potter Bath Book* (London: Frederick Warne, 1989), n.p.

17. Here I discuss the video, *The Tale of Peter Rabbit and Benjamin Bunny* (Grand Slamm Partnership/Frederick Warne, 1993), and the CD-ROM, *The Adventures of Peter Rabbit and Benjamin Bunny* (Novato, Calif.: Mindscape, 1995).

18. Francis Joseph. *The Bunnykins & Beatrix Potter Price Guide: Royal Doulton, Beswick, Royal Albert* (London: Francis Joseph Publications, 1998).

19. *A Catalogue of Children's Books, Being a Collection of Fairy Tales, Stories & Verse and Beatrix Potter with Peter Rabbit* (Stroud: Ian Hodgkins & Co., Catalogue 109, Summer 2000).

20. Peter Lunenfeld, "Unfinished Business," in *The Digital Dialectic: New Essays on New Media*, ed. Peter Lunenfeld (Cambridge, Mass.: MIT Press, 2000): 6–22.

BIBLIOGRAPHY

A Catalogue of Children's Books, Being a Collection of Fairy Tales, Stories & Verse and Beatrix Potter with Peter Rabbit. Stroud: Ian Hodgkins & Co., Catalogue 109, Summer 2000.

Hately, David, adapter. *The Tale of Peter Rabbit.* Loughborough: Ladybird Books in association with Frederick Warne, 1987.

Joseph, Francis. *The Bunnykins & Beatrix Potter Price Guide: Royal Doulton, Beswick, Royal Albert*. London: Francis Joseph Publications, 1998.

Lunenfeld, Peter. "Unfinished Business." Pp. 6–22 in *The Digital Dialectic: New Essays on New Media*, edited by Peter Lunenfeld. Cambridge, Mass.: MIT Press, 2000.

Mackey, Margaret. *The Case of Peter Rabbit: Changing Conditions of Literature for Children.* New York: Garland, 1998.

Peter Rabbit: A Beatrix Potter Bath Book. London: Frederick Warne, 1989.

Rudd, David. *Enid Blyton and the Mystery of Children's Literature*. Basingstoke: Macmillan, 2000.

Seabrook, John. *Nobrow: The Culture of Marketing—The Marketing of Culture*. New York: Alfred A. Knopf, 2000.

Seiter, Ellen. *Sold Separately: Parents and Children in Consumer Culture*. New Brunswick, N.J.: Rutgers University Press, 1995.

Tales of Beatrix Potter. Dancers of the Royal Ballet in association with the Royal Opera House, Covent Garden. EMI Film Productions, 1971, videocassette.

The Adventures of Peter Rabbit and Benjamin Bunny. Novato, Calif.: Mindscape, 1995, CD-ROM.

The Parables of Peter Rabbit: Faith over Fear. Brentwood, Tenn.: Brentwood Music, 1995, videocassette.

The Parables of Peter Rabbit: Friends. Brentwood, Tenn.: Brentwood Music, 1994, videocassette.

The Tale of Peter Rabbit and Benjamin Bunny (Grand Slamm Partnership/Frederick Warne, 1993), videocassette.

Trachtenberg, Bonnie, adapter. *The New Adventures of Peter Rabbit*. New York: Sony Wonder, 1995, audiotape, picture book and video.

13

Peter Rabbit in Japan and My Approach to Beatrix Potter's World

Shin-ichi Yoshida

Peter Rabbit is now one of the most popular children's literary characters in Japan, along with Winnie-the-Pooh, Miffy, the Little Prince, the Snowman, and other classic characters. His popularity, I suppose, might be stimulated a little by the Peter Rabbit merchandise, which flourishes in Japan too. This popularity is, however, short-lived—only thirty years as compared with the far longer lifetime of the original Peter in the English-speaking countries.

Beatrix Potter's original *Peter Rabbit* in translation first appeared in Japan in 1971. Before then we had several translated versions of the "Peter Rabbit books" but they were published with different illustrations from Beatrix Potter's originals. The earliest of these to appear, as far as I know, was *The Tale of Tom Kitten,* which appeared in *Kodomonotomo* (*Children's Friend*), a magazine for children, in February 1926. It was published as an article in a magazine, not as a separate book form, and the illustrations were poorly traced from the originals by a Japanese artist (name unknown). The Japanese title was *The Naughty Kittens and the Ducks Who Lost Their Dresses*.

I will explain here about the circumstances of the introduction of foreign children's books through translations in modern Japan. Foreign (translated) books have played a predominant role both in the development of modern Japanese literature and in the building up of modern ideas of life. Japan realized modernization in 1867 (a year after Beatrix's birth) after the long national isolation. The modern Japanese government after that time adopted the policy of "catching up and passing the Western advanced countries," at least until the end of World War II. With that end in mind, they tried to cut off their old feudalistic ideas and vigorously to take in European advanced cultures. Therefore, modern Japanese children's literature has developed by the support of translations of many European classics, including Grimms' *Fairy Tales,* Andersen's *Fairy Stories,* Stevenson's *Treasure Island,* Lord Tennyson's *Enoch Arden,* Burnett's *Little Lord Fauntleroy,* Kipling's *Jungle Book,* Lewis Carroll's two *Alices*, Sewell's *Black Beauty,* Mark Twain's *The Prince and the Pauper,* and so on. These stories were translated along with the Russian, French and Italian literatures by the end of the nineteenth century. That tendency continued and accelerated after 1900—except in the case of picture books. Their regular introduction began far later, after World War II. The above-mentioned introduction of *The Tale of Tom Kitten* in 1926 was an exception indeed.

Before the publication of the translated versions of Beatrix's original books by Fukuinkan Publishers after World War II, we had four separate versions of Beatrix's works. These, however, were not as picture books but in the form of illustrated storybooks whose illustrations by Japanese illustrators were completely different from the originals. There was one exception, which was entitled *The Adventures of Peter Rabbit* (that is, *The Tale of Peter Rabbit*), translated by Eriko Kishida, poetess, illustrated by Sekiya Miyoshi, and published by Kaiseisha Publishers in April 1968. The illustrations are unique. They so closely follow Peter's course of movements throughout the book that his image appears several times on each page. On the same page we see a variety of Peter's figures—in other words, a flow of different times is drawn on the same page. We see the animated picture of the hero's movements all through the work. The pictures are in line and watercolor. They are another work as compared with the originals, but I judge it an interesting variation of Peter Rabbit picture book, qualitatively different from what we call a pirated edition.

The other three versions were more truly pirated works: in April, 1966, by Kodansha Publishers; in May, 1971, by Obunsha Publishers; in August, 1977, by Kodansha Publishers.

The first of these was *Peter Rabbit* based on *Altemus' Wee Books for Wee Folk,* by the American Henry Altemus Company. It contained three stories, *The Tale of Peter Rabbit, When Peter Rabbit Went A-Fishing,* and *When Peter Rabbit Went to School,* translated by Tatsuzo Nasu, illustrated by Saburou Yamada. Correctly speaking, these are not the works by Potter, except *The Tale of Peter Rabbit,* but the title page says the works are by Beatrix Potter, which is very misleading.

The second example was the translation of *The Tailor of Gloucester*. The translator is Isoko Hatano, and the illustrator Hiroshi Inoh. This version has a comment about the author by the translator at the end, in which it is said that Beatrix wrote a story about a baby elephant—another misleading error.

The third book has two stories, *The Tale of Peter Rabbit* and *The Tale of Benjamin Bunny,* translated by Yoshiko Yagita and illustrated by Katsumi Oofuru. This was published six years after the licensed versions of the two *Tales* were published by Fukuinkan Publishers. As most Japanese knew by then what the originals looked like, it was a shame that such a false *Peter Rabbit* was published. I suspect it was not copyrighted.

Such is the history of the introduction of *Peter Rabbit* in Japan before the Fukuinkan Publishers' authorized edition appears. Fukuinkan began to publish the Japanese versions, first with six books, *Peter Rabbit, Benjamin Bunny, The Flopsy Bunnies, Tom Kitten, Miss Moppet,* and *The Fierce Bad Rabbit,* in November 1971. These were followed by *Mrs. Tittlemouse, Johnny Town-Mouse,* and *Two Bad Mice* in May 1972; *Squirrel Nutkin, Jemima Puddleduck,* and *Ginger and Pickles* in January 1973; and *Mr. Tod, Samuel Whiskers,* and *Gloucester,* in February 1974. After a gap, *Timmy Tiptoes, Mrs. Tiggy-Winkle,* and *Jeremy Fisher* appeared in June 1983, followed by *Pigling Bland, The Pie and the Patty-Pan,* and *Sly Old Cat* in June 1988; *Yours Affectionately, Peter Rabbit* in April 1992; *Appley Dapply* and *Cecily Parsley* in May 1993; *Little Pig Robinson* in September 1993, and *Fairy Caravan* in June 2000.

We now have an official Japanese version of almost all the works by Beatrix Potter. We are proud that no non-English speaking country except Japan has such a complete set of translations of Potter's works. This citation is ample proof of how popular Peter Rabbit is in Japan.

I have explained how we Japanese have had a close relationship with modern European literature. Especially in children's literature, we have had translations of almost all modern classics and a variety of contemporary literature. Each individual book has its own identity and characteristics, but at the same time has a human universality. *Peter Rabbit* is quite English and also very universal. We are not so familiar with, for instance, a hedgehog, but we have no difficulty in appreciating *Mrs.*

Tiggy-Winkle because of other characteristics of the universality of human beings—the amiable, reliable, and kind-hearted nature of a washerwoman who is faithful in service. We have so assiduously and avidly adopted foreign children's books as part of our own literary heritage that we can easily grasp the charm of foreign originals even through the translations. We have been able to receive *Peter Rabbit* with a natural affection. We take great delight in these little books, setting aside many picture books by our own Japanese writers. I am sure that our enthusiasm is mainly owing to the literary excellence of Beatrix Potter's literature, and especially to the way it speaks to human beings everywhere.

THE TALE OF ONE JAPANESE READER

At this point, I would like to talk about my own history of attachment and relationship to Beatrix Potter, her life and literary works. I took a great interest in children's books for the first time when my oldest child, then three years of age, showed a keen interest in books. It was in 1966. He seemed very, very pleased when I read picture books, so I myself was pleased to read the text over and over again. Before long, I too became absorbed in picture books while reading to him. This engagement led me to acknowledge that English people have many of the most excellent children's books in the world. I realized that I was in the kingdom of children's books as a student of English without knowing it. I had so far been teaching adult literature to students who major in English literature in Rikkyo University in Tokyo. But at this point I began positively to appreciate English children's books and eventually came upon *Peter Rabbit*. As we had yet no Japanese version at that time, I showed my son the originals, reading the text to him in my extemporarily translated Japanese. Of course, he rejoiced over it, and I was also delighted to see my son so pleased.

Just then in my university, we suffered student unrest, as many other universities elsewhere did at that time. We could not hold our regular class activities at all for a full year. We were obliged to develop some new and original curriculum for the students in order to reopen our classes for the next school year. I proposed to open a new class of English children's literature. This proposal was supported without any objection by the staff, so I started my course of the study of English children's literature in my university in 1970. But I worried about my lectures for the first year on account of my insufficient preparation and lack of information. As soon as I finished my lectures for the year, I set out to obtain information and materials for study early in 1971, first to the New York Public Library to meet Ms. Baker, and then to "The Boys' and Girls' House" and "The Osborne Collection" in Toronto.

In Toronto, I met Ms. Lillian H. Smith in her later years and was given much information by the staff—Ms. Bagshaw, Ms. St. John, Ms. Johnston, Ms. Scott, and others. Above all, I owed very much to Ms. St. John, Chief Curator of the Osborne Collection. While I studied many materials there, day after day, I happened to focus upon Beatrix Potter on a certain day. Ms. St. John told me that the same sights as Beatrix drew for her picture books three quarters of a century ago still remained. She herself had not had the chance to visit there yet, but, as I was to go to the United Kingdom after Toronto, she strongly advised me to visit the Lake District if at all possible.

Now, it happened to me most luckily that a very long postal strike was occurring in England at that time in the early spring of 1971, and the Osborne Collection could not make a necessary contact with its English "Friends" for a long time. So when I left Toronto, I was asked to deliver letters to the English Friends, including letters for Mr. Brian Alderson, recently President of the Beatrix Potter Society, and for Mr. Leslie Linder. It was far better than any letter of introduction for me.

Thus I most fortunately was privileged to make an acquaintance with Mr. Leslie Linder in his last years. He invited me to his charming residence at Buckhurst Hill in the suburbs of London. He was mild, amiable, and kind. He showed me many original drawings, paintings, sketches, and letters by Beatrix, which were all treasured under his own bed! He also introduced me to Mr. Stephens of Freckerick Warne, so I had a chance to see the original illustrations of *The Tale of Peter Rabbit*. I was deeply impressed to see for the first time those pictures that had been so long present in my mind. Moreover, Mr. Linder advised me to visit the National Book League to see Beatrix's original paintings and drawings, and the first editions of her works there, all of which had been collected, arranged, and recently deposited by him. There Mr. Keith Clark, who was to write a guide titled *Beatrix Potter's Gloucestershire* later in 1988, showed the collection to me and explained each item. Later he kindly sent me a copy of *The Linder Collection of the Works and Drawings of Beatrix Potter* (compiled perhaps by him), published in 1971 after I came back to Japan.

When I first met Mr. Linder, his *A History of the Writings of Beatrix*

Potter was in the midst of printing and not yet published. He took out a hand-drawn map and gave it to me, saying, "This is a Map of Sawrey. I drew two kinds of map for the Introduction of the *History,* but left the choice about which map the Publishers would use for the book. This map was the one not chosen by them and has been sent back to me. It is unnecessary to me now. This may be helpful to you when you visit Sawrey, so I will let you have it."

My first visit to Sawrey just after Easter Monday in 1971 proved to be unexpectedly fruitful, owing to his Beatrix-associated map with the kindest suggestions for seeing Sawrey. I keenly realize how lucky and happy I was at meeting with the most valuable instructions by Mr. Leslie Linder. I have treasured the map given to me; it is basically the same as you see on page xxiii of the Introduction to *A History,* with a few small differences.

In Near Sawrey, Hawkshead, and Keswick, I took many photographs of the places associated with Beatrix and her works. Especially I made photographic records of the same scenes as in the illustrations of the *Peter Rabbit* picture books. After returning to Tokyo, I sent my selections of the pictures to Ms. St. John in Toronto as a token of my thanks for her assistance. It was a great pleasure to me that she kindly put my photographs on display for a time in the hall of the Osborne Collection.

While I was away, Ms. Momoko Ishi's translations of the first issue of the Fukuinkan Japanese versions of *Peter Rabbit* books had been in progress in Japan, and they were finally published in November 1971. As soon as I returned to Japan, I was asked to write about my impressions of Beatrix Potter's Lakeland and about Beatrix and her works for *The Mothers' Companion,* a monthly magazine by Fukuinkan. I wrote an article entitled "The World of Beatrix Potter" for its October issue, 1971. That article was translated into English and appeared in No. 5, 1973, of *The International Library Review,* entitled "The World of Beatrix Potter As Seen through the Eyes of a Japanese Visitor." In it I stressed the factual side of Beatrix's works more strongly than their fanciful side, writing "It is my impression that if we really want to understand the world of Miss Potter's work, we should visit her home, because to visit that area means to enter her works. Her pictures seem as if they were drawn by an ecologist after long and careful observation." And I was so deeply impressed with the activities of the National Trust and Beatrix's contributions to it too, that I wrote, "Of course it is hard for present-day children to find around them in London the things which Miss Potter drew. English children, however, still have the Lake

District; they will find beautiful areas which have been protected by the National Trust if they only go halfway up the River Thames. Beatrix Potter's works, which appeal to us to return to nature quietly but strongly, are all the more valuable in the present society where industries are developing and cities are expanding quickly. I am sincerely glad that Miss Potter's picture books are translated into Japanese at last, but on the other hand, I cannot deny a certain fear in my mind. Have we Japanese and our children the beauties of nature to which we are able to return? This is the question I have been asking myself since I left Sawrey village." This impression of mine remains unchanged at the end of the twentieth century.

After this experience, I published three books on Beatrix and her works—*From Peter Rabbit's Countryside* (December, 1989), *The Letters from Peter Rabbit* (April, 1990), and *The World of Peter Rabbit* (October, 1994). Now I have finished translating Judy Taylor's *Beatrix Potter: Artist, Storyteller and Countrywoman* (new edition) into Japanese. It was published early in 2001 through Fukuinkan Publishers, and has been very well received so far. With this publication, my introduction of Beatrix Potter and her world to Japanese readers, which started in 1971, is virtually complete.

About the Contributors

Alice Byrnes is an associate professor of communication arts and English at Molloy College in Rockville Center, New York. She received a doctor of arts degree in English from St. John's University in Jamaica, New York. Dr. Byrnes is the author of *The Child: An Archetypal Symbol in Literature for Children and Adults,* published by Peter Lang in 1995.

June Cummins is an assistant professor in the Department of English and Comparative Literature at San Diego State University, where she specializes in children's literature. Interested in both American and British literature, she has written about Laura Ingalls Wilder, the *Curious George* series, and Virginia Woolf. She is currently working on a book about twentieth-century American children's literature and the American national identity.

Eliza T. Dresang, an associate professor at the School of Information Studies of Florida State University, is the author of *Radical Change: Books for Youth in a Digital Age* (Wilson, 1999) as well as numerous other scholarly publications that analyze literature for children and young adults. Her research, teaching, and service focus on the information needs and behaviors of youth, the resources and services that meet these needs, and the political and social context in which the information/user match occurs.

Melissa Gross is an assistant professor with the School of Information Studies at Florida State University. As part of her research specialty in information-seeking behavior, she has a special interest in children as a user group and the information resources developed specially for them. Dr. Gross' research on imposed information-seeking has been widely published, as has her work evaluating resources for children that deal with sensitive issues such as HIV/AIDS, sexuality, and child abandonment.

Peter Hollindale retired in 1999 as a reader in English and educational studies at the University of York in England. While he was there, he introduced one of the earliest undergraduate courses on children's literature in British universities. In 1997 he gave the annual Linder lecture to the Beatrix Potter Society. Entitled "Aesop in the Shadows," it has since been published in *Signal* and by the Society. He has also twice lectured at the Society's biennial study conference at Ambleside in Cumbria. His extensive publications on children's literature include a study of the vocabulary of children's literature criticism, *Signs of Childness in Children's Books* (Signal, 1997), and critical editions of J. M. Barrie's *Peter Pan* texts. He is now a freelance writer and lecturer, with special interests in children's theater and drama.

Margaret Mackey teaches at the School of Library and Information Studies of the University of Alberta in Canada. She is the North American editor of *Children's Literature in Education* and author of *The Case of Peter Rabbit: Changing Conditions of Literature for Children* (Garland, 1998). She has published and presented widely on topics relating to children's literature in print and other media. Her current research involves the behavior of young readers in response to texts in different media.

Lissa Paul teaches children's literature at the University of New Brunswick in Canada, where she is a professor in the faculty of education. She writes for journals in Canada, the United States, and Britain, including *Canadian Children's Literature, The Horn Book,* and *Signal*. Her book *Reading Otherways* (Signal, 1998) was short-listed for the F. Harvey Darnton Award for historical criticism in children's literature.

Scott Pollard and Kara Keeling both work in Newport News, Virginia. He earned his Ph.D. in comparative literature from the University of California at Irvine and currently serves as chair of the English Department at Christopher Newport University. She earned her Ph.D. in English from Indiana University and is the children's and young adult literature specialist at Christopher Newport University, where she also directs the Childhood Studies Program.

Carole Scott is dean of undergraduate studies and professor of English at San Diego State University in California. She has published articles in *Children's Literature, Children's Literature Association Quarterly, Children's Literature in Education, The Lion and the Unicorn,* Australia's *Papers: Explorations into Children's Literature, Orana,* and in collections of essays published in Denmark, South Africa, Sweden, the United Kingdom, and the United States. Her book *How Picturebooks Work* (co-authored with Maria Nikolajeva) has recently been published by Garland Publishing.

Lawrence R. Sipe is an assistant professor with the Graduate School of Education at the University of Pennsylvania in Philadelphia, where he teaches courses in children's literature in the Reading/Writing/Literacy Program. With nineteen years of involvement in public education, he has taught from kindergarten through eighth grade and has been a supervisor of language arts for a school board. His doctoral studies were in children's literature, emergent literacy, and literacy criticism at Ohio State University. His research concerns the development of young children's literary understanding.

Judy Taylor was a publisher for thirty years with The Bodley Head in London, specializing in books for children. She is chairman of the Beatrix Potter Society and the author of a number of books about Beatrix Potter, including *Beatrix Potter: Artist, Storyteller, and Countrywoman*. She has edited and annotated *Beatrix Potter's Letters* and *Letters to Children,* and is the coauthor with Patrick Garland of the one-woman play *Beatrix,* which starred Patricia Routledge. She has recently published a selection of sketches from the letters of the artist Edward Ardizzone, creator of *Little Tim*. For ten years she has worked with Volunteer Reading Help, an organization that helps children in primary schools with their reading on a one-to-one basis. She is now on the national committee of that organization.

Joyce Irene Whalley was for many years on the staff of the National Art Library, Victoria and Albert Museum, in London. Part of her responsibility for rare books and manuscripts included the library's collection of early children's books. She was there when the Leslie Linder bequest of Beatrix Potter material entered the library, and that, together with the fact that she had worked on the Museum's Beatrix Potter exhibition the year before, gave her a wonderful opportunity to study all aspects of the work of the famous writer and illustrator. As a result of this close association with the work of Beatrix Potter and the public interest in it, she joined the curator of the Leslie Linder Collection at the National Book League to found the Beatrix Potter Society in 1980, and has continued her involvement with the society to this day. Her books include *"Cobwebs to Catch Flies": Illustrated Books for the Nursery and Schoolroom, 1700–1900* (Elek, 1975) and, with Tessa R. Chester, *A History of Children's Book Illustration* (John Murray and the V & A Museum, 1988). She has also written several books on the history of western calligraphy and related topics, in addition to books and articles on Beatrix Potter.

Shin-ichi Yoshida was born in Tokyo in 1931. He taught at Rikkyo University in Tokyo, where he is now a professor emeritus, and also at the Japan's Women's University in Tokyo. He has served as president of the Japan Society for Children's Literature in English, and also as president of Ehon-gakkai (picture-book study) Associates. He is a member of the Beatrix Potter Society.